Remembering the Phallic Mother

Remembering the Phallic Mother

PSYCHOANALYSIS, MODERNISM, *and the* FETISH

MARCIA IAN

Cornell University Press

ITHACA AND LONDON

First published 1993 by Cornell University Press.

Excerpts from "The Hollow Men" in Collected Poems 1909–1962 by T. S. Eliot, copyright 1936 by Harcourt Brace Jovanovich, Inc., copyright ©1964, 1963 by T. S. Eliot, reprinted by permission of the publisher.

Excerpts from "Burnt Norton," "East Coker," and "Little Gidding" in Four Quartets, copyright 1943 by T. S. Eliot and renewed 1971 by Esme Valerie Eliot, reprinted by permission of Harcourt Brace Jovanovich, Inc., and Faber and Faber Ltd.

Excerpts from "Lines Composed a Few Miles Above Tintern Abbey" in Selected Poems and Prefaces of William Wordsworth, Riverside Edition, ed. Jack Stillinger. Copyright © 1965 by Houghton Mifflin Company. Used with permission.

Lines from Charles Baudelaire, "Correspondences," from Les Fleurs du Mal, translated by Richard Howard. Translation copyright ©1983 by Richard Howard. Reprinted by permission of David R. Godine, Publisher, Inc.

Extracts from The Standard Edition of the Psychoanalytic Works of Sigmund Freud, ed. James Strachey, published by W. W. Norton and Company, Inc., 1966 by arrangement with Sigmund Freud Copyrights, The Institute of Psycho-Analysis, London, and The Hogarth Press Ltd. Reprinted by permission.

International Standard Book Number 0-8014-2637-5
Library of Congress Catalog Card Number 92–33381

Printed in the United States of America

Librarians: Library of Congress cataloging information appears on the last page of the book.

⊗ The paper in this book meets the minimum requirements of the American National Standard for Information Sciences–Permanence of Paper for Printed Library Materials, ANSI Z39.48-1984.

For my parents
Seymore and Ada Goldwasser

It's not just that "god" is dead; so is the "goddess."

—Donna Haraway

CONTENTS

PREFACE

Two intellectual crises may account for the coming into existence of this book: the first occurred in seventh grade, when I suddenly realized, for a variety of reasons personal and cultural, that I had to choose between science and literature or else risk a split personality; and the second came about when I returned to college and literary study after ten years away from it (spent reading Henry James, *Mother Earth News*, and "getting back to the land"), to discover that language, which used to refer to things like "the land," had stopped referring to anything except itself. In this book I attempt to make sense of these two puzzling moments by reading them "large" as cultural problems and symptomatic histories of ideas not mine alone.

In *Remembering the Phallic Mother: Psychoanalysis, Modernism, and the Fetish* I present literary modernism as a movement characterized by an essentially romantic or metaphysical conception of language. I contest and contend with the postmodern truism that language is "material," and that "language speaks us," rather than the other way around, as if language caused people. This notion of language is ultimately mystical. According to Genesis, the act of speaking creates the world, but I concentrate on the more recent history of this idea, focusing on the specifically modernist view of language and its implications for contemporary literary theory.

I do not, however, suggest that we either could or should attempt to recreate foundationalist notions of reference. I agree, rather, with Donna Haraway's insistence that the distinction between fact and fiction becomes irrelevant in the "world system of production/reproduction and communication called the informatics of domination." As Haraway argues, "The boundary-maintaining images of base and superstructure, public and private, or material and ideal never seemed more feeble."[1] The so-called phallic mother functions as the very archetype of such "boundary-maintaining images" in British, European, and American literary modernism, and related social discursive practices. I seek to root out the phallic mother from her real and imaginary place at the heart of what I call psychoanalytic modernism. I do not try to cover the entire American, British, and European terrain but concentrate mainly on American and British literary modernism as it has been "institutionalized" (William E. Cain's term) in recent theoretical and pedagogical practices.

According to the modernist view, language, or as we now say, "representation," was understood to be its own subject, object, and instrument, to constitute reality rather than refer to it. Language, in particular literary language like that, for example, of James Joyce, was theorized as basically self-referential and reflexive, a symbol of itself, as Samuel Beckett put it. To describe the literary or artistic works of the so-called high modernists as self-referential or even autonomous during the early years of the twentieth century was polemical and provocative; but by the 1960s to describe modernist works in these terms had become a pedagogical cliché that severely restricted discussions of modernism to its most aestheticized aspects.

I argue here that this modern idealization of language represents not so much the Nietzschean avant-gardism its champions so often claimed for it as it does the literary historical continuation of romanticism with its inherent Christian humanism intact, and with only its "referentiality" to an empirical social world erased. In literary modernism, the linguistic and the material trade places so that language, paradoxically, becomes the real. Thus literary modernism, with

---

[1] Donna J. Haraway, *Simians, Cyborgs, and Women: The Reinvention of Nature* (New York: Routledge, 1991), 163, 165.

its implicit romanticization of the powers of language, becomes the "natural" prelude to academic postmodernism, in which discourse itself becomes fetishized as if it possesses a power or agency that particular human subjects themselves lack.

Even though the modern conception of language is in general an idealization, the science of psychoanalysis "naturalized" this conception with its explicit claims that naturally, always, and at all times, whether awake or asleep, the human mind produces symbolic discourse. From the point of view of Freudian psychoanalysis, every mind is a self-sufficient language-producing machine and every individual a unique lexicon of symbols and stories. This view grounded and authorized literary modernism's most ambitious claims about itself. I use the term "psychoanalytic modernism" to emphasize the inseparability of these phenomena and suggest that psychoanalytic theory is itself a genre of literary modernism. The so-called phallic mother of the title of this book symbolizes both the unique claims to aesthetic autonomy made by the literary modernists and the specific fantasy of corporeal completeness (the symbolic reunion with mother), which Freud claimed lurked deep in every psyche as an innate idea.

In Chapter 1 I explore the significance and ramifications of the symbol of "the phallic mother" within early psychological and psychoanalytic discourse and later feminist theory and gender theory, together with the ambivalences about maternity, sexuality, individuality, and mortality this history reveals. Because the phallic mother is an idealization, fetish, trope, or symbol whose evolution mirrors a broader literary and cultural history, the discussion in this chapter serves to set up and map out the argument of the book as a whole. In Chapter 2 I explain in more detail the logic of articulating together the social and literary meanings of the fetish, discussing, for example, Henry James, Karl Marx, Richard von Krafft-Ebing, and André Breton. In Chapter 3 I concentrate on the fantastic concreteness of fictional characters in relation to the idea of the fetish, again beginning with James, and moving through E. M. Forster, D. H. Lawrence, and Jean Genet. In Chapter 4 I make of modernist poetry an occasion for proposing the poetic version of the fetish, which I call, to subvert T. S. Eliot's famous phrase, the *subjective correla-*

tive, or what Samuel Beckett, inspired by Baudelaire and Proust, called the *autosymbol,* both indicators of a hyperbolic belief in a logos meant to replace superannuated god-concepts. In Chapter 5 I return to the subject of psychoanalysis to analyze how it serves as the exemplary modernist discourse, teaching us to think of language as not only symbolically, but naturally, even biologically, real. In Chapter 6 I continue this argument by tracing how the "curious ontolinguistics" of Lacanian psychoanalysis permit the biological bottom to drop out of contemporary literary theory, leaving it oddly depoliticized just when theorists are longing to "intervene" in their respective academic institutions on behalf of projects like multiculturalism.

I have worried long and often about how to thank adequately the friends, colleagues, and loved ones who have supported me and this project in our various incarnations. I will have to accept the fact that, if I cannot thank them adequately, I can at least thank them.

Thank you to Barbara Harman and Bill Cain, who taught me that thought and feeling need not be strangers; to Arthur Gold (may he rest in peace), the soul of wit; to Walter Sokel, whose intellect and grace taught me the meaning of "ego ideal"; to Dan Albright, a most astonishing teacher; to Paul Cantor for real help when it was most needed. Thank you to my brother, Richard Goldwater, whose philosophical and psychological critiques have helped me to clarify my own thinking.

Thank you to my friends and colleagues (that they are both means more than I can say) here at Rutgers for their support, encouragement, good humor, intellectual interlocutions, and fun parties: Emily Bartels; Wesley Brown; Elin Diamond; Sandy Flitterman-Lewis; Marjorie Howes; Cora Kaplan; Marianne de Koven; Marc Manganaro; John McClure; to Barry Qualls, special thanks. Many thanks to George Levine and Carolyn Williams (Myth U), for an invigorating year at the Center for the Critical Analysis of Contemporary Culture; and to Diana Fuss for her invaluable comments on subjects scholarly and not so scholarly. Thanks to John Gillis for his generous friendship and a mind-expanding year at the Rutgers Center for Historical Analysis. Thank you to Ed Cohen, for great phone, and for knowing that anything is possible—even in academia.

Thank you to my students, for laughing, for thinking, for doubting; thanks especially to Kera Bolonik, Alison Bowman, and David Toise.

I thank Cornell University Press for its support of this project. I am particularly grateful to Bernhard Kendler for his constructive advice and good taste, to Carol Betsch for her wry humor and technocratic expertise, and to Lou Robinson for her persistence.

I thank my darling daughters, Nikki and Shayna, whose strength and creativity delight and inspire me, and who (I hope) will find this book, or at least the title, a source of amusement; and my dear father, Seymore Goldwasser, who has been most unreasonably supportive, and who still makes me look up words in the dictionary.

Portions of Chapter 3 appeared in an earlier version in "The Text/Body Connection: Character as Fetish in *The Plumed Serpent*," *The Psychoanalytic Review* 78 (Summer 1991): 279–300; I thank the editors for permission to use this material in expanded form here.

MARCIA IAN

New Brunswick, New Jersey

Remembering the Phallic Mother

[1]

On Being and Having:
De-cathecting the Phallic Mother

Hate is not the opposite of love. The real opposite of love is individuality.

     —D. H. Lawrence, "Love Was Once a Little Boy"

What we desire is to bring into a world founded on discontinuity all
the continuity such a world can sustain.

     —Georges Bataille, *Death and Sensuality*

The formidable image of the phallic mother—a grown
woman with breasts and a penis—occupies the symbolic center of psychoanalytic theories of sex and gender, as well as
the center of many of the controversies these theories have
provoked. According to psychoanalytic doctrine, the phallic
mother is the archetypal object of desire, every psyche's "wet
dream." Freudian analyst Robert C. Bak calls her the "ubiquitous fantasy," the "main position," in all the perversions.[1]
And, insofar as "perversion" characterizes *every* psyche according to psychoanalysis, we must assume Bak's statement is
meant to apply to each of us. As Juliet Mitchell points out, at

---

[1] Robert C. Bak, "The Phallic Woman: The Ubiquitous Fantasy in Perversions," in *The Psychoanalytic Study of the Child*, ed. Ruth S. Eissler et al.,
25 vols. (New York: International Universities Press, 1968), 23:15–36. Bak
out-Freuds Freud in this study by believing so firmly in "phallic primacy"
and the concomitant autonomy of the ego, and by dismissing so thoroughly
the importance of research into the pregenital preoedipal phase that he
argues as if fetishism and other perversions were ego functions rather than
symptoms of their lack.

least since the original publication of Freud's *Three Essays on the Theory of Sexuality* in 1905, psychoanalysis has insisted on "the final indivisibility of normality and abnormality."[2] In *Three Essays* Freud contends that "normality" per se does not exist because "the extraordinarily wide dissemination of the perversions forces us to suppose that the disposition to perversions is itself of no great rarity but must form a part of what passes as the normal constitution."[3] It follows that the "ubiquitous fantasy" of the phallic woman "must form a part of what passes as the normal constitution" as well.

The "revival of the maternal or female phallus," Bak continues, is the "primal fantasy [that] constitutes the psychological core of the bisexual identification"(16). As much of the recent work on Freud reminds us, originary bisexuality has from the start, like perversion, characterized the "normal" psyche according to psychoanalysis.[4] But the very idea of bisexuality, and the feelings associated with it, apparently complicated matters for Freud more than he could bear; he was more comfortable theorizing about perversion than about bisexuality. For starters, bisexuality committed the psyche to an orgastic repertory of subject "positions." In a letter to

[2] Juliet Mitchell, *Psychoanalysis and Feminism* (New York: Vintage, 1974), 5. Here Mitchell defends Freud: "Most politically revolutionary writers would outbid Freud in their stress on the final indivisibility of normality and abnormality, forgetting that this was one of Freud's starting points."

[3] Sigmund Freud, *Three Essays on the Theory of Sexuality*, vol. 7 of *The Standard Edition of the Complete Psychological Works of Sigmund Freud*, trans. James Strachey (London: Hogarth Press, 1953), 171. The *Standard Edition* is hereafter abbreviated *SE* in text and notes.

[4] Much of the feminist critique of Freud finds his repressed identification with women—his mother, his daughter, his patients—to be the root of his myopic masculinism. See, for example, the extensive critical literature on the Dora case. One might begin with Madelon Sprengnether's amply documented "Enforcing Oedipus: Freud and Dora," in *The (M)other Tongue: Essays in Feminist Psychoanalytic Interpretation*, ed. Shirley Nelson Garner, Claire Kahane, and Madelon Sprengnether (Ithaca: Cornell University Press, 1985), 51–71, and Mary Jacobus, "*Dora* and the Pregnant Madonna," in *Reading Woman: Essays in Feminist Criticism* (New York: Columbia University Press, 1986), 137–93. On the subject of Freud's relation to his mother, see Estelle Roith, *The Riddle of Freud: Jewish Influences on his Theory of Female Sexuality* (London: Tavistock, 1987).

Wilhelm Fliess dated 1 August, 1899, Freud wrote: "But bisexuality! You are certainly right about it. I am accustoming myself to regarding every sexual act as a process in which four individuals are involved."[5] He was still so convinced in 1901 of the importance of bisexuality that he wrote to Fliess on 7 August that he thought his next work would be called "'Human Bisexuality.' It will go to the root of the problem"(448). When push came to shove, however, he declined to burrow that deep. Writing to Fliess in July 1904, as he was finishing *Three Essays,* Freud confided that in this work he "avoid[ed] the topic of bisexuality as much as possible" except where it seemed to him unavoidable, namely, in the discussion of homosexuality. Freud was evidently uncomfortable with the idea of bisexuality, partly, it now appears, because he got the idea from Fliess, with whom he had a complicated love/like relationship, and partly because the psychologically unstable Otto Weininger, who claimed to have gotten the idea of bisexuality from Freud, had recently killed himself out of fear of his "criminal nature" (464).

Bisexuality was to figure more prominently in *Three Essays on the Theory of Sexuality* than Freud had indicated to Fliess. But it figured there paradoxically, as it does in psychoanalytic theory as a whole, as a central, germinal concept that remains rooted, but never sprouts; that is, Freud never explores its logic with the same rigor he applies to concepts such as "hysteria," "anxiety," "repression," "the unconscious," or a whole glossary of others. Generations of readers have noticed its attraction for Freud and sensed its unexamined gravity at the core of psychoanalytic theory, but have for the most part allowed it to rest. Judith Butler, one theorist who has recently considered the issue, suggests that Freud's notion of bisexuality never amounted to more than "the coincidence of two heterosexual desires within a single psyche" since, whether the child identified with the parent of the same or of the opposite sex, he or she still ended up desir-

[5] Sigmund Freud, in *The Complete Letters of Sigmund Freud to Wilhelm Fliess, 1887–1904,* trans. and ed. Jeffrey Moussaieff Masson (Cambridge: Harvard University Press, 1985), 364.

ing the parent whose sex was opposite to that identification.[6] The girl as girl must repudiate "the mother as an object of sexual love" unless she thinks of herself as a "man" by identifying with her father, just as the boy who desires his father does so from the "feminine" subject position through an identification with his mother. Either way, as Butler puts it, "only opposites attract." There is no homosexual desire in this model, Butler argues, only an inverted heterosexuality; and without acknowledging homosexual desire as such, the supposedly radical new science of psychoanalysis could never have subverted the "culturally mandated heterosexuality" it tried to deconstruct (75).

This critique makes sense, however, only if one assumes, as Freud did, that identification and desire cannot coexist in one psyche. A man who desired another man, according to this logic, only appeared to do so, whereas what he was "really" doing was identifying with his mother; analogously a woman who desired a woman did not really desire her sexually but rather wished to be like her father. This logic denies not only same-sex desires but also heterosexual identifications, as if a man and a woman must automatically desire each other as other, and never respond to each other as in some way the "same." But it now appears that this assumption was one of Freud's great mistakes as well as one source of his inveterate melancholy. Compulsive heterosexuality depends on—in fact, it could even be defined as—the enforced heteronomy of identification and desire, the mutual exclusivity of being and having. For this very reason the factitiousness of their distinction has come under intense scrutiny of late, for example, in Wayne Koestenbaum's account of the origin of psychoanalysis in Freud's erotic identifications with his early mentors and collaborators Fliess and Breuer.[7]

Even Freud's editor in the *Standard Edition* noted the in-

[6] Judith Butler, *Gender Trouble: Feminism and the Subversion of Identity* (New York: Routledge, 1990), 61.
[7] Wayne Koestenbaum, "Privileging the Anus: Anna O. and the Collaborative Origin of Psychoanalysis," *Genders* 3 (Fall 1988): 57–81. See also his *Double Talk: The Erotics of Male Literary Collaboration* (New York: Routledge, 1989).

consistency with which Freud assigned narrative priority
here to identification, there to desire, as if the priority of one
over the other could be established (as if it mattered). In the
Three Essays (1905) and *Totem and Taboo* (1912–13) identification emerges during the "cannibalistic oral phase" of instinctual appetite; in "Mourning and Melancholia" (1917)
identification appears as "a preliminary stage of object
choice"; whereas in *Group Psychology* (1921) identification
"precedes object-choice and is distinct from it" (*SE* 14:241).
Mikkel Borch-Jacobsen, however, considers the relation of
identification to desire only apparently problematic because,
he argues, for all intents and purposes identification simply *is*
the erotic engine of the subject.[8] Accordingly he sets out to
"follow the outlines of the mimetology that Freud's texts at
once include and evade," finding mimesis to come before
desire in every case (53): "The so-called subject of desire has
no identity of its own prior to the identification that brings
it, blindly, to occupy the point of otherness" (48).

I would support the view that bisexuality represented for
Freud no dualism, simple or complex, of selves and others,
identifications or desires, but rather a relation of nondualistic
fluidity. This fluidity Freud associated with the polymorphous sexuality he believed every "normal" individual was
compelled to give up as he or she matured, but which he sus-
pected was not exclusively infantile or regressive, but, possibly, a route to the freedom of sexual feeling he resigned himself to thinking civilization inevitably took from us.[9] What
Freud did instead of exploring bisexuality or any of its possible permutations was, as we all know, to impose upon the
multiplicity of sexual desire the depressing teleological narrative of reproductive heterosexuality.

[8] Mikkel Borch-Jacobsen, *The Freudian Subject,* trans. Catherine Porter
(Stanford: Stanford University Press, 1988).
[9] Butler argues that such a polysexuality (as suggested by Gayle Rubin) is a
utopian notion supported only by its association with prelapsarian infantile
bliss seen from a point of view always already inscribed as gendered; she sees
no reason to think gender would disappear too if we got rid of compulsory
heterosexuality (*Gender Trouble* 75).

Ambivalence vs. Equivalence: Biting the Umbilical
Cord That Feeds Us

This chapter, then, is a reading of the phallic mother as the
symptom of a compulsion to resolve ambivalence by dissolv-
ing it into a specious equivalence. Two decades or so before
the invention of psychoanalysis, Karl Marx argued that the
workers in any capitalist society suffer from the fetishistic
compulsion of the bourgeoisie to translate differential production values into general, abstract equivalents. About one hundred years after the publication of *Capital*, feminism identified patriarchal society as a whole—Marxism included—as
locus classicus for a universal equivalence compulsion whereby sexual difference disappeared in the spurious equivalence
of "Man" and "man." I take here as my specific task, however, the critique of psychoanalytic theory in the context of literary modernism and interpret psychoanalytic discourse as I
might any exemplary modernist text. My purpose is to historicize both psychoanalysis and literary modernism as twin manifestations of a new attitude toward "representation" at once
scientist and romantic. I recognize the peculiar symbiosis of
literary criticism and psychoanalysis; perhaps "parasitism"
would be a more accurate term, since literary interpretation as
we know it has been sponsored at least in part by psychoanalysis, whereas Freud could probably have adduced his theorems without his literary examples (although he would then
have to have been somebody else—and so would I).

Because literary criticism and theory sustain themselves on
poisonous stereotypes of sex "naturalized" by psychoanalysis,
my argument tries to chew through the umbilical cord that
connects certain quasi-foundational assumptions of literary
theory to psychoanalysis. This umbilical cord connects what I
call, using Freud's own term, the "navel" of the psychoanalytic dream of sex and gender to its spectral other, the phallic
mother.[10] But insofar as our cultures, our planet, our relations

[10] This phrasing is meant to resonate with Madelon Sprengnether, *The
Spectral Mother: Freud, Feminism, and Psychoanalysis* (Ithaca: Cornell Uni-

to ourselves and to one another continue to be systemically tainted by these poisonous stereotypes, the argument attempts to "signify" beyond itself to indicate the long reach of the phallic mother and the extent of her hold on us. To my mind the phallic mother represents the conflation, compaction, and concretion of all the most primitive fears and desires of hegemonic heterosexist white bourgeois patriarchy (i.e., home sweet home). But—and this may be the more fundamental problem— she is furthermore the very "type" of idealization itself, and therefore more pernicious and persistent than we thought.

Psychoanalysis represents both the endpoint and the origin for an astonishing number and variety of trends and themes in Western intellectual history, not all of which have to do with sex and gender. Freud was usually willing to confront and articulate the contradictions he and others continually found either inherent in or revealed by his work. But, as feminist critics both inside and outside psychoanalysis have pointed out virtually from the beginning, on the subject of female sexuality Freud was disingenuously obtuse, admitting he knew little about this "dark continent" but always turning from such disclaimers to make precise authoritarian claims about its location, its nature, and its history.[11] Freud has little of use to say about women; but then, psychoanalysis is not *about* women. At best, as Luce Irigaray put it, the institution of psychoanalysis "maintains itself paradoxically in sexual indifference, inasmuch as, for that analysis, the female sex is always understood on the basis of a masculine model."[12] Neither is the image of the phallic mother *about*

---

versity Press, 1990). Sprengnether shows how the figure of the mother functions as a palpable and constitutive "absence" in Freudian theory.

[11] One could perhaps chart this critique from the Freudian to the Lacanian, from, for example, Karen Horney's vigorous thrust against Freud's phallocentrism in "The Denial of the Vagina" (1933), reprinted in *Feminine Psychology,* ed. Howard Kelman (New York: Norton, 1967), 147–61, to contemporary feminist film theory, beginning with Laura Mulvey, "Visual Pleasure and Narrative Cinema," *Screen* 16 (Autumn 1975), reprinted in *Feminism and Film Theory,* ed. Constance Penley (New York: Routledge, 1988), 57–68.

[12] Luce Irigaray, *This Sex Which Is Not One,* trans. Catherine Porter (Ithaca: Cornell University Press, 1985), 146.

women; it does not *refer* to women or to mothers. It does not refer at all, except to the possible collapse of sign and referent—a collapse represented as and replaced by the fetishization of their phantom connection to the mother. The image of the phallic mother purports to embody immanence as mother, as a woman who inseminates and lactates, as if to be woman is simultaneously to mean and to be, to be like a poem an end in itself for another, to cause and to continue in some enviable way. It pretends to offer the simultaneous ontological resonances of being and having as a fantasy of continuity, the satisfaction of hungers not yet felt, the fulfillment of desires prior even to their failure to appear.

Deconstructing the image of the phallic mother, then, will not teach us about women or mothers, although it will shed light on the historical construction of them as categories, and, to a certain extent, on how these categories have been invoked to oppress women and other "others". If I were asked, however, to say what is to me the most useful gift of the many psychoanalysis has offered us, I would answer that it is Freud's definition of the psyche as the realm where the law of noncontradiction does not apply. In the psyche, both any idea *p and* its opposite not-*p* are true, and may either together or separately cause or prevent, animate or agitate, signify or deracinate, inspire or terrorize—or deaden. The phallic mother is a (if not *the*) case in point. She is, according to psychoanalysis, at once the object of every psyche's secret fear and its deep desire. She represents the absolute power of the female as autonomous and self-sufficient; at the same time she is woman reduced to the function of giving suck. She is neither hermaphrodite nor androgyne, human nor monster, because she is emphatically Mother. And yet she hardly resembles anyone's actual mother—except in one's own fervid imagination, and that is precisely the problem. She is a fantasmatic caricature, and a caricature of the fantasmatic. Neither fully object nor fully subject, she is, to use Freud's term for the symbolic-and-therefore-real contents of the unconscious, our most fiercely guarded "psychical object," as well as our role model and the very "type" of the

autonomous self. By having a penis, she defies the psychoanalytic "fact" of woman's castration, at the same time she
attests to the "fact" of every other woman's castration but
hers; she is the girl who has everything and the one "we" for
that reason desire and wish "we" could be.[13] In short, she
has, she bears, she is, the fetish—but whose?

Here we have another conceptual knot in psychoanalysis to
chew through before proceeding. It is not quite true that the
phallic mother represents the suspension, in the psyche, of
the rule of noncontradiction; she does not embody contradiction, although she may arouse contradictory feelings. Because
she is not two, but one, she does not embody or represent
ambivalence, although she may arouse ambivalent feelings in
others, feelings that are *their* problem and not hers. Rather
she represents the wish for the end of contradiction and the
end of ambivalence. Ambivalence is the psychic analog for
what you have when the law of noncontradiction is suspended. Ambivalence is the law of antinomial affect, that is, of
"both/and"-ness, the coexistence of opposites, but not their
merger; ambivalence is not ambiguity. (And male and female
are not "opposites.") Antithetical affects in the psyche may
oppose and conflict with each other but do not diminish,
negate, or cancel each other. They are not equivalent, but
*ambi*valent—a peculiarly psychoanalytic neologism.

In fact, Freud, in a footnote to "Instincts and their Vicissitudes" (1915), credits Eugen Bleuler with the invention of the
term *Ambivalenz,* which Freud then applies to the psycho-
physics of instinct, whose behavior he compares to that of
waves in order to show that numerous instincts can be in flux
at the same time and still not lose their separate identities.[14]

[13] See, for example, Freud, "Female Sexuality," in *SE* 21:229: "Quite different
are the effects of the castration complex in the female. She acknowledges the
fact of her castration, and with it, too, the superiority of the male and her own
inferiority; but she rebels against this unwelcome state of affairs."

[14] Freud, "Instincts and Their Vicissitudes," in *SE* 14:131. Eugen Bleuler, born
the year after Freud (1857), directed the Burghölzli sanitorium in Zurich, where
he did pioneering research. The works Freud cites are "Vortrag über Ambivalenz" (Berne, 1910) and *Dementia Praecox, oder Gruppe der Schizophrenien*
(Leipzig and Vienna, 1911).

In this paper Freud discusses two of the four "vicissitudes" of the sexual instinct (momentarily putting aside repression and sublimation), namely, what he calls "reversal [of an instinct] into its opposite" and "turning round [the instinct] upon the subject's own self" (126). His primary examples are the opposing but reversible poles of sadism and masochism, scopophilia and exhibitionism, love and hate. A detailed reading of this paper is not necessary here, but Freud's principal findings are relevant because they typify the conceptual ambivalence that structures psychoanalytic discourse on sex and gender and which Freud feels obliged to "resolve": that ambivalence which opposes the teleological narrative of reproductive heterosexual complementarity to the chaotic poetics of the individual's polymorphous search for pleasure.

In "Instincts and their Vicissitudes" Freud suggests that "we shall come to a better understanding of the several opposites of loving if we reflect that our mental life as a whole is governed by *three polarities,* the antitheses Subject (ego)— Object (external world), Pleasure—Unpleasure, and Active— Passive. (*SE* 14:133)." Freud shows how the sexual subject moves easily from the first of these polarities to the second, and thence to the third, occupying in the course of these movements the full range of antithetical "subject positions." The phenomenology of these shifts is most simply demonstrated in the case of those "instincts whose respective aim is to look and to display oneself (scopophilia and exhibitionism, in the language of the perversions). Here again we may postulate the same stages": "(*a*) Looking as an *activity* directed towards an extraneous object. (*b*) Giving up of the object and turning of the scopophilic instinct towards a part of the subject's own body; with this, transformation to passivity and setting up of a new aim—that of being looked at. (*c*) Introduction of a new subject to whom one displays oneself in order to be looked at by him" (*SE* 14:129). It may seem at first that although the dialectic of the scopophile and the exhibitionist does include as Freud promised the two "polarities" of subject/object, and active/passive, the middle polarity of pleasure/unpleasure is missing. But this omission disappears if one assumes that the subject is launched from one "pole" to the next by the synaptic discharge of unpleasure as identification oscillates with desire in what Lacan will call a "libidinal dynamism."[15]

If this is true, then I could rewrite Freud's scenario as follows: the scopophile looks desirously at an object (or other), identifies with that object, becomes the object, sees him or herself as object; and then seeks a subject to behold him or her in turn as object. At that point the object becomes the subject again by watching others watch. (Presumably the other subject is oscillating analogously.) In this manner the ambivalent poles of identification and desire structure erotic need nonhierarchically. Power flows from pole to pole, as it were, in the "healthy" organism without a hitch. As in the case of bisexuality, however, Freud characteristically avoids extrapolating "too far" along that "unbroken chain," which he tells us "bridges the gap between the neuroses in all their manifestations and normality" (*SE* 7:171). Instead, he historicizes the otherwise nonteleological erotics of instinct by identifying as their proper domain the early years of psychosexual development, during which (in his view) the infant psyche is roughly analogous to a primitive organism barely differentiated from its environment. Thus the eruption of unruly or "perverse" sexuality during adulthood would constitute regression to earlier stages when infantile wishes and fantasies held sway.

On behalf of the nonteleological aspects of eros, Freud asserts that our "numerous" sexual instincts "emanate from a great variety of organic sources." They arise "inside" us. In fact, according to Freud it is our painful inability to defend ourselves against stimuli arising from inside that first teaches us to distinguish between "inside" and "outside."[16] From external stimuli, Freud says, we can flee (oddly forgetting here, con-

---

[15] Jacques Lacan, "The Mirror Stage," in *Écrits: A Selection*, trans. Alan Sheridan (New York: Norton, 1977), 2. Lacan first presented versions of this paper in 1936 and 1949.

[16] Freud's detailed mythic biohistory, in Section 4 of *Beyond the Pleasure Principle*, of this distinction of the "little living vesicle" from what threatens to demolish it is astonishing, depressing, and charming (*SE* 18:24–34).

cerned as he is with protozoa and the like, that human babies cannot even lift their heads at first); but when stimuli arise inside us we can only suffer. We experience urgent "needs," which clamor for "satisfaction" (*SE* 14:119) in the form of "organ-pleasure" (*SE* 14:125–26). As time passes, however, Freud observes, we narrow the range of our search for organ pleasure. Or, speaking from the deeply cynical point of view of works such as *Beyond the Pleasure Principle* (1920), *The Future of an Illusion* (1927), or *Civilization and Its Discontents* (1930), we widen the gap between our "organs" and the satisfaction of their needs to an abyss bridgeable only by death, or by the self-induced psychoses of intoxication, romance, or religion. We inveterately displace the location of the object likely to satisfy us, sublimate the sexual energy of our quest for it, and postpone allowing ourselves to enjoy it. More than likely, we fear the sight of it, because in it we read our own death.

This, I submit, is what history is to Freud—a psychical road movie, intermittently if drily amusing, ending in the grave—a movie whose story can be infinitely varied since every "organism wishes to die only in its own fashion" (*SE* 18:39), but a movie that can have no sequel in any "afterlife." As Samuel Beckett put it when explaining *Waiting for Godot* to a cast about to perform it, this story "is about man, who is shrinking—about man, who is dwindling."[17] Furthermore, the story logically must run backward if it is not to dwindle out of sight; it begins in multiplicity and polymorphousness but diminishes toward the decided absence of "morph": "If we are to take it as a truth that knows no exception that everything living dies for internal reasons—becomes inorganic once again—then we shall be compelled to say that '*the aim of all life is death*' and, looking backwards, that '*inanimate things existed before living ones*'" (*SE* 18:38; Freud's emphasis). In other words, history is a continuous narrative

---

[17] From Walter D. Asmus, "Beckett Directs *Godot*," in *Beckett: Essays and Criticism*, ed. S. E. Gontarski (New York: Grove Press, 1986), 283. I suppose one could describe *Waiting for Godot* as a kind of road movie whose main characters have run out of gas.

only in retrospect, because death is the only prospect. Yet if one looks too far into the past, one sees the human being dwindle or disperse yet again, back into the "inanimate." If life is a short chain of sentience inexplicably suspended between two poles of the elemental inanimate, it is no wonder that the image of the mother occupies such an important position in psychoanalytic phenomenology.

The phallic mother, seemingly all productivity and reproductivity, flows with milk and semen, and yet stands like a screen between us and our prehistory as "inanimate things"; she stands at the beginning of our psychic, cultural, and specific history as Death's mirror image as well as death's symbolic negation. Insofar as human history is the history of men, and insofar as Freud is a man in fear of shrinking, it is no wonder that he obsessively prevents Mother from moving about either the psychological or the cultural landscape with subjectivity and sadness of her own. It is no wonder that he produces nutty anthropological narratives like *Totem and Taboo*. And it is no wonder that the joy Freud communicates when he explores pregenital sexuality and the unconscious, dissipates in the gloom of his peculiarly depressing descriptions of relations between the sexes and that heterosexual reproductivity which seems to presage our return to the elements. In retrospect the glorious search for organ pleasure turns out to be a kind of false advertisement, as polymorphous desire betrays us into reproducing the species. It is the species which is "immortal," not the individual. The individual "carr[ies] on a twofold existence: one to serve his own purposes and the other as a link in a chain, which he serves against his will, or at least involuntarily. The individual himself regards sexuality as one of his own ends; whereas from another point of view he is an appendage to his germ plasm, at whose disposal he puts his energies in return for a bonus of pleasure."[18] The species, on the other hand, is "immortal" thanks to the *germ plasm*, which links generations of individuals each to each along

[18] Freud, "On Narcissism: An Introduction," in *SE* 14:78.

the "chain" of heredity.

"Germ plasm" was a term apparently coined by August Weismann, an evolutionary biologist and speculative entomologist to whose work Charles Darwin (a former mentor), among others, would later refer. Germ plasm is the "hereditary substance" in the "germ" cells of multicellular organisms, the substance that, Weismann hypothesized, "possesses a fixed architecture . . . which has been transmitted historically" and which "contains the primary constitutents of all the cells in the body in its determinants."[19] It appears that Freud borrowed not only the term "germ plasm" from Weismann, but indeed the whole wry vision of the individual as a mere "appendage to his germ plasm," which appears in the passage quoted above from "On Narcissism" (1914).[20] In the introduction to his *Germ Plasm* (1892), Weismann refers to his earlier essay "On Heredity" (1883), in which he contested "the possibility of the transmission of acquired characters," arguing instead that, although the body "in the narrower sense" or "soma" is mortal, the "reproductive substance" "is always passed on from the germ-cell in which an organism originates in direct continuity to the germ-cells of the succeeding generations" (9): "[I] maintained that the germ-cells alone transmit the reproductive substance or germ-plasm in uninterrupted succession from one generation to the next, while the body (soma) which bears and nourishes the germ-cells, is, in a certain sense, only an outgrowth from one of them" (9). For Weismann the term "germ-plasm" denotes the potentially immortal hereditary substance of an animal or a plant whether or not the cell's nucleus "is sexually differentiated" (35). Either way, the individual could be described impersonally as an "outgrowth from" (or in Freud's image an "appendage to") the "ancestral germ-plasm" (11).

[19] August Weismann, *The Germ-Plasm: A Theory of Heredity*, authorized trans. W. Newton Parker and Harriet Ronnfeldt (New York: Charles Scribner's Sons, 1898), 35,61.
[20] In *Beyond the Pleasure Principle*, Freud finally credits Weismann and his theories and discusses Weismann's distinction between the mortal soma and the immortal germ plasm (*SE* 18:45–50).

But for Freud sexuality is precisely the point. For the sake of a "bonus of pleasure" the individual will put "his energies" at the "disposal" of the immortal germ plasm; but in return the germ plasm disposes of the mortal individual to reproduce the species. Freud did not seem to mind fatherhood; he is his most endearing when he speaks as a father, for example when recounting little Anna Freud's hungry dream of "wild stwawbewwies, omblet, pudden," or about other fathers, such as the man who dreamed of his little dead son crying, "Father, don't you see I'm burning?"[21] Freud does not take personally either what he takes to be the facts: that life has no end other than reproducing itself at the expense of the individual; and that individuals have no "ends" in the end but one: "Seen in this light, the theoretical importance of the instincts of self-preservation, of self-assertion and of mastery greatly diminishes. They are component instincts whose function it is to assure that the organism shall follow its own path to death" (*SE* 18:39). We balk at Freud's biological determinism in part at least because he explains as biological necessity behavior we now think of as culturally determined—and this we take personally. To put this another way, where Freud saw sex, we see gender.

For example, to return briefly to "Instincts and their Vicissitudes," in the child's earliest years (according to Freud) the instincts operate "independently of one another," but over time natural selection for instincts narrows the play of pleasure until the vicissitudes of sex come under the rule of gender, which then retroactively confers meaning upon sex. The sexual instincts, Freud writes, "achieve a more or less complete synthesis at a late stage" when "the antithesis active/passive coalesces later with the antithesis masculine/feminine, which, until this has taken place, has no psychological meaning" (*SE* 14:125,134). The human organism, then, confers meaning upon its ambivalences when and only insofar as they all coalesce into the "antithesis masculine/feminine." Two more passages from Freud will, I think, illustrate even more clearly

[21] Freud, *The Interpretation of Dreams,* in *SE* 4:130, 5:509.

how Freud rewrites as necessity the plastic poetics of sex. First, in the *Introductory Lectures on Psychoanalysis* (1915–1917), Freud again describes the vicissitudes of sexual instinct, calling it "libido." He uses striking new metaphors, but asserts as fact the familiar ambivalence of the polymorphous and the dualistic: "Sexual instinctual impulses are extraordinarily *plastic*, if I may so express it. . . . "One of them can take the place of another, one of them can take over another's intensity; if the satisfaction of one of them is frustrated by reality, the satisfaction of another can afford complete compensation. They are related to one another like a network of intercommunicating channels filled with a liquid; and this is so in spite of their being subject to the primacy of the genitals—a state of affairs that is not at all easily combined in a single picture."[22] The reader can readily agree that Freud has not succeeded in creating a "single picture" here. Freud has elsewhere speculated that libido is probably one chemical substance subject to thermodynamic and hydraulic pressure; yet the idea of libido as a "liquid" filling intercommunicating channels inside us, squirting about from one to another suggests rather the laboratories of mad scientists in old horror movies or perhaps medieval maps of the innards. How this seething plastic liquidity could be connected with, let alone subject to, the genitals of males and females, is mysterious at best.[23]

Yet how well we recognize Freud's wish to reason it out, to subject the chaos of desire to the rule of His and Her Majesties, the genitals; we recognize his wish to resolve the ambivalence of desire and its irrelevance in an antithesis of masculine and feminine, which is no antithesis at all but, as Jane Gallop pointed out, an algorithm of "one" and "zero."[24]

---

[22] Freud, *Introductory Lectures on Psychoanalysis*, in *SE* 16:345.

[23] Peter Amacher shows that Freud's teachers Ernst Brücke and his student Sigmund Exner both described "nervous excitation" as traveling through nerve fibers much as fluid would travel through interconnecting pipes. See Peter Amacher, *Freud's Neurological Education and Its Influence on Psychoanalytic Theory* (New York: International Universities Press, 1965), 14, 45.

[24] Jane Gallop, *Reading Lacan* (Ithaca: Cornell University Press), 1985.

We also recognize what Freud means when he says that one impulse "can take the place of another," and that "if the satisfaction of one of them is frustrated by reality, the satisfaction of another can afford complete compensation." He is referring to the recourse every subject has to perverse aims and objects when the "proper" genital ones are not available. In "'Civilized' Sexual Morality and Modern Nervous Illness" (1908), he makes it clear that the plastic libido's becoming at last "subject to the primacy of the genitals" does not mean so much that sexual pleasure locates itself centrally there as that the libido must come under the rule of reproductive function.[25] Just as the "several opposites" of instincts in their vicissitudes have "psychological meaning" only when they have "coalesced" into the "antithesis" of masculine/feminine, so must "the autonomy of the erotogenic zones" yield to "their subordination under the primacy of the genitals, which are put at the service of reproduction" (*SE* 9:188).

Inevitably, however, some "of the sexual excitation which is provided by the subject's own body is inhibited as being unserviceable for the reproductive function." This excess of excitation, Freud tells us, is *perverse;* and the development of what we think of as culture depends on its successful suppression or sublimation. Freud reasons implicitly that species and culture can be distinguished from each other just as reproductive sexuality can be distinguished from the perverse. According to this logic, species immortality may depend on the "involuntary" reproductive service of male and female genitals, but the production of culture depends on the perverse plasticity of that libido *not* coalesced into the (speciously) antithetical masculine and feminine. If psychological meaning inheres in the resolution of ambivalence in the equivalence of gender, then culture is a refuge for the free-form, the multiplicitous, the fluidly combinatory. This view of culture as the refuge of Eros, depends, alas, on the assumption that nature and culture are distinct and uncon-

[25] Freud, "'Civilized' Sexual Morality and Modern Nervous Illness," in *SE* 9:188–89.

nected realms. If we use Freud's categories of Eros and Thanatos to organize the two ambivalent realms of bios and culture in the terms we've been considering here, then, contrary to Freud's own assertions, Eros is allied with culture, libido, perversion, plasticity, organ-pleasure, and autonomy, and Thanatos is allied with nature, life, the inanimate, domesticity, subordination, genitality, and binarism.

But if there's one large lesson to learn from psychoanalysis, it is that the realms of nature and culture are neither "realms" nor distinct. On the contrary, what is "natural" to us is to live in a state of continuously politicized culture complexly governed by the interactions of interconnected networks of personal, impersonal, and interpersonal systems of representation, knowledge, and power, which, to our consternation, seem to have been organized according to an antithetical gender paradigm! (It is as if society were secretly ruled by an infernal mainframe that used a binary code whose digits were *m* and *f*.) The question remains: how did all that interesting ambivalence, all that multiplicity and difference "coalesce" into the tightly packed, fantasmic fetish of totality, the phallic mother? Of course I can't answer *that* question, so I will ask instead, what happens if we unpack the fetish? What does one find in a container whose contents are itself?

This task will prove both interpretive and historical, insofar as history can be defined, as Donna Haraway defines it, as "a corrosive sense of the contradictions and multiple material-semiotic processes at the heart of scientific knowledge."[26] In other words, although the image of the phallic mother is as old and varied as culture itself, I do not aspire to write its variorum, but rather to contextualize and rationalize the image and its persistent fascination, to show how it functions as a switch point among the several coexisting but incompatible psychoanalytic ideologies, which have their own histories. Irigaray's *Speculum of the Other Woman* probably remains

[26] Donna J. Haraway, *Primate Visions: Gender, Race, and Nature in the World of Modern Science* (New York: Routledge, 1989), 172.

the best study (of the Harawayan kind) of how masculinist Western philosophers such as Plato and Freud "constructed" women in their own image. Another, more recent essay, "The Phallic Mother: Platonic Meta-physics of Lacan's Imaginary" by Lorraine Gauthier, expands the Irigarayan critique of Platonic metaphysics to include Lacan's concept of the Phallus. In it Gauthier shows how "Lacan's conceptualization of the maternal has merely reiterated, in the language of modern linguistics, an age-old devaluation and exclusion of the mother."[27]

But the fate of the maternal is not my primary concern here so much as the *function* of the maternal in psychoanalysis as an "equivalence" or "totalizing" effect. By "equivalence effect" I mean how a concept that has become loaded with symbolic value may, in the words of Jean-Joseph Goux, come to "retain only what is common to diverse representations, effacing the differences among singular images," becoming by means of this effacement "metaphysical" and "detached," and, like money in circulation, a "'general equivalent that exists for itself and that persists in itself.'"[28] By "totalizing effect" I echo Ernesto Laclau and Chantal Mouffe, who describe such effects as the focal points of condensed social relations that seem to emanate from one center of hegemonic power, but which in fact circulate around a "variety of hegemonic nodal points," which may be highly overdetermined economically, historically, and symbolically, but which possess "ontology" only if we make the mistake of thinking of them that way.[29] A prime example of an equivalence effect would be the psychoanalytic "sex/gender system" as described above, in which the

[27] Lorraine Gauthier, "The Phallic Mother: Platonic Meta-physics of Lacan's Imaginary," in *The Hysterical Male: New Feminist Theory*, ed. Arthur Kroker and Marilouise Kroker (New York: St. Martin's, 1991), 213.

[28] Jean-Joseph Goux, *Symbolic Economies: After Marx and Freud*, trans. Jennifer Curtis Gage (Ithaca: Cornell University Press,1990), 99. Goux is quoting Marx, *Contribution à la critique* (Paris: Sociales, 1957), specifically, for the French edition of *Zur Kritik der politischen Oekonomie* contains material not found in the English translations.

[29] Ernesto Laclau and Chantal Mouffe, *Hegemony and Socialist Strategy* (London: Verso, 1985), 139.

phallus replaces and subsumes "diverse representations," "effacing the differences among" them as they "coalesce," and becoming by means of this effacement "metaphysical" and "detached."[30] Thus the phallus functions as general equivalent in the sex/gender system, whereas the phallic mother embodies its totalizing effects as the unitary signifier of nondifference. Desiring, as I do, to critique the totalizing equivalence effects of psychoanalysis itself, I use the psychoanalytic term "fetish" to denote those effects which depend on erasing difference and relation and to signal as well their psychologically primitive ideation and ideology, which masquerade as humanist, abstract, and symbolic.

The scope and application of the term "fetish" may seem to broaden as my argument proceeds, until one may feel inclined to ask if there is anything that is not a fetish. I will ignore this question for now. In Chapter 2 I will begin to map out the recent literary history of the romantic fantasy that language is "constitutive," roughly from Wordsworth to Lacan, paying special attention to the role of psychoanalysis in theorizing, scientizing, and materializing this fantasy. Finally, in an attempt to sort out the usefully discursive from the suspiciously idealistic or positivistic, or at least to consider on what basis such a distinction might be made, in my concluding chapter I will take up Freud's notion of "construction" in relation to some contemporary usages of the term.

Epistemophobia: Freud Fails to Contemplate His Navel

In psychoanalysis, the significance of the Mother to the psyche is precisely the seductive totalization she seems to offer, the promise that she and "I" are, at the deepest level, equiva-

---

[30] The phrase "sex/gender system" is from Gayle Rubin, "The Traffic in Women: Notes on the 'Political Economy' of Sex," in *Toward an Anthropology of Women,* ed. Reyna Reiter (New York: Monthly Review Press, 1975), 168.

lent, connected as if by a psychical umbilical cord that can never be severed, but which the Father must try to sever again and again with his blunt and never wholly effectual instrument.[31] The Mother seems, to our peril, to volunteer to dissolve in the fluid materiality of her body all the troubling questions attendant upon individuation and triangulation. By contrast, the significance of the phallus, from the point of view of psychoanalysis, seems to be whether or not it is detachable from the mother, whether it signifies the aggressivity of the individuated ego or its vulnerability. A father, having been a child himself, is still attached to Mother at the root of his repressed "feminine" identifications. These two questions taken together—whether the individual or the phallus is psychologically detachable from Mother—leads to that peculiar equation "penis = child," which is explicitly the core of psychoanalytic sexual ideology from Freud to Lacan. André Green explains this equation as follows: "It is psychoanalysis which gives to the child, woman born, a significance bearing on his entire development: namely, that he is a substitute for the penis of which the mother is deprived, and that he can only achieve his status as subject by situating himself at the point where he is missing from the mother on whom he depends. This substitute is the locution and link of exchange between the mother and the father who, possessing the penis, still cannot create it (since he *has* it)."[32]

If we psychoanalyze psychoanalysis, we begin to suspect that the phallus might be a screen image, a phobic substitute for something else. That something else would be the umbilical cord; for it is the umbilical cord after all, and not the penis, which constitutes the historic "locution and link of

---

[31] One ought—and one would if the emphasis of this chapter were different—to take to task the many theorists (e.g., Jacques Lacan, Nancy Chodorow, Janine Chasseguet-Smirgel, and occasionally Julia Kristeva) who participate in promulgating, either explicitly or implicitly, this terrorist ideology of the engulfing mother from whom the father must rescue the child.

[32] André Green, "Logic of Lacan's object (a) and Freudian Theory: Consequences and Questions," in *Introduction to Interpreting Lacan*, ed. J. H. Smith and William Kerrigan (New Haven: Yale University Press, 1983), 166.

exchange" from which the subject must be "missing" if he is to be a subject and not a permanent appendage of the mother.

Psychoanalysis has resolutely turned away from this obvious biological fact. Freud's response to Otto Rank's book *The Trauma of Birth* (1924) is a case in point. Rank argued that the universally traumatic experience of birth is the true origin of all anxiety, not the fear of castration. Extrapolating from his own practice, as well as from case histories by other analysts, works of art and literature, and religion and philosophy, Rank claimed both that "the child's every anxiety consists of the anxiety at birth . . . and [that] the child's every pleasure aims at the reestablishing of the intrauterine primal pleasure."[33] Rank was well aware of the extent to which his theory, if accepted, would displace the canonical primacy of castration anxiety. But for Rank the birth trauma alone explained castration anxiety. It was the birth trauma that made it "intelligible" for "childish primal anxiety" as it developed to "cling more especially to the genitals just on account of their vaguely imagined (or remembered) actual biological relation to birth (and procreation)" (20). Rank argued that the female, not the male, genitals really worry us, and that castration anxiety was a substitute formation in which the phallus served as "a 'symbol' for the umbilical cord": "It is conceivable, indeed obvious, that precisely the female genitals, being the place of the birth trauma, should soon again become the chief object of the anxiety-affect originally arising there. Thus the importance of the castration fear is based . . . on the primal castration at birth, that is, on the separation of the child from the mother. . . . But it does not seem quite appropriate to speak of 'castration' where, as yet, there is no clearer relation of anxiety to the genitals, than is given by the fact of birth from the (female) genitals" (20). As Peter Gay reminds us, Rank felt that in *The Trauma of Birth* he was merely pursuing a few offhand remarks of Freud's: one concerning the "act of birth as source of anxiety" Freud made in 1908 following a paper Rank gave on the mythic

[33] Otto Rank, *The Trauma of Birth*, translator unnamed (1929, authorized facsimile, Ann Arbor: Xerox University Microfilms, 1976), 20.

births of heroes; Freud's informing the Vienna Psychoanalytic Society in 1909 that "the child has anxiety from the act of birth on"; and a footnote Freud added in 1909 to *The Interpretation of Dreams* asserting that "birth is the first experience of anxiety and therefore source and model of the affect of anxiety."[34]

Rank was, in some respects, more Freudian than Freud, and for good reason. Since 1905 when Rank first visited him, Freud had like a fond father lavished material and professional aid upon this self-taught man, who in turn had worked indefatigably for Freud, his committee, and the "cause" of psychoanalysis. Eventually, however, Freud came to agree with those who for years had "warned" him that Rank was a secretly hostile neurotic with a father-complex, a defector, a fanatic, a tyrant, a moneygrubber, and an egotist. As Gay points out, this diagnosis was long in coming. For years Freud had maintained an almost "Olympian neutrality" amid considerable infighting. On many occasions he allayed the suspicions of Karl Abraham, Ernest Jones, and others who mistrusted Rank, and remained Rank's friend and patron even when, for example, with Sandor Ferenczi, he published *The Development of Psychoanalysis* (1924), in which he hinted that in the interest of shortening a patient's analysis it was worth spending less time scrutinizing his childhood experiences. Freud was the last of the inner circle to view Rank as having, like Adler and Jung, irrevocably decamped, and the last to join the general character assassination of the formerly "dear Otto." But, Gay writes, he became "increasingly quizzical" about Rank's revisionist ideas, until, "upon reflection, he came to read Rank's emphatic, almost fanatical harping on the birth trauma as an intolerable abandonment of time-tested psychoanalytic insights" (476). In the end, Rank, together with his theory of the birth trauma, was effectively ejected from the European psychoanalytic community and shunted back to the United

[34] Peter Gay, *Freud: A Life for Our Time* (New York: Norton, 1988), 475. The paragraph that follows this citation is a synopsis of Gay's account of the Rank episode (470–89).

States, where he had already begun to earn considerable respect and a good living.

On the surface, at least, the outcome of the Rank affair can be read as a kind of "decision" handed down after due consideration by the high court of psychoanalysis on the subjects of the birth trauma and the general psychic primacy of Mother. In retrospect, however, this decision appears but symptomatic of Freudianism's own anxiety formations and repetition compulsions, thanks to which it effectively repressed or short-circuited its own train of associations whenever they led to woman, birth, or biological individuation. It is obvious that getting rid of Rank did not get rid of the question of the psychic significance of birth, or of the extra-oedipal meanings of woman. We are far from being "rid" of (although we are still ridden by) such questions. Indeed, sometimes it seems the only way to rid ourselves of the "question" of woman is to agree with Lacan, although not for the reasons he offers, that there is no such "thing" as woman. The only way to cease to be a problem may be to cease to be. Freud was relatively skilled, however, at keeping the problem of woman at bay. He managed to defend at least the manifest content of psychoanalytic discourse from most theoretical challenges to his precious "sexual aetiology."

Georg Groddeck was another of Freud's contemporaries who saw birth as more psychically significant than Freud did. Like Rank, Groddeck believed the intrauterine experience to be both the source of primal anxiety and the origin of primal pleasure. In his *Book of the It*, Groddeck wrote that behind the "Oedipus situation" is the "fear of incest with the mother," "the vilest of crimes, worse even than matricide."[35] Although, Groddeck argued, some "races . . . allow marriage between brother and sister," and others "give the marriageable daughter to be sexually initiated by her father," "never, since the beginning of the world and so long as it shall stand, is a son permitted to lie with his mother" (88):

[35] Georg Groddeck, *Das Buch vom Es* (Vienna: Psychoanalytischer Verlag, 1923). Translated by V. M. E. Collins as *The Book of the It* (London: Vision Press, 1949), 88. See Lawrence Durrell's introduction to the translation.

"Why should this be so? Tell me. Perhaps woman can throw more light on this than man. One fact remains: because every erection is desire for the mother, every erection, without exception, following the law of transference, is accompanied by the dread of castration" (88). Groddeck also "reasoned" that beginning life inside the mother made bisexuality natural. After all, as he put it, "not even the most passionate pederast has escaped the destiny of staying for nine months in the body of a woman" (202).

Groddeck was a physician who more or less converted to psychoanalysis. He came to believe that both "what we call physical, organic disease" and all "mental life is one continuous symbolization" expressed through us by an immanent cellular intelligence, which he called the "It" (230). Speaking in terms at once reminiscent of Freud, Lacan, and D. H. Lawrence, he disparages what he calls the "I"-consciousness:

> I am speaking intentionally of the "I"-consciousness as we grown-ups feel it. It is not absolutely certain that the newborn child is entirely without the consciousness of being an individual; indeed, I am inclined to think that he is so conscious, only that he cannot express himself in speech. I go so far as to believe that there is an individual consciousness even in the embryo, yes, even in the fertilized ovule, and in the unfertilized one too, as well as in the spermatozoon. And from that I argue that every single separate cell has this consciousness of individuality, every tissue, every organic system. In other words, every It unit can deceive itself into thinking, if it likes, that it is an individuality, a person, an "I." (239)

Freud admitted, and others have been happy to acknowledge, that his *es*, translated into "English"as the Latin *id* in *The Ego and the Id* (1932), is adapted from Groddeck. Freud's *id*, however, denotes the deepest psychic "unconscious," whereas for Groddeck every single cell has "consciousness" and is conscious of this consciousness, so that the body is in reality an infinite collection of "selves" already "thinking long before the brain comes into existence . . . thinking with-

out the brain" (223). Groddeck was "forced . . . to accept the
hypothesis" that the body is made of innumerable "It beings
belonging to the individual cells," each of which "conceals
within itself a male and a female It, as well as the tiny It
beings of the ancestral chain" (222). Groddeck's mention of
the "ancestral chain" recalls Weismann's "ancestral germ
plasms." Like Freud, Groddeck does not credit Weismann
where appropriate. In fact, in *The Germ-Plasm* Weismann
spoke of what he called "ids," a term meant to recall Nägeli's
cellular "idioplasms" but to expand upon their significance
by suggesting that "each idioplasm is composed of several or
many ids, which are capable of growth and multiplication by
division" (63). Weismann, then, uses the term "ids" to describe something like what we now know as the chromo-
somes, which he hypothesized must transmit "architectural"
information from one generation to the next. Weismann
made no mystical claims about cellular consciousness or
inherent sexuality. Perhaps this is why neither Freud nor
Groddeck saw fit to credit him.

In certain, at least superficial, respects Freud as a theorist
had more in common with Weismann, the rigorous yet imaginative biologist, than with Groddeck, the self-proclaimed
hysteric who told his readers that as a child he enjoyed pretending to be a girl by standing before the mirror with his
genitals tucked between his legs, and who as an adult became
an effective therapist when he realized how much he identified with his mother.[36] Groddeck's *Book of the It* takes the
form of an epistolary novel and explains to a general audience
that everything from breast cancer to syphilis is the work of
that "capricious, unaccountable, entertaining jester," the It
(238). Freud kept his distance from Groddeck, commending
his successes as an analyst, but never approving of his mysti-
cism or his reductionism. In effect, Freud steered a middle
course between the evolutionary materialism of Weismann
and the wild romanticism of Groddeck, writing in a letter to
Groddeck dated 18 June 1925, for example: "Everything from

[36] In the last quarter of *The Book of the It*, Groddeck explores these and
related subjects.

you is interesting to me, even if I may not follow you in detail. I do not, of course, recognise my civilised, bourgeois, demystified Id in your It. Yet you know that mine derived from yours."[37] Freud's "civilised, bourgeois, demystified Id" prefers not to recall its uncivilized beginnings inside the womb, let alone to its "ancestral" beginnings as ungendered idioplasm.

Both of these unthinkables continue to constitute the historically "abjected" truth of psychoanalytic discourse, even in the recent work of the psychoanalyst and theorist who invented this use of the word "abject." In *Powers of Horror* (1980) Julia Kristeva defines "the abject" as if it were the direct personal experience of what she named in *Revolution in Poetic Language* (1974) the *chora*.[38] *Chora* refers to the semiotic chaos of the subject who has not yet made the "thetic break" from the imaginary connection to the mother's body into the "symbolic" realm of language: "Language learning can therefore be thought of as an acute and dramatic confrontation between positing-separating-identifying and the motility of the semiotic *chora*. Separation from the mother's body, the *fort-da* game, anality and orality . . . all act as a permanent negativity that destroys the image and the isolated object even as it facilitates the articulation of the semiotic network, which will afterwards be necessary in the system of language where it will be more or less integrated as a *signifier*" (*Revolution* 47). Kristeva's discursive agenda in *Revolution* was the importance of the preoedipal mother-child relationship to establishing the subject's relation to the self, language, and the "world." As a theorist she helped expose the autocratic "paterialism" (Goux's term) of psychoanalytic narratives of subjectivity and its development. She redefined the "semiotic" as bodily rooted in the *chora* of the

---

[37] Georg Groddeck, *The Meaning of Illness: Selected Psychoanalytic Writings including His Correspondence with Sigmund Freud*, trans. Gertrud Mander, ed. Lore Schacht (London: Hogarth Press, 1977).

[38] Julia Kristeva, *Powers of Horror: An Essay on Abjection*, trans. Leon S. Roudiez (New York: Columbia University Press, 1982), and *Revolution in Poetic Language*, trans. Margaret Waller (New York: Columbia University Press, 1984).

mother's *materiality* and promised that no matter what tricks patriarchy might try to play on us the semiotic *chora* would continue, like the unpredictable body itself, to erupt into language.

Part of Kristeva's strategy in *Revolution* and elsewhere has been to distinguish between the phallus and the penis, taking seriously the idea that the phallus is not an organ but "a symbolic function—*the* symbolic function" which, upon "the discovery of [mother's] castration" (*Revolution* 47) "is established without regard to the anatomical difference of the sexes" (*Écrits* 282).[39] If, Kristeva implies, the phallus truly signifies the symbolic function itself, then as Lacan says neither sex has a privileged relation to it. If the phallus defines or governs relations among signs and signifieds as essentially (and essentialized, one might add) *linguistic* relations, then the "subject" too must be a function of syntax, in which case, again, female subjects have equal claim to the phallus. Indeed, recent work on the lesbian phallus explores this provocative line of reasoning.[40] I would like to point out, however, that this definition of the phallus as transcending gender, as potentially gender-neutral, depends not only on flirting with or ignoring the denotative and connotative history of the word, but also on affirming the myth of sexual nondifference upon which phallocratic culture has depended for its power over women and others.

Regarding the phallus as a symbol—as not referring to the penis—also affirms the pernicious reduction of difference per se to mere gender difference by claiming that language is a realm where difference is no longer anatomical or material. To make anatomical difference meaningless is, ironically, to erase psychoanalysis but not, alas, gender; but to say that anatomical difference just *is* the meaning of difference is to be a fundamentalist. Both of these extremes, however, are implied by

---

[39] Lacan, "The Signification of the Phallus," in *Écrits*, 281–91.

[40] Physically, the lesbian phallus can be represented as a dildo or other instrument or agent of penetration of woman by woman. Discursively, the lesbian phallus signifies lesbian subjectivity with full access to the so-called symbolic realm of language, family, sexuality, and culture.

what David Macey has called the "curious ontolinguistics" of
Jacques Lacan, which brings "man" into reflexive and narcissistic relation with "himself" as signifier.[41] The effect of this
ontolinguistics is, as Andrew Parker has suggested, to make
the body itself the "abject" of Lacanian theory, that is, "that
very 'something' which it cannot recognize as a thing and
still preserve its disciplinary integrity."[42]

To illustrate this point, on which I agree with Parker, I
quote the same passage he uses from Lacan's "Signification
of the Phallus" to show how Lacan, like any patriarchal auto-
crat, counts on the biological reference to the "turgid" penis
implicit in the supposedly logical signifier "phallus": "It can
be said that this signifier is chosen because it is the most
tangible element in the real of sexual copulation, and also
the most symbolic in the literal (typographical) sense of the
term, since it is equivalent there to the (logical) copula. It
might also be said that, by virtue of its turgidity, it is the
image of the vital flow as it is transmitted in generation"
(287). Kristeva, in turn, herself depends on this occultation
of the penis by the phallus, which she then rediscovers, tri-
umphantly as it were, inside the mother's body. The subject
in Kristeva's theory does not fare as well as the mother (who
is better off than the father, since she has her phallus and
eats it too). The subject-as-child finds itself defined as a
"twisted braid of affects," reminiscent, I would say, of an
umbilical cord pulsing with emotion, but not connected to
any reliable other, an umbilical cord to which the phallic
mother as much as the autocratic father denies being related
(*Powers of Horror* 1). No one wishes to claim, to "appropriate," even to identify with, the subject position of the child—
it is just too painful. But anyone can claim the "logical"
phallus and feel a certain heroism inheres in the act, like
Wart reaching for Excalibur.

Kristeva, in bad faith, speaks in *Powers of Horror* in the
voice of the semiotic subject mourning its phalluslessness,

---

[41] David Macey, *Lacan in Contexts* (London: Verso, 1988), 175.
[42] Andrew Parker, "Mom," in *Sexual Difference*, Special Issue of the
Oxford Literary Review 8, nos. 1–2 (1986): 102.

not recognizing the extent to which she has vilified her own vision of the body as defined by an otherness that precedes its entrance into the symbolic. Mary Jacobus suggests that according to Kristeva the child colludes with the mother's "imaginary desire for the phallus," an "archaic paternal space," in order to open a necessary space between itself and the mother. Insofar as the child identifies itself with that void rather than with the phallus, and feels itself to be, as a result, "not yet a subject" in relation to a mother who is "not yet an object," the child is the "abject": "The 'abject' is the most fragile, the most archaic, sublimation of an 'object' at the point where it is inseparable from instinctual drives; that is, the mother. . . . [There follows, however] a 'close combat' between a sort of subject that is not yet a subject and a mother who is not yet an object—'Repelling, rejecting; repelling itself, rejecting itself. Ab-jecting'—marks the self-differentiating movement which will install difference, and at the same time narcissism."[43] The abject is "at the border of [its] condition as a living being" at the very moment that its "body extricates itself, as being alive, from that border" (*Powers of Horror* 3). It seems disingenuous to claim as Kristeva does that the abject, defined as a state of liminal individuation, can find no "correlative, which, providing me with someone or something else as support, would allow me to be more or less detached and autonomous." This description fits perfectly if the placenta is taken as the first "something," the mother or other primary caretaker, as the first "someone," who functions as "correlative" and support for the "more or less" autonomous liminally individuated fetus, and the cutting of the umbilical cord as the moment when "necessary space" is inserted between mother and child.

Instead, once again the concept of the mother kowtows to the paternal, the patriarchal, the phallus it longs to be and have. This should come as no surprise, given that *Powers of*

---

[43] Mary Jacobus, "Madonna: Like a Virgin; or, Freud, Kristeva, and the Case of the Missing Mother," in *Sexual Difference*, 43.

Horror reads filth and abjection as represented in biblical and literary language as proto-sacral, a pit-stop on the road to the fulsomely religious and patriarchal representation of psychoanalysis and the analyst in her book *In the Beginning Was Love*. Kristeva suggests that Freud embodied the "culmination of the nihilist program" to "objectify man's being" and that it therefore devolves upon the psychoanalyst now to offer the patient faith in new beginnings, the hope of a new birth in the Father:[44] "Consubstantiality with the father, and identification with his name? Patients aspire to nothing else, and the process is at once essential to psychic maturation and a source of pleasure (through assumption of the father's power and elevation to the summit of authority). More than any other religion, Christianity has unravelled the symbolic and physical importance of the paternal function in human life. Identification with this third party separates the child from its jubilant but destructive physical relation with its mother and subjects it to another dimension where . . . language unfolds" (40). In this passage Kristeva manifests a retrograde misogyny and a complacent theodicy that call attention to the central concerns of this chapter (and of the book as a whole).

First, that in this passage Kristeva brands as dangerous the physical relation to the mother, but represents as natural the wish for "consubstantiality with the father, and identification with his name," indicates the phobic terror of the mother's body that psychoanalytic theory institutionalizes but neither addresses nor treats. Clearly, however, this fear is not peculiar to psychoanalysts, men, or fetishists, but is pandemic. Second, we see that psychoanalysis enables Kristeva to feel safe from the mother, and from herself as mother, by allowing her to feel that she, priestlike, confers upon her patients the experience of consubstantiality with the father through her ministrations. This patriarchal grandiosity casts yet more doubt on psychoanalysis as an extension of reli-

---

[44] Julia Kristeva, *In the Beginning Was Love: Psychoanalysis and Faith*, trans. Arthur Goldhammer (New York: Columbia University Press, 1987), 60.

gion in disguise, an extension that reaches right into the academy by means of literary theory's fascination with Lacanianism.[45] Third, the view of language sometimes implied by so-called high theory like Kristeva's, a view of language as the privileged medium, which permits identification to occur as a kind of "safe intercourse"[46] free from the trammels, taints, and politics of sexed bodies, is entirely unacceptable from a materialist, feminist, democratist perspective.

The penis may be as Lacan calls it, *a* (but not *the*) "logical copula" insofar as it does make possible conjunctions between one man's body and the body of another, male or female, in relation to which fantasies abound. Nevertheless, to assign, as psychoanalysis does, to the penis, "raised" to the symbolic function of the phallus, the status of universal signifier, the signifier of all possible conjunctions of bodies, is to make of it a fetish against the threat of its loss, and against the threat of the presence of the umbilical cord, eerily attached to us at the center of our physical being, yet attached at the other end to what or to whom—to God? to a soulmate? to chemistry? to, as the advertising slogan for one "900 number" promises, "your friend on the other end?"—we do not know. The phantom umbilical cord signifies our connection, or lack of it, to that which is and is not us. Do you feel "cut off" from others? (You are.) Do you feel that your very being leaks out of you every time you let down your guard? (It does, it does—even when your guard is up.)

The penis is not and never was the universal organ of connection. It is never even a temporary organ of connection between mothers and daughters, or women and women, or even, and this is most to the point because it is this relation upon which all psychoanalysis is based, between mothers and infant sons. Every single human being ever born, however, has been joined to its mother by an umbilical cord; or

[45] This seems to me true despite, not because of, Freud's efforts to free people from religion, efforts for which I for one remain grateful.

[46] Henry James uses "safe intercourse" to describe polite but relatively intense conversation in novels such as *The Ambassadors.*

rather, every single human being has been joined by an umbilical cord to a placenta, an organ discarded at birth and thus not even permanently part of the mother's body. Thanks to the umbilical cord, during gestation, the bodies of mother and baby are linked, but thanks to the selectivity of the placenta they are not identical. The umbilical cord thus defines difference in two ways which are not mutually exclusive, but rather co-constitutive. In utero the umbilical cord defines difference as separation. During a healthy pregnancy, "the embryo and foetus are quite well marked as 'other' by all the ordinary immunological critera." The fetus depends on this otherness to develop, but also on special antibodies manufactured for the occasion by the mother's immunological system to suppress recognition of this otherness and subsequent rejection of the fetus as foreign."[47]

Before continuing to explore the phenomenology of the umbilical cord, I shall complicate the discussion further by referring to the one location in psychoanalytic discourse in which an ambivalent interchange is described as structural rather than repressed or resolved into an equivalence. This discussion occurs in Freud's "Project for a Scientific Psychology" (1895), and it has nothing to do with sex or gender, but rather "neurones," which is no doubt why the ambivalence in question does not make Freud too anxious to speculate about it. Freud's plan in the "Project" is "to represent psychical processes as quantitatively determinate states of specifiable material particles, thus making those processes perspicuous and free from contradiction."[48] (In this case, getting rid of contradiction does not mean erasing ambivalence, but foregrounding it.) Although Freud did not have the technology to prove or disprove his theories, by means of inference and deduction he drew a picture of what he thought must go on in the nervous system, much of which has turned out to be quite to the point. In general it seemed to him that

[47] See Donna J. Haraway, *Simians, Cyborgs, and Women: The Reinvention of Nature* (New York: Routledge, 1991), 253 n. 8. I thank Ed Cohen for this reference.
[48] Freud, "Project for a Scientific Psychology" in *SE* 1:295.

energy must be circulated in the nervous system as the "flow" of "neuronal excitation," which alternately charged or "cathected" each neurone and then was released by it.

The movement of energy from neurone to neurone, as opposed to within the neurone, Freud thought, must take place across what he called "contact barriers": "The first justification for this hypothesis arises from the consideration that there the path of conduction passes through undifferentiated protoplasm instead of (as it otherwise does, within the neurone) through differentiated protoplasm, which is probably better adapted for conduction. This gives us a hint that conductive capacity is to be linked with differentiation, so that we may expect to find that the process of conduction itself will create a differentiation in the protoplasm and consequently an improved conductive capacity for subsequent conduction" (*SE* 1:298–99). In trying to figure out what goes on in the nervous system Freud's reasoning powers operate at full tilt, unhampered by his phobic masculinism, and perhaps even aided by it as he exercises his prerogative for "objectivity." When he imagines the objective material processes of the psyche, he conceives of it as an evolving economy driven by the ambivalence of neurones, that is, their conductivity and their differentiation. Furthermore, their conductivity, their capacity to communicate, to transmit energy and information, depends on their differentiation from one another. Not only that, but they contribute to one another's development: "Conduction itself will create a differentiation in the protoplasm and consequently an improved conductive capacity for subsequent conduction."

The conductivity-in-differentiation that Freud attributes to the neurones could also describe the interchange through the umbilical cord and placenta between the bodies of mother and child. Moreover, it offers a suggestive ungendered model, I think, for the democratic human interaction toward which we are working and thinking our various ways. At birth, of course, the umbilical cord is severed; from this point on the baby is not separated, but "individuated." The word "individual" originally meant indivisible, which is what one remains (give or take the loss of a limb or the addition of a prosthesis or two) until death. Individuation is a physical fact of existence, although we may experience ourselves emotionally as "separate" from a community of others with whom we might identify, or from loved ones.[49] The biochemical link of mother to infant diminishes after birth, as other foods replace breast milk. Since not all babies are breastfed by their mothers, *the umbilical cord is the only universal biological organ of connection.* Why hasn't this organ been fetishized, let alone included, in psychoanalytic organ phenomenology?

The most obvious answer has to do with the masculinism of psychoanalysis, for which "the penis is always the leading erogenous zone" for both sexes, and what seems to be in psychoanalysis as in our culture as a whole "the narcissistic impossibility . . . of calling back into question the value of the phallus, and only of the phallus, that penis with which benevolent and tender Nature has endowed her sons."[50] Even the cultural gynophobia to which theorists beginning with Karen Horney attributed this masculinism, represents only a reflection not the cause or explanation of phallocentrism. Psychoanalysis does attribute structural symbolic significance to the primal organic connection of the infant to the mother, but only in terms of a return to the womb. This psychoanalytic myth may differ in many respects from the surreal misogyny of the Christian vision of the womb as the first of death's incestuous haunts, and yet Kristeva's way of thinking reminds us that the two views have much in common.

In his self-styled funeral sermon called "Death's Duel" (1630), for example, which he delivered a few days before his death wrapped in his burial shroud, John Donne described birth as the first step toward reentry into that grave from which he just emerged. Death is but the final insult since

[49] Richard Goldwater's "Maieutic Psychiatry" explores, as an aspect of dualism vs. monism, the distinction between *separation* (as the self/other relation of identification) and *individuation* (as the sexual/aggressive mode of the every ego for itself).
[50] Sarah Kofman, *The Enigma of Woman: Woman in Freud's Writing,* trans. Catherine Porter (Ithaca: Cornell University Press, 1985), 134, 92.

there he will be forced to share the womb with his relatives
in the "miserable incest" involuntarily suffered in the grave,
"when the same worm must be my mother, and my sister
and myself! . . . when I must be married to my mother and
my sister, and be both father and mother to my own mother
and sister."[51] This horror follows inevitably from the fact of
birth, which was, after all, according to doctrine, but the
introitus in mortem. Birth is but issue and deliverance "from
that death, the death of the womb, is an entrance, a deliver-
ing over to another death, the manifold deaths of this world;
we have a winding-sheet in our mother's womb which grows
with us from our conception, and we come into the world
wound up in that winding-sheet, for we come to seek a
grave" (169–170). Donne sees the umbilical cord as the
"winding sheet" with which every fetus is equipped from the
moment of conception. From that moment until resurrection, as it seems to Donne, "man" is cannibalized by a series
of involuntary identities with parents and siblings, to be re-
deemed only by a "blessed dependency . . . upon him that
hangs upon the cross. . . . [and] there suck at his wounds . . .
till he vouchsafe you a resurrection and an ascension" (189).

It would be easy to read these passages from a Kleinian perspective, which might see Donne's redemptive itinerary as a
movement from the "bad breast" of woman to the "good
breast" of Jesus. Like Freud, Ernest Jones speculated at length
concerning what he took to be the psychosexual etiology of
religion, and from a point of view different from Freud's,
since he was not Jewish. But Jones, like Kristeva, seems less
to explain religion from the point of psychoanalysis, than to
construct the two as twinned ideologies. Jones, writing in
1914, stated that "Protestantism . . . ma[de] this final step in
the evolution of a purely androgenic procreation myth, which
has ended in a universal feminine protest in the countries
professing this faith,"[52] protest, presumably, such as Klein's.
Protestantism, according to Jones, revolted in horror from

51 John Donne, in *Devotions upon Emergent Occasions* (Ann Arbor:
University of Michigan Press, 1959), 176.
52 Ernest Jones, "Madonna's Conception through the Ear: A Contribution

earlier kinds of Christian faith, which were too close to their psychosexual roots. The Holy Ghost of the Catholic Trinity, for example, according to Jones, who seems to think he speaks as a post-Protestantist, represented a masculine transmutation of the phallic mother who had been highly visible in the ancient religions, but a transmutation not masculine enough for the highly gynophobic Protestants.

The anguished ecstasy with which Donne clings to a bleeding Christ as to a nursing mother would perhaps, according to Jones's interpretation, be evidence of his early training as a Catholic. Be that as it may, I add my voice to the "protest" within psychoanalytic theory by protesting against the resacralization of the phallic mother by anyone. Donne's nightmare vision of helpless entanglement in the umbilical cord, and involuntary incest in the womb, are terrors not far below the "surface" of Christian theology or psychoanalytic theory. The fantasy of coupling and commingling, which Donne calls anathema, Freud calls human nature. When Freud, in his essay "The 'Uncanny,'" tells us stories about the return to the womb, they are always confirmations or inversions of the repressed wish to go "home" to the mother's genitals rather than to Jesus: "It often happens that neurotic men declare that they feel there is something uncanny about the female genital organs. This *unheimlich* place, however, is the entrance to the former *Heim* [home] of all human beings, to the place where each one of us lived once upon a time and in the beginning. There is a joking saying that 'Love is home-sickness.'"[53] In this fairy tale a little tiny neurotic man gets to go back to where we all lived once upon a time, the place, Freud implies, toward which every man in love is headed in his dreams. He is headed home, ostensibly to reproduce heterosexuality in the Freudian version of a salvation narrative, albeit the salvation of the species defined in Darwinian terms. This is one dream woman can have too, although, of course, she *is* the home in

---

to the Relation between Aesthetics and Religion," in *Essays in Applied Psychoanalysis* (New York: International Universities Press, 1964), 2:326.

[53] Freud, "The 'Uncanny,'" in *SE* 17:245.

question. (If you lived *here*, you'd be [the] home now.) In *The Interpretation of Dreams*, for instance, Freud offers several examples of "pretty" dreams by female patients about water, which he claims are about giving birth (*SE* 5:400–404). Males, on the other hand, who fantasize literally about being inside their mothers' wombs, according to Freud in "From the History of an Infantile Neurosis," identify with the mother and desire to replace her in the primal scene by receiving the father's penis (welcome home, Dad) and giving *him* a child—as if the penis *could* enter the womb![54]

One reason we find these stories of incestuous habitation of the mother repulsive may be our repressed knowledge that indeed we have been there before. Each of us performed an involuntary intercourse with the mother as we emerged through her, linked by the umbilical cord, an organ that protrudes at birth from the mother's "forfended place" like a bloody phallus with a child at the other end. Does the boy child fantasize that his penis is a remnant of this "copula"? (Otto Rank thought so.) Is that why he feels so "implicated" in the sinful materiality of femininity?

More to the point, should we replace the phallus with the umbilical cord as the universal "copula," so that where phallus was, there umbilical cord shall be? Yes *and* no. First, yes for if we must have an organic "objective correlative" for the phantasmic connection human beings can feel or miss, the umbilical cord is a much more logical choice than the phallus; *everybody* had one and *everybody* lost one. Next, yes for feminist reasons. The phallus has been and remains the sign of hierarchical patriarchal positivist oppression and no amount of "appropriating" the phallus can change that; the phallus cannot include woman—it can only "govern" her "relations" (Lacan "The Signification of the Phallus," 289). Yet, fortunately, the umbilical cord is too ugly, too abject, too parasitical, too much like tripe to essentialize as the phallus has been essentialized. Admitting its universality and the universality of its loss might help put Mother and the

[54] Freud, "From the History of an Infantile Neurosis," in *SE* 17:100–104.

Governor in perspective. Both need to be relieved of their status as essentialized and vilified. But, no because one must always say "no" to a universal signifier, "no" to any fantasy of totality—the umbilical cord is discarded at birth. Humanity has had plenty of universal signifiers, and none have turned out to be either universal or as significant as promised.

One recurrent theme in the critiques of psychoanalysis over the years has been that psychoanalysis fancies itself the totality fit to replace God. The case of Dora's analysis is perhaps the most familiar instance of Freud's hermeneutic authoritarianism. Freud's insistence on the transparent meaning of her every word, every dream, every gesture, despite her protests that he did not understand her or do her justice, cost him her trust and that of many readers. In *The Interpretation of Dreams*, the foundational text of psychoanalysis, Freud contends that the mind is by nature formal and formalist (*SE* 4:329). It reacts "to everything that is simultaneously present in the sleeping mind as currently active material" by manufacturing its coherence (*SE* 4:228). The mind cannot do otherwise. To manufacture this coherence constitutes "necessity" in the unconscious: "The dream-work is under the necessity of combining into a unity all instigations to dreaming which are active simultaneously" (*SE* 4:228).

But in section 7 of *The Interpretation of Dreams*, Freud admits that "the question whether it is possible to interpret *every* dream must be answered in the negative" (*SE* 5:524). It may be "always possible to go *some* distance" in interpreting it, enough, at least "to convince ourselves that the dream is a structure with a meaning," and probably "far enough to get a glimpse of what that meaning is" (*SE* 5:25). But "there is often a passage in even the most thoroughly interpreted dream which has to be left obscure; this is because we become aware during the work of interpretation that at that point there is a tangle of dream-thoughts which cannot be unravelled and which moreover adds nothing to our knowledge of the content of the dream. This is the dream's navel, the spot where it reaches down into the unknown" (*SE* 5:525). The dream's navel is its "unplumbable spot," the spot where the dream thoughts "cannot, from the nature of things, have any definite endings"(*SE* 4:111n). On the contrary, they "branch out in every direction" into the psyche from which, if the "meshwork" of thought is "particularly close," the "dream-wish grows up, like a mushroom out of its mycelium" (*SE* 5:525).

The dream sprouts like a mushroom out of the complex darkness of the dream thoughts, a darkness that even Freud's night vision cannot always penetrate. Freud describes the point at which his insight fails as the "navel" of the dream, "the spot where it reaches down into the unknown" and he cannot reach down after it. Invoking the "navel" as the privileged figure of the uninterpretable cannot fail to be significant in the discourse that above all others finds anatomical detail significant. Given the phobic unknowability of the mother in psychoanalysis, given the fishy silence on the part of these erudite physicians concerning the organ that connects mother to baby, it matters that Freud chooses the "navel" as the figure of the unknowable, the untouchable, the untranslatable "spot" in the psyche. Even when Freud does not know he knows better than anyone. He puts his finger on the very spot he has spotted with utmost clarity as unrecognizable: the spot where psychoanalysis stares blankly at what it chooses not to know. For what else could be at the other end of this umbilical cord, were Freud to haul it in, hand over hand, following the line of its logic backward to his origin, but the mother and the placenta, the image of his own ambivalent likeness to the inorganic.

When Is a Weltanschauung Not a Weltanschauung?
When It's a Fetish.

According to psychoanalysis, which, at least in its Freudian version, insists upon the consubstantiality of *psyche* and *soma*, the very processes of "stimulus, substitution, conversion and discharge" Freud attributes in the "Project for a Scientific Psychology" to the activities of neurones, also characterize the psychosexual imagination (*SE* 1:295). Relative to *The Interpretation of Dreams*, Freud's earlier papers articulate such processes more in terms of systems of "ideas" and "conceptions" than of words, images, and syntax. It is not surprising, therefore, that literary theory often ignores the early papers of psychoanalysis, which seem cluttered with quasi-Lockean perceptual vocabulary rather than the more familiar twentieth-century language of "representation" and "construction."[55] Nevertheless, the early pieces reveal that from its inception psychoanalysis has understood the fundamental activity of both the "normal" infantile psyche and that of the adult "pervert" to be the production of equivalence through those processes of substitution we now think of loosely as "identification." In this concluding section of the present chapter I sketch the poetics and problematics of the taxonomy of equivalence effects—and in particular their totalization as "the fetish"—which I take to be paradigmatic of psychoanalysis (and of literary modernism generally), effects to be explored in greater detail in the chapters to follow.

In an early encyclopedia entry titled "Hysteria" (1888), Freud points out that hysterical paralyses cannot be attributed to organic causes because "hysterical paralyses take no account of the anatomical structure of the nervous system which, as is well known, shows itself most unambiguously in the distribution of organic paralyses."[56] In "Some Points for a Comparative Study of Organic and Hysterical Motor Paralyses" (1893), Freud responds even more emphatically to those physicians who were still hunting for organic lesions to explain hysterical phenomena: "I, on the contrary, assert that the lesion in hys-

[55] One early work that still enlightens, especially in feminist contexts, is Sigmund Freud's *Studies in Hysteria* (1895), written with Josef Breuer. Frank J. Sulloway's book *Freud, Biologist of the Mind: Beyond the Psychoanalytic Legend* (New York: Basic Books, 1979) has reminded readers of the early "crypto-biological" work.

[56] Freud, "Hysteria," in *SE* 1:46. Freud's editors attribute this entry to Freud and include it in the *Standard Edition* because of its characteristic style, concerns, and the evidence in it of Freud's recent studies under Charcot and Breuer. The point I take from it is reiterated elsewhere in Freud's early work.

terical paralyses must be completely independent of the anatomy of the nervous system, since *in its paralyses and other manifestations hysteria behaves as though anatomy did not exist or as though it has no knowledge of it.*"[57] It is this conviction which enables Freud to "move on to psychological ground," where he follows Janet in asserting that hysteria follows the "popular conception of the organs and of the body" rather than anatomical fact (*SE* 1:170).

Rather than a lesion in the organic tissue, a lesion in "the *conception,* the *idea,* of the arm," rather than in the arm itself is the cause of hysterical paralysis, a lesion which corresponds to "the abolition of the associative accessibility of the conception of the arm," which "behaves as though it did not exist for the play of associations." He emphasizes that the arm can be inaccessible to association "without its material substratum (the nervous tissue of the corresponding region of the cortex) being damaged" (*SE* 1:170). The reader can no doubt see the problems that arise from a statement like this. On the one hand Freud describes the activity of mind as if it were independent of its material substratum, yet on the other, he describes the activity of mind as having physiological consequences, suggesting, perhaps, that mind and body have an ambivalent, and not an equivalent, relation to each other. At the very least, this account of the "hysterical lesion" disrupts the correspondences between mind and body, idea and referent, upon which medicine, including neurology, had relied for its understanding.

Disrupting correspondence is precisely what Freud means to do when, also in the "Comparative Study," Freud declares that the term *representation paralysis* describes cerebral paralyses better than, say, "projection paralysis" because, although "each element of the periphery [of the body] corresponds to an element in the grey matter of the [spinal] cord," "the reproduction of the periphery in the cortex is no longer a faithful reproduction point by point[;] . . . it is no longer a

---

[57] Freud, "Some Points for a Comparative Study of Organic and Hysterical Motor Paralyses," in *SE* 1:169; Freud's emphasis.

true projection" but much more complex (*SE* 1:161; Freud's emphasis). Hysteria does not, as indicated above, "correspond," "project," or, we might add, refer or express, in any simple determined way; it is a form of representation paralysis in which what is manifest results from a local cessation of what should ideally be the unblocked conductivity of ideas. The "Project for a Scientific Psychology" complicates this picture of wounded conceptions further with the information that "ideas which in other people have no consequences and of whose importance we can make nothing" can become "excessively intense" in the mind of the compulsive hysteric to the point that this idea seems incongruous or absurd to anyone not so affected (*SE* 1:348).

Upon analysis, however, Freud tells us, the "excessively intense" idea turns out to be a substitute for some other, quite sensible one. The schematization of substitution and symbol formation Freud offers at this point is so lucid (if suspiciously so) and so fundamental to the rest of psychoanalysis and psychoanalytic theory in all its variants that I shall quote it here at length. In what follows Freud shows how excessively intense idea *A* comes to stand in for the "real" problem, idea *B*, a substitution formation "cured" by its analysis:

> Before the analysis, *A* is an excessively intense idea, which forces its way into consciousness too often, and each time gives rise to weeping. The subject does not know why he weeps at *A*; he regards it as absurd but cannot prevent it.
>
> After the analysis, it has been discovered that there is an idea *B*, which justifiably gives rise to weeping and which justifiably recurs frequently so long as a certain complicated psychical action has not been performed against it by the subject. The effect of *B* is not absurd; it is intelligible to the subject and can even be combated by him.
>
> *B* stands in a particular relation to *A*.
>
> For there has been an occurrence which consisted of *B* + *A*. *A* was an incidental circumstance; *B* was appropriate for producing the lasting effect. The reproduction of this event in memory has now taken a form of such a kind that it is as though *A* had

stepped into *B*'s place. *A* has become a substitute, a *symbol* for
B. Hence the incongruity. (*SE* 1:349; Freud's emphasis)

The last part of this passage is the most important here: "It is
as though *A* had stepped into *B*'s place. *A* has become a substitute, a symbol for *B*." The accessibility of the patient to
his own thought process is blocked by a symbol that has
stepped in to conceal or disguise an idea by representing it
otherwise. Idea *A* is thus whisked out of circulation and its
absence is concealed by idea *B* to which it remains clandes-
tinely connected.

In this formulaic description it is easy to see how *A* has
come to substitute for *B*. That is, Freud makes it seem simple with the word "incidental": "*A* was an incidental cir-
cumstance; *B* was appropriate for producing the lasting
effect." No one has yet figured out what such an incidental
relation between an idea and its symbol might be, although
plenty, including Freud, have tried. In every case something
remains unexplained or undescribed. Nevertheless, in the
case of psychoanalysis itself, this very argument is "an excessively intense idea" that symbolizes the "not absurd," the
"intelligible," idea that the phallus, itself an "excessively
intense idea," has been substituted for the umbilical cord.

In *The Interpretation of Dreams*, the reader can see the
lack of this umbilical cord between the mother and the
infant, who, unable to reconnect with the mother's body at
will, finds a hallucinatory substitute for her in thumbsuck-
ing and fantasy, which psychoanalysis regards as the subject's first acts of symbolization. In its earliest instances of
wishing, Freud hypothesizes, the infant, who retains a "mne-
mic image" of (possibly mythical) occasions when his instincts were satisfied, revives and "recathects" the memory
of satisfaction in the hope this will bring about a repetition of
the happy event. When the external world fails to respond, as
it inevitably does, the infant will try to establish a "perceptual identity" between the wished-for and the experienced by
traveling "the short path of regression" toward hallucination,
where ideas are thing-like, more like "presentations" than

"representations" (*SE* 5:565–66). The need, however, will persist, since substitution is never complete.

The theoretical example of the infant seeking a "perceptual identity" between a mental representation, and its mother, is for Freud the beginning of a lifetime of such wishes active in the psyche as chains of substitutions. In her accounts of infantile psychosexuality Melanie Klein describes the normal babe as a sadistic cannibal for whose psyche such substitutive satisfactions are the usual fare. This preoedipal stage is "a period when sadism predominates," inaugurated "by oral sadism (with which urethral, muscular, and anal sadism associate themselves)."[58] The child's dominant desire at this time is to destroy the mother, to rip her open to find her imagined contents (i.e. the father's penis, excrement, children, food) and also implicitly to destroy the father, whom he expects to find inside the mother, as well as himself, who is also "inside" her. Preoedipal erotism is active "at all the various sources of libidinal pleasure," Klein argues, expanding the "classic" psychoanalytic equation penis = child to include penis = child = feces = food = nipple = father (219).[59] Klein, perhaps more than any other theorist, demotes the phallus from its position as His Majesty the Signifier, contending instead that infants of both sexes identify most intensely with the mother's breasts and nipples, thus privileging *them* as signifiers. Klein does not see babies or even children as particularly concerned with the genitals of either sex, but sees "the deprivation of the breast as the most fundamental cause of the turning to the father," not the mother's lack of a penis.[60]

58 Melanie Klein, "The Importance of Symbol-Formation in the Development of the Ego" (1930), in *Love, Guilt, and Reparation and Other Works 1921–1945*, vol. 1 of *The Writings of Melanie Klein* (New York: Free Press, 1984), 232.

59 For classic Freudian formulations of this classic equivalence, see Sigmund Freud, "On the Sexual Theories of Children," in *SE* 9:205–26; "Some Psychical Consequences of the Anatomical Distinction between the Sexes," in *SE* 19:241–60, especially 256–57; and "Female sexuality," in *SE* 21:221–46.

60 Melanie Klein, "Early Stages of the Oedipus Conflict" (1928), in *Writings*, 1:186–98.

Here Lacan's notion of the "logical copula" is handy to describe not the phallus or any particular organ but rather the "=" that refers to their shared substitutibility. In Klein's fantastical equation the subject indeed includes itself as a signifier interchangeable with the father's penis, the mother's breast and nipple, with its and its parents' excrement, with its mother's real and possible children all lumped together, and all of these in turn with edible (and excretable) substances. According to Klein, this is as it should be. The psychosexual appetite of the infant must be enormous to satisfy the ravenous "metabolism of images" responsible for the growth and development of individual consciousness and personality.[61] Again, Klein has written more unflinchingly than anyone about this hungry "metabolism" in "The Importance of Symbol-Formation in the Development of the Ego" (1930), in which we learn that the "earliest defense set up by the ego is directed against the subject's own sadism and the object attacked, both of these being regarded as sources of danger" (232). These sadisms, these anxieties, Klein argues, contribute to the formation of the ego and the symbolizing faculties peculiar to the healthy creative human consciousness. Not only simple libidinal interest, but also the anxiety arising in this phase of oral/anal sadism, sets in motion the mechanism of identification and, in turn, of symbol formation:

> Since the child desires to destroy the organs (penis, vagina, breasts) which stand for the objects, he conceives a dread of the latter. This anxiety contributes to make him equate the organs in question with other things; owing to this equation these in their turn become objects of anxiety and so he is impelled constantly to make other and new equations, which form the basis of his interest in the new objects and of symbolism.
>
> Thus, not only does symbolism come to be the foundation of all fantasy and sublimation but, more than that, it is the basis of the subject's relation to the outside world and to reality in general. (220)

[61] Jacques Lacan and Wladimir Granoff, "Fetishism: The Symbolic, the Imaginary, and the Real," in *Perversions: Psychodynamics and Therapy*, ed. Sandor Lorand and Michael Balint (New York: Gramercy, 1956), 267, 268.

The mother's body (together with its imagined contents) is therefore both the object of sadistic fantasies and the source of anxious concern. The child normally, necessarily, equates the mother's body with the outside world, which, in Klein's view, becomes "the mother's body in an extended sense" (232).

Development requires "sadistic appropriation and exploration of the mother's body and of the outside world." To accomplish this the subject establishes "symbolic relation to the things and objects representing the contents of the mother's body and hence . . . [its] relation [to its] environment and to reality" (232). This structural impulse to explore and appropriate objects by establishing symbolic relations to them Klein terms "epistemophilia," or love of knowing. The curiosity of a child is thus felt as the need to scan the world for symbols, which according to Klein, enables the child to feel he knows things. The healthy epistemophiliac finds and makes ever new symbols and thus feels securely connected to its "environment and to reality" because mental health encourages the development of "kindly imagos" that is, of highly individualized, even idiosyncratic, yet variable symbols.[62] Klein's theory is the inverse of Freud's. According to Freud's theories of sexual development, the significance of the boy's penis and the fear of losing it propel him to sublimate his desires for the Mother and head off into the "world" to become a cultural worker where he may reencounter his old wishes in the form of the uncanny. If we listen to Klein with an equally reductive ear, we may feel that the best the child can aspire to is to lay claim to the world as an uncanny place to be explored at leisure. Both Freud and Klein offer a surreal vision of the world as a uterus from which there is no exit and a breast to which there is no return. Both assume that every child begins the world as half of a luxuriously intimate reflexive dyad that remains the model for knowing, being, desiring, and doing ever after.

Needless to say, as the passage from Donne showed, this vision is not new or unique to psychoanalysis, nor did psy-

[62] See Melanie Klein, "Personification in the Play of Children" (1929), in *Writings*, 1:199–209.

choanalysis invent the imaginary interchangeability of body parts. Just one passage from Wendy Donager O'Flaherty's compendium of the "use of sexual metaphors and animal symbols to express religious concepts of the relationships between men and women, gods and goddesses, and humans and deities" (ix) suffices to disabuse us of such a notion: "In Australian puberty rites, the male undergoes both circumcision and, a year later, subincision, to open a 'penis womb,' a symbolical male vagina. . . . Géza Røheim even suggests that by means of this ritual 'a vaginal father' replaces the 'phallic mother' of the infantile situation. . . . (This interpretation, it must be cautioned, has been open to challenge; some have suggested that the subincision wound is intended to simulate the pocket of a kangaroo.)"[63]

A kangaroo? In the set of rituals and rites known as psychoanalysis, then Freud and Klein may be the phallic mother and vaginal father (though which is which I cannot say). Together, they epitomize the psychoanalytic view of the Anglo-European nuclear family as seen self-consciously from complementary "masculine" and "feminine," patriarchal and maternal, perspectives. To see them this way is to historicize psychoanalysis as being the specific self-reflection of the overripe bourgeois nuclear family as it entered its decadence at about the turn of this century.

On the other hand, there being no radical discontinuity between the present and the recent past in which the institutions of the family and psychoanalysis both evolved, we might as well make use of those ideas and vocabularies we have. "Epistemophilia" is one term too useful to discard, for it dignifies work as the search for "kindly imagos," a gently driven adult form of work as play. In relation to epistemophilia, a brief comparison between Freud's and Klein's understandings of the term reveals one more ambivalence in psychoanalysis, an ambivalence "resolved" by means of yet another equivalence effect, this time between "perversion" and "infantilism." [64] The

[63] Wendy Donager O'Flaherty, *Women, Androgynes, and Other Mythical Beasts* (Chicago: University of Chicago Press, 1980), 288-89.
[64] In "Notes upon a Case of Obsessional Neurosis," for example, Freud pos-

ambivalence in question concerns the status and even the ethics of abstract thinking, which in turn calls attention to certain persistent problems in our critique of ideology, and our ideology of critique. No one has determined the precise relation between ideas and their "material substratum" or between language and the world. *Is* language the world? Can abstract language be political? Is language more material when it is about "experience" or history or economics than when it is about language? Are theorists perverts? (Are perverts the real theorists?) Are anti-theorists perverts? Both? Neither?

By using the term epistemophilia the way she does, Klein valorizes the human propensity to seek and make meaning as a variety of the instinct for self-preservation, what Donna Haraway might call our need for "survivable stories."[65] According to Kleinian logic we ourselves make the psychic road we travel as we leave "home," laying down brick after brick of symbols and substitutions. For Freud epistemophilia signifies the perverse eroticization of thinking that all too easily tempts us to stray too far away from "home" and Mother in search of one idea with which to replace her. In "The Project for Scientific Psychology," when Freud describes hysteria as compulsive symbol formation, he confesses that noncompulsive symbol formation normally goes on all the time. For the hysteric the symbol replaces the thing for which it ostensibly stood: "The knight who fights for his lady's glove *knows*, in the first place, that the glove owes its importance to the lady; and secondly, he is in no way prevented by his adoration of the glove from thinking of the lady and serving her in other respects. The *hysteric*, who weeps at *A*, is quite

---

ited "the sexual instinct of . . . knowing" and called it the "epistemophilic instinct." He argued that in an "obsessional patient" given to "brooding" and dominated by his "epistemophilic instinct," the thought process itself becomes sexualized, for the sexual pleasure which is normally attached to the content of thought becomes shifted on to the act of thinking itself" (*SE* 10:248).

[65] A phrase Haraway used in a talk titled "Theory in the Figure: Feminist Figures for Unmanly Worlds," given 9 April, 1991 at Rutgers University sponsored by the Center for the Critical Analysis of Contemporary Culture.

unaware that he is doing so on account of the association
A–B, and B itself plays no part at all in his psychical life. The
symbol has in this case taken the place of the *thing* entirely"
(*SE* 1:349; Freud's emphasis). At first sight Freud's example of
the knight who fights for his lady's adorable glove seems
more suitable as an example of the fetishist than of the "normal" man. But his sly comment that the knight is not "prevented by his adoration of the glove from thinking of the lady
and serving her in other respects" puts the emphasis squarely
back on the normalcy, from the point of sexology, of these
other forms of service. The whole passage is a near parody of
Richard von Krafft-Ebing's definition of the fetishist.

Krafft-Ebing, professor of psychiatry and a colleague of
Sigmund Freud at the University of Vienna, was considered
by most of his contemporaries to be "the true founder of
modern sexual pathology."[66] The first edition of his famous
Psychopathia Sexualis, a clinical analysis and formal classifi-
cation of the major perversions, was published in 1886, the
year Freud, then thirty years old, married and opened his
medical practice in Vienna, and twelve years before the publication of Freud's first work directly concerned with sexuality. In
the section of *Psychopathia Sexualis* concerned with *fetishism*,
a term first applied to psychopathology by the French psychologist Alfred Binet (1857–1911),[67] Krafft-Ebing describes the behavior of thirty-six "pathological" fetishists, men whose sexual interest is limited exclusively to "the idea of certain portions of the female person, or . . . [to] certain articles of
female attire."[68] These men carry to violent extremes their
partialities: the lover of kid-gloves, the collector of ladies'

---

[66] See Chapter 8, "Freud and the Sexologists," in Sulloway, *Freud, Biologist of the Mind* (New York: Basic Books, 1979), for an introduction to "the
nascent science of sexology," in which "almost every element of Freud's theory of child sexuality was exactly anticipated, or in some way implied or suggested, before him" (279).

[67] Alfred Binet, "Le Fétichisme dans l'amour," in *Revue Philosophique* 24
(1887): 143–67, 252–74.

[68] Richard von Krafft-Ebing, *Psychopathia Sexualis: With Especial
Reference to the Antipathic Sexual Instinct, a Medico-Forensic Study*, 12th
ed., trans. Franklin S. Klaf (New York: Bell, 1965), 143.

handkerchiefs, the despoiler of feminine tresses, the shoe fetishist, the lover of fur-pieces, all have their places in this taxonomy, and seem by turns tragic and comical.

Yet it is unjust, Krafft-Ebing writes, in accord with Binet, absolutely to distinguish "them" (i.e., perverts) from "us" ("normal" folk). What he calls the "physiological" or normal fetishist differs only in degree from the "pathological" one. The "physiological " fetishist is any man—in effect, every-man—who prefers a certain part of the female body having a "direct relation to sex (as have the breasts and external geni-tals)" and "particularly . . . a certain form of this part" (143–44). Every man, Krafft-Ebing tells us, in other words, who is a "thigh man" or a "breast man," or who prefers cer-tain womanly shapes over others, is a "physiological" fe-tishist. This kind of fetishism may even be regarded "as the real principle of individualism in love"(143). Furthermore, any man may carry his enthusiasm to such a pitch that his sexual fervor may remind us of the "worship . . . [of] relics, holy objects, etc., in religious cults" without seeming unduly romantic (143).

When Freud, in *Three Essays on the Theory of Sexuality,* writes in passages partly quoted earlier in this chapter, that normality, neurosis, and perversion abide together on one con-tinuum, one "unbroken chain," he warns us, using the same categories as Krafft-Ebing, not to invite the "insoluble diffi-culties [we face] as soon as we try to draw a sharp line to dis-tinguish mere variations within the range of what is physio-logical from pathological symptoms" (*SE* 7:161). Perversion is to some extent, then, by definition, normal; even so, in cer-tain cases most of us would feel entirely justified in cutting the "chain" that links the normal with the perverse. This is especially so, Freud writes, "where (as, for instance, in cases of licking excrement or of intercourse with dead bodies) the sexual instinct goes to astonishing lengths in successfully overriding the resistances of shame, disgust, horror, or pain" (*SE* 7:161). These acts "are so far removed from the normal in their content that we cannot avoid pronouncing them 'patho-logical.'" But just what is it that makes these acts seem unequivocally pathological? Freud suggests, in the lines just quoted, two possible answers to this question, neither of which is, as far as he is concerned, the right one. One is simply the "content" of these perversions, which is "so far removed from the normal" that its perversity is self-evident. The logic of this explanation is, of course, circular; it is not enough to say that something is perverse because it is not normal. The second explanation is a bit more precise: an act is perverse when it is performed in vigorous defiance of "the resistances of shame, disgust, horror, or pain." Here too, however, the logic is circular. This second explanation is merely a moralized version of the first; it is not enough to say that an act is perverse because it negates those resistances which we consider "normal."

To answer the question of what constitutes "pathological" perversion we return to Krafft-Ebing, who suggests that we can distinguish between "physiological" (or normal) fetishism and "pathological" (or perverse) fetishism "through gradual transitions" from one to the other because the pathological fetishist concentrates his sexual interest "on a certain portion of the body that has no direct relation to sex."[69] The pathological fetishist, in other words, is he who ceases to be "physiological," he whose sexual interest strays "through gradual transitions" away from "breasts and external genitals" toward "the idea" of a part of a female; he strays from an entity we presumably would all agree was "physiological" to something that took its place as the object of desire: an "idea." He who replaces the real with the ideal—the actual with the symbolic—is, in short, perverse.[70] Furthermore, the farther he strays toward the "ideal" the more perverse he is. As Freud puts it, "it is perhaps in connection precisely with the most repulsive perversions that the mental factor must be regarded as playing its largest part in the transformation of the sexual instinct" (*SE* 7:161).

[69] Krafft-Ebing originally argued that fetishism, like other perversions, was congenital, caused by "hereditary taint," until, in response to Binet's objections, he began to claim that fetishism, unlike other perversions, was caused "environmentally" and seemingly by "chance."

[70] By this logic Jacques Lacan's psychoanalytic theory posits the perverse

It is the "mental factor," Freud would have us believe, that is, the unusual degree to which the "mind" is involved, which characterizes perversity according to this logic, and not that perverts act out what the rest of us merely fantasize. It is, furthermore, the degree to which the ideal replaces the so-called real (or physiological) as the object of our desire and interest, and the possibly excessive value with which we invest our favorite ideas, which makes our "mental work" perverse. Alfred Binet, who first used the term "fetishism" to link religious practices to sexual rituals, found "abstraction" and "idealization" to characterize the mental habits of the pathological fetishist. "Abstraction" refers to how the fetishist "isolates" the "loved object, even if it is part of a person's body," so that for him it constitutes "an independent whole."[71] "Idealization" indicates the excessive value with which the fetishist invests the abstraction he adores. Binet noticed that the intelligent patient ("un malade intelligent") was especially vulnerable to the inevitable disappointments of idealization, and thus to this kind of pathology. One of his patients was a hand fetishist for whom even the loveliest hand "remained always inferior to the image he had made of it."[72]

"Abstraction" and "idealization" are terms that show at a glance that Binet conceived of fetishism as if it were an intellectual disorder, as if fetishism were actually a pathological metaphysical passion, or even a pathological passion for metaphysics. And this makes a degree of sense if we think of fetishism as an excessive belief in the symbols we make, or rather a denial of the fact that they are symbols. Fetishism expresses the desire to take these symbols literally; it insists

---

as the normal, since it posits as necessary the fact that we all live in the realm of the "symbolic" from the moment we become aware that we are not fused with our mothers.

[71] From Binet, "Le Fétichisme dans l'amour," 271: "Le fétichisme tend à l'*abstraction,* c'est–a–dire a l'isolement de l'objet aimé, qui, alors même qu'il n'est qu'une fraction du corps d'une personne, se constitue *en un tout indépendant*" (Binet's emphasis).

[72] Binet, "Le Fétichisme dans l'amour," 150: ". . . car la réalité reste toujours inférieure a l'image qui'il s'en était faite."

violently that symbols not just "mean," but "be." Fetishism, therefore, is a kind of materialistic idealism. Fetishism con- flates the physiological with the ideal (in Krafft-Ebing's terms), the "reality" with the "image" (in Binet's terms), and the signified with the signifier (in current terms) so that the ideal may replace the physiological, the image may replace the reality, and the signifier may replace the signified. This may seem counterintuitive: the lingerie-fetishist, for exam- ple, may seem, upon first consideration, to be far as possible from "idealizing" his beloved since he has, on the contrary, reduced all the qualities of his "beloved" to underwear. Never- theless, he has reduced his beloved to this tangible object by means of "abstraction" and "idealization." He does not caress the lingerie in order to fantasize about its wearer; he takes her garments and enjoys them in private so he does not have to bother with the actual woman. He has reduced her via "lustful substitution" to a tangible symbol, embod- ied her in a concretized "idea," which is the end product of a series of imaginative associations, which itself constitutes his "perversion."

This, at any rate, is the sexologist's understanding of per- version, namely, that perversion is any substitution for geni- tal heterosexuality. Genital heterosexuality serves as the "material substratum" of psychosexuality, it would seem, and any sexual behavior that does not "correspond" to this substratum is considered an incongruous abstraction, a kind of "representation paralysis." The reader may have noticed, however, that this is also the psychoanalytic profile of the infant who ostensibly learns properly to tolerate his autono- my by substituting the hallucination of satisfaction for the person of the mother. Whereas psychoanalysis sees the "per- vert" as fixated at, or having regressed to, a stage of psycho- sexual infancy, we see this diagnosis of deviance as itself per- nicious heterosexist ideology posing as science. The psycho- analytic description of the infant, however, appears to us as more or less acceptable child psychology. If the infant is a natural epistemophiliac, then perhaps the fetishist is an epis- temophobe, afraid to know, afraid to make new symbols, new meanings, to try new substitutes. Fetishism then would be more a rejection of the "partialness" of experience than a reduction of experience to a mere part. The fetish expands in the mind of the fetishist to become ontologically as well as erotically sufficient: it grows from an equivalence effect to a totalizing effect.[73] It replaces the "conductivity and differentiation" of subjects in relation to each other and to themselves with the reified metaphysics of presence in which the subject loses itself. And it disguises as possession the conditions of separation and individuation in which we live even *in utero*.

As a discourse psychoanalysis could be accused of being both epistemophilic and epistemophobic—of being, in short, ambivalent about its claims to knowledge and truth. I have paid special attention in this chapter to the epistemophobia of psychoanalysis, to its avoidance of diverse sexualities, its compulsive resolution of ambivalence into equivalence, its refusal to contemplate its own navel out of fear of individuation, and its refusal to accept epistemophilia as the positive eros of culture. These phobias coexist with the epistemophilic eagerness of psychoanalysis to diagnose, document, and diagram the structure and behavior of the psyche in relation to its objects, to language, to culture. Freud's long essay on Leonardo da Vinci (1910) brings these together when he portrays the artist as both epistemophobe and epistemophile, qualities which in this case curiously cancel each other out. "The craving for knowledge in Leonardo" was so strong that he was "to investigate instead of loving." His libido was not repressed, but sublimated; he had vast psychical energy available for his research, yet he had no interest in "sexual themes."[74] At the same time, according to Freud, da Vinci's psyche was obsessed by the image he cherished and feared of his mother as a woman with a phallus, like the Egyptian goddess whose "body was female" but which "had a male organ

---

[73] Subsequent chapters explain in more detail what must remain for now more or less an assertion on my part.

[74] Freud, "Leonardo da Vinci and a Memory of His Childhood," in *SE* 11:77.

in a state of erection" (*SE* 11:94). As time passed, Freud spec-
ulates, this image and "his infantile past had gained control
over him," as did "insatiability, unyielding rigidity and the
lack of an ability to adapt to real circumstances," causing
him to abandon his art (*SE* 11:133). Finally neither knowing
nor loving was possible for him as the creative psychic motility of epistemophilia yielded to the epistemophobic overin-
vestment in the memory of the phallic mother.

At least, this is the story according to Freud, for whom the
phallic mother is the object of both epistemophilic and epistemophobic impulses. In "The Sexual Theories of Children"
(1908), he describes a dream he attributes rather vaguely to
"adults": "The dreamer, in a state of nocturnal sexual excitation, will throw a woman down, strip her and prepare for
intercourse—and then, in place of the female genitals, he
beholds a well-developed penis and breaks off the dream and
the excitation."[75]

The violent man in the dream stops cold when "he beholds
a well-developed penis" where "the female genitals" should
be. The reader can only speculate that perhaps the penis he
encounters is his own since, as Freud mentions, the dreamer
is "in a state of nocturnal sexual excitation," which is broken
off when he finds his phallus broken off and in the place of
the other. The problem for this dreamer seems to be that in
his world there is an extra phallus, or one which is figured as
excess instead of lack, the opposite problem from that of phobic Little Hans, who needed to assume that everyone male or
female had a "widdler." In fact, says Freud, "it would have
been too shattering a blow to his *Weltanschauung* if he had
had to make up his mind to forgo the presence of this organ
in a being similar to him."[76]

The little boy's weltanschauung anxiously includes the
female phallus as present; the "adult" man's weltanschauung
wishes to expel the female phallus, and with it the little boy,
if at all possible. These two conceptions of the world taken
together exemplify the dialectic algorithm of patriarchy. In his

[75] Freud, "The Sexual Theories of Children," in *SE* 9:216.
[76] Freud, "Analysis of a Phobia in a Five–Year–Old Boy," in *SE* 10:106.

"New Introductory Lectures on Psychoanalysis" (1933) Freud delivers a paper titled, "The Question of a *Weltanschauung*," in which this conceptual algorithm expands to fill the intellectual horizon. Freud defines weltanschauung as "an intellectual construction which solves all the problems of our existence uniformly on the basis of one overriding hypothesis, which, accordingly leaves no question unanswered and in which everything that interests us finds its fixed place. It will easily be understood that the possession of a *Weltanschauung* of this kind is among the ideal wishes of human beings."[77] In the weltanschauung "all the problems" of boy and man are solved "on the basis of one overriding hypothesis, which, accordingly, leaves no question unanswered and in which everything that interests [them] finds its fixed place." In this lecture, however, Freud wishes to persuade his audience that psychoanalysis is not so simple, that it is not a weltanschauung, that it is not a dream of a discourse motivated by an "ideal wish." To that end he presents religion and science as alternative views of the world, only the former of which is a welstanschauung. Religion from the psychoanalytic point of view is a magnified projection of infantile belief in the omnipresence and omnipotence of the phallic parents, together with a denial of the facts of life; whereas science takes the more enlightened view that wishes are not horses, and that seeing the phallus everywhere is something only children, dreamers, and perverts do. Religion in Freud's view is a bonafide delusion, which cannot admit of change, and is therefore merely a "wishful world" (*SE* 22:168). Science on the other hand welcomes change and difference; it is not a weltanschauung, not a causal narrative about a prime mover, not a bid for mastery, for all of which Freud praises it. Science is, rather, "the intellectual working-over of carefully scrutinized observations," the rejection of "revelation, intuition or divination," and as such it does "not differ in its nature from the normal activity of thought" (*SE* 22:159, 170). Here Freud dismisses religion as a cosmic totalizing effect,

[77] Freud, "New Introductory Lectures on Psychoanalysis," in *SE* 22:158.

but praises science for the unsentimental historicity and empiricism which makes it resemble "normal thought"— surely a tergiversation, on Freud's part, on what characterizes "normal thought"! In the end all of civilization for Freud is thus divided into two antithetical paradigms—one pathological, epistemophobic, fixated on its cultural past, and the other epistemophilic, interested in "research" and cultural change—locked in titanic struggle for the souls or minds of the world, and about which Freud is, so far as he can tell, not ambivalent.

[2]

Self-Reference and the
Fetish of Autonomy

Man is a column of blood, with a voice in it.
—D. H. Lawrence, *The Plumed Serpent*

In the preceding chapter I argue that the image of the phallic mother represents certain eroticized ambivalences toward materiality, individuality, and mortality that Freudian psychoanalysis was unable to "own," ambivalences that in historical terms we can also understand as entrenched cultural conflicts about the meanings of motherhood and female sexuality. For centuries the figure of the phallic woman served as an icon of sexuality and fertility for diverse religions and cultures. Psychoanalysis, a cultural tradition (if not a religion) in its own way, was perhaps unique among them for adducing her as a scientific fact of sorts. The phallic mother apparently emerged as central to the symbology of a sufficient number of analysands for analysts to conclude that they had discovered what amounted to an innate sexual idea, namely, that of embodied sexual nondifference. As a psychical object, the phallic mother represents both self-sufficiency and limitless succor. Uniting male and female sexualities, she needs no other to complete her, yet one can always be completed by her (and her alone), no matter one's subject position.

I pursue this line of reasoning to argue that the phallic mother is emblematic of certain magical beliefs about meaning as immanent in its representation, beliefs both explicit and implicit in psychoanalytic discourse specifically and literary modernism more generally. Psychoanalysis in this respect may even be taken as the exemplary manifestation of literary modernism. Insofar as she seems to represent autonomy and dependence as consubstantial, the phallic mother is the image of reflexivity as the immanent signifier of itself. Such reflexivity, masquerading as autonomy, I argue, is privileged to such an extent by the discourses of psychoanalysis and literary modernism that I feel justified in calling it their shared epistemological "fetish." I proceed intertextually, that is, by interpreting both literary and psychoanalytic texts, especially those that bear directly on the subject of fetishism or immanent meaning. I admit that my argument capitalizes on the idea of the "fetish" as a term connecting two kinds of discourse, one ostensibly scientific and the other aesthetic. In so doing I follow Freud, who in *The Interpretation of Dreams* and elsewhere relies on the multiple meanings of overdetermined "switch words" in the dreams he analyzes in order to connect different, seemingly unrelated chains of signifiers and symbols.

But this use of the fetish as a bridge across difference is justified by the history of fetishism and fetish-discourse itself. The fetish has always been cross-cultural. In a series of rich and fascinating historical and theoretical essays, William Pietz has shown that the fetish originated as an "idea," a "problem," and "a novel object . . . in the cross-cultural [mercantile] spaces of the coast of West Africa during the sixteenth and seventeenth centuries." The fetish was always a material object, for example a shaped piece of gold alloy, usually worn close to the body. It was "proper to neither West African nor Christian European culture," but was used to make commercial transactions possible "between cultures so radically different as to be mutually incomprehensible."[1] These cultures included indigenous African groups, the Protestant Dutch, Catholic Portuguese, and

---

[1] William Pietz, "The Problem of the Fetish, I," *Res* 9 (Spring 1985): 5, and "The Problem of the Fetish, II," *Res* 13 (Spring 1987): 24. See also Pietz, "The Problem of the Fetish, IIIa," *Res* 16 (Autumn 1988): 105–23.

some Jews and Moslems.

The "translatability" of fetish objects fostered "noncoercive" commercial relations between "bewilderingly different cultures," but at the same time, a racist and monotheocentric European discourse grew up to explain the metaphysical significance of the fetish and the perversity of its supposedly benighted African worshippers. In "The problem of the fetish, II," Pietz shows that a "complex of themes focused around this central idea," all of which expressed "the problem of how any personal or social value could be attributed to material objects whose only 'natural' values were instrumental and commercial" (45). Discourse about the "theory of fetishism," Pietz argues, was fully established in Europe by 1800, "having been formulated during the period of the Encyclopedists (the 1750s and 1760s)," and then appropriated and extended by subsequent theorists (23). It is Pietz's sense of the fetish as originally cross-cultural I wish to extend, although mainly to bring together the "cultures" of psychoanalysis and academic literary criticism. "Fetish discourse" is enjoying an exciting new vogue in critical theory, especially in critical writing about film and popular culture, which springs directly from the psychoanalytic use of the term. I particularly enjoy the irony of defining the fetish as cross-cultural when what it seems to embody, from the point of view of high modernism, is antithetical to the idea of social relations, namely, autonomous agency, personal perversity, and immanent beauty.

Within these two cultures—psychoanalysis and literary modernism—I wish to exploit the social meanings of the fetish, that is, as Pietz puts it (following Marx), its "dependence . . . for its meaning and value on a particular order of social relations, which it in turn reenforces" (23). In the twin cases of psychoanalysis and literary modernism, the order of social relations on which the fetish depends, and which it reinforces, is specifically oedipal and patriarchal. It is also linguistic, for, as we know, patriarchal hegemonies have maintained themselves for centuries in part by obfuscating their material operations while reproducing them through "imma-

terial" discursive strategies. Because of how our thinking
about representation has changed during the modern period
(again, thanks in part to psychoanalysis), we now understand
that ideas, representations, and discursive structures have
material consequences; we are prepared to view language as
a form of politics, or perhaps as formalized politics. For this
reason, I am differently concerned with Pietz's assertion
that, historically, one of the fetish's necessary attributes has
always been its "untranscended materiality." In the case of
modern and postmodern theories about language, one of our
most puzzling questions about language remains whether,
and to what extent, language is "material." The question of
the materiality of language is central, for it is precisely by
attributing an untranscendable materiality to "discourse"
that we are unwilling to claim for ourselves that we fetishize it.

Some may protest that I argue by metaphor or analogy
rather than logically. In my defense I admit to relying on
what Donald P. Spence calls "isomorphism."[2] Discussing the
problematic nature of psychoanalytic "truth," Spence (rather
cynically) claims that the three criteria for a good psychoanalytic interpretation seem to include: the "'mapping' of many
results onto relatively few causes"; medieval-style analogical
reasoning in which "similarity of form suggests similarity of
content"; and the assumption that "all pattern matches are
indications of cause and effect"(144–45). Spence does not dispute the therapeutic effectiveness of psychoanalytic constructions, but he laments their lack of scientific rigor, for
"finding a match is not the same thing as discovering a
cause" (155). He apparently finds it frustrating not to be able
to find the "causes" for his patients' behaviors. In this case,
however, I am trying to construct a suggestive isomorphism,
not find a cause for behavior, but to identify a historical
"match" between psychoanalysis and literary modernism. I
do not claim to be constructing a causal narrative linking one
to the other.

[2] Donald P. Spence, *Narrative Truth and Historical Truth: Meaning and
Interpretation in Psychoanalysis* (New York: Norton, 1982).

In the present context, the "match" in question is between the heterogeneous ambivalent identities "fixed" in the psychoanalytic fetish of the phallic mother and the heterogeneous hierarchical linguistic relations "fixed" in the modernist fetish of "sensuous thought" or autonomous art. In the case of psychoanalysis, the symbol is thought to be biologically immanent in the unconscious. In the case of literary modernism, a certain precious materiality or sensuous fleshliness is thought to inhere in and exude from the "body" of language. In both cases, an unquestioned if sometimes illogical biological realism serves to ground, locate, or validate the meaning of meaning. This biologism, or rather what could be called "the form of biologism," is one of the isomorphisms I shall foreground.

As the name for a form of sexual perversion, as well as the name for certain lapses of artistic judgment, the term "fetishism" came to figure prominently, and self-consciously, in both literary and psychiatric texts during the last quarter of the nineteenth century. A fascinating fictional example of fetishism crops up in Henry James's *Roderick Hudson,* first published in 1875, the earliest novel he felt merited inclusion in the New York edition of his collected works.[3] James was later, mainly through his brother William, to learn a great deal about what the psychiatric community thought of such forms of psychopathology as fetishism.[4] But in 1875 when he published *Roderick Hudson* such developments were more than a decade in the future. Nevertheless, the fetishism of which James's narrator accuses Mrs. Light in the novel not only fits Pietz's historical definitions of the fetish, but also the sexological taxonomies of those who like Alfred Binet (1888) and Richard von Krafft-Ebing (1886) were later to describe fetishism as a pathological erotic dependency on some overvalued symbolic object. In the passage below from

---

[3] Henry James, *Roderick Hudson* (1878; Harmondsworth: Penguin, 1986). *Watch and Ward* (1870), his true first novel, embarrassed James, and for good reason. In this book the author, even more than the hero, appeared to be a fetishist and a pedophile.

[4] This interesting history is the focus of my work-in-process.

Roderick Hudson, as my reading of it will suggest, James seems to effect a complex transition between older and newer ways of thinking about the fetish. He seems to be moving specifically toward the psychoanalytic understanding of the fetish as the personal pathology of a partial self that must be "read" as its quasi-linguistic symbolic self-expression. In addition, James even preempts what we tend to think of as the peculiarly post-psychoanalytic, post-semiotic insight that culture as a whole is a symbolic, indeed symptomatic, discourse, to be "read" as an intersubjective intertext that we misinterpret as being about "us." The partial self in question is one Mrs. Light, and her "fetish" is the "sacred parcel" that represents her "maternal hopes."

Mrs. Light is the mother of an extraordinarily beautiful daughter, whom she idealizes and on whom she has lavished obsessive and manipulative care. From the first moment she realized that her daughter "was to be a beauty of beauties, a priceless treasure," she coddled her; she raised her to bring a handsome return on the marriage market. "I lived only for my daughter," she explained to Rowland Mallet, the wealthy American aesthete whose impecunious protegé, Roderick Hudson, is unfortunately enamored of the young woman. "I watched her, I fondled her from morning till night, I worshipped her" (209). By the time she was ten she was so beautiful, so noticed everywhere they went, that Mrs. Light "had to make her wear a veil like a woman of twenty" (209). It was a "wonderful rigmarole," the narrator confesses, like "a pious duty":

> Mrs. Light evidently, at an early period had gathered her maternal hopes into a sacred parcel, to which she said her prayers and burnt incense—which she treated generally as a sort of fetish. These things had been her religion; she had none other, and she performed her devotions bravely and cheerily, in the light of day. The poor old fetish had been so caressed and manipulated, so thrust in and out of its niche, so passed from hand to hand, so dressed and undressed, so mumbled and fumbled over, that it had lost by this time much of its early freshness, and seemed a rather battered and disfeatured divinity. (207)

Mrs. Light fetishizes her "maternal hopes" as if they formed a "sacred parcel." This parcel is the only object of her only religion, an object before which and with which, at least in the narrator's imagination, she has for years performed her devotions.

James describes this fetish, as an abstraction ("maternal hopes") that is paradoxically tangible: she has caressed it for years, mumbled and fumbled over it. Furthermore, it is a kind of phallic doll she "dressed and undressed," "caressed and manipulated," and "thrust in and out of its niche." And, even though at last "rather battered and disfeatured," she still "brought [it] forth in moments of trouble, to have its tinselled petticoat twisted about and be set up on its altar" (207). Within the context of this passage, Mrs. Light's fetish seems to "mean" narcissistically and reflexively, for her alone. To the narrator, Mrs. Light's relationship to her daughter seems to involve only one "real" person, namely the pushy mother, for whom this relationship seems to resemble ritualized play. Furthermore, it seems to the reader that, according to this passage, when the mother looks at her daughter she sees only her own image, the image of her own "hopes," which she fetishizes like some "disfeatured divinity." Using her daughter thus to conjure a kind of hallucinatory wish-fulfillment, Mrs. Light is a woman who feels incomplete and manipulates her daughter for phallic self-fulfillment.

But Mrs. Light's fetishism is not only brilliantly prescient psychoanalytic thinking, but also a representation of the kind of cross-cultural interaction Pietz described as the fetish's original context. The plot of *Roderick Hudson*, like that of so many of James's novels, comprises a series of crosscultural interactions. As the novel opens, we meet Rowland Mallet, a reasonably affluent, educated, and relatively cosmopolitan Massachusetts man of both Dutch and "primal Puritan" ancestry. Mallet becomes the patron of Roderick Hudson, an unschooled but gifted American sculptor who now lives in Northampton, Massachusetts, but came from Virginia. As the narrator makes clear, Mallet and Hudson already represent vastly different "cultures." Northampton represents the "peaceful [dull], rural [provincial] New England community *quelconque* [there are, unfortunately, lots more like this one]" (40). Mallet, like James is privately educated in diverse settings, but unlike James has a consciousness "not . . . *too* acute" (46). Mallet takes Hudson away from these provincial surroundings, however, to Europe to expose him to the great art of the older cultures. To Mallet's consternation, there Hudson meets and falls madly in love with Christina Light, the mysterious Catholic American *fille fatale* whose unmistakably vulgar mother has bred her up to be married off to the wealthiest prince she can snag. Christina represents, in other words, both her mother's and Roderick's *personal* fetish, and, in Pietz's wider social sense, a *commercial* fetish on the marriage market. She is the locus of mercantile and cultural exchange among American Catholics, American Protestants of various persuasions, and Italian aristocrats possessed of various degrees of social status. She has even been veiled by her mother like a Mahometan, and "been taken to the Jews and bidden . . . [to] put up her veil" to raise money (209). Christina is thus, just like Pietz's historical fetish, a natural "object" to which considerable "personal or social value" is "attributed" proportional to her "instrumental and commercial" worth in the eyes of diverse cultural representatives.

Christina is perfectly aware of how her mother seeks to capitalize on the desire of others for her. Mrs. Light desires that others desire Christina, who *should* be other to Mrs. Light, but seems to be instead an idealized and displaced self-image. But Christina is, on top of (or underneath) everything else, an intelligent and self-conscious individual who is sick of being fetishized. She prefers to view herself as a "subject" rather than as an object, and is far more sophisticated than any other character in the novel, except, of course, the narrator. No degree of self-consciousness can protect her from the exigencies of the society in which she finds herself, however. She is finally obliged to marry according to her mother's wishes, thereby to reproduce and perpetuate the hierarchical social relations her fetishistic mother has caused to be inscribed on her and through her. The marriage comes off because Christina is misrecognized by the other characters as in herself valuable, a misrecognition she encourages by representing herself as indeed the image of all their desires, cannily playing the role of hallucinatory wish fulfillment. To the reader she embodies in one overdetermined, selfconscious and reflexive signifier the spurious resolution of several conflicting aesthetic, religious, and social meaning systems, whose conflicts take place in that linguistico-cultural realm we now call, in Lacanian shorthand, "the symbolic."

As Laurence Holland has pointed out, James's prose throughout his career is characterized by the commingling of aesthetic, religious, and economic vocabularies, so that the easy "slippage" from one meaning system to another, a characteristic of the fetish, typifies James's writing as well.[5] Furthermore, James's body of work includes such a wealth of fetishized abstractions and symbolic rituals (more numerous and various than I can suggest here) that James just may be the quintessentially fetishistic novelist. Be that as it may, what I wish to emphasize is how James's fetishizing extends Pietz's historical continuum. The fetish "slid" from religious to commercial to aesthetic signifier, ultimately concealing or "forgetting" its origins in the relations of material production. In the James passage, however, it has slid even further, to the point that it "means" primarily as part of one woman's personal psycho-syntax. The only substance left to the fetish at this point is its linguistic or symbolic force; what was once a set of material relations has become *concretized as an abstraction,* and thus principally as a "psychical object."

By the turn of the century, psychoanalytic theory had "forgotten" or lost interest in the cross-cultural or social meanings of the fetish, preferring instead to interpret retroactively all fetishes as always having been phallic symbols, thus rigidly fixing or reducing its multiple references. Paradoxically psychoanalysis privileged the act of symbol-

---

[5] Laurence Bedwell Holland, *The Expense of Vision: Essays on the Craft of Henry James* (Princeton: Princeton University Press, 1964).

ization itself as infinitely repeatable—as even coterminous with the history of civilization. Just as in the case of Mrs. Light's private religion, the meaning of the fetish came to seem perverse and antisocial even as it was discovered to be at the root of sociality. In an essay entitled "Mom," Andrew Parker points out that to date what literary theory has found most useful about psychoanalysis has to do not with its litany of complexes, oedipal or otherwise, or syndromes (including fetishism), but rather with its valorization of symbolic process.[6] At its extreme, despite its usefulness, this valorization veers into what Parker calls semiosis, the hypertrophic overvaluation of representation (which I would call the fetishization of representation). This "malady of representation" fosters what Parker has called the accretion of "a purely intransitive realm of representations" (99). An "intransitive representation"—that is, a symbol that is finally a symbol of itself—seems to me to be how we still perceive modernist works that, like Mrs. Light's fetish, represent meaning as private and interior rather than social and necessarily interpersonal.

We have institutionalized this view of literary modernism as a canon of quintessentially symbolist, or rather autosymbolic, works, in critical narratives that equate the symbolic with the human. This view is exemplified by *The Norton Anthology of English Literature*, that repository of the canonical teachings of the New Criticism, which promulgates the romantic myth about language from which it remains a challenge to deviate.[7] It still serves as a standard introduction to great works of English literature and to their associated conventional wisdoms, modern texts included. In its section on writers of the twentieth century, it devotes more pages to the work of James Joyce and D. H. Lawrence than to any other individuals (which would perhaps be surprising in Lawrence's case, except that F. R.

[6] Andrew Parker, "Mom," in *Sexual Difference*, Special Issue of the *Oxford Literary Review* 8, nos. 1–2 (1986): 96–104.

[7] M. H. Abrams, gen. ed., *The Norton Anthology of English Literature*, 4th ed. (New York: Norton, 1962).

Leavis named him part of the Great Tradition), and this is apparently because both are acclaimed as having produced works at once radically symbolic and profoundly "human." The *Norton Anthology* offers about a hundred pages from the work of each, twice as many as from the next most copiously represented writers (W. B. Yeats and T. S Eliot), so that Joyce and Lawrence become the lords of modernism as the *Norton Anthology* defines it. Both are presented as freakish individuals whose stylistic genius was nevertheless normative for the period: Joyce is the manic-depressive "genius, given to fits of sudden gaiety and of sudden silence," whose amazing creations "are not freaks or historical oddities" (2051–52); Lawrence "cannot be dismissed as merely a great eccentric," because he is essentially an artist, not a prophet, whose *"rendering"* of life matters rather than his admittedly eccentric ideas about it (2144).

The *Norton Anthology* presents Joyce as more comic and more cosmic than Lawrence, and Lawrence as more concerned than Joyce with the themes of marriage, class relations, and the environment. Nevertheless, these two wildly different, idiosyncratic, and individualistic writers are narrativized by the *Norton Anthology* in remarkably similar ways: both are exiles from their native lands who are above all artists; both are supersaturated with a detailed concrete sense of daily life back "home" from which both forge brilliantly innovative *symbolic* prose styles that are at once "poetic""and "deeply human." The reader of Joyce, advises the *Norton*, must "set aside" "all preconceptions" in order to appreciate the work of this artist/exile who gradually "gave up realism altogether" (2054), paradoxically using his "fascinating linguistic virtuosity" (2053) to write a masterpiece "embracing all of human history" (2055). Similarly, readers of Lawrence must not seek out his work "with the conventional categories of 'plot' and 'characters' in mind," despite the fact that there are "more and bitterer lovers' quarrels in Lawrence's novels than anywhere else in English literature" if they are to meet the "challenge" of this artist/pilgrim who uses "high poetic symbolism" from "the deepest recesses of his being" to define "the essential reality" of people (2143–44). Both writers appear in these descriptions as individuals who dissociated themselves from the world to create in poetic prose symbolic representations of normal depth psychology. In Joyce it is "always . . . the punning language, extending significance downwards—rather than the plot—that bears the main load of meaning" (2056), whereas Lawrence's "radically" new novel shows "uncanny psychological precision" beneath the "acute surface realism" (2143).

It is hardly necessary to point out (yet again) what have since come to seem the inadequacies of the New Criticism; suffice it to say that we now think twice before we advise our students to approach a text with "no preconceptions" or to look beneath or behind or down into language for some essential humanity. But what interests me is this normative description of modernism with its faith in the autonomy of the artist in physical and spiritual "exile," alone with his subjectivity and his *sprezzatura*, and in that of the resulting work, an autonomy taken to be generically and authentically human because transhistorical. Furthermore, this sense of autonomy is displaced onto language itself by modern artists such as T. S. Eliot in his early essays with his concept of the text as "objective correlative" and by those critics who best explicate and enact modernist poetics. Hugh Kenner ascribed to language an organicist autonomy that made it seem independent of cultural conventions, definitions, and limitations, when he said that "the poetic of our time grows from this [modern] discovery" that words are not "fixed upon a rigid and authorized grid,"nor are "linguistic contracts . . . arbitrary."[8] Language thus seemed to offer both the scope and the lawfulness we once got from religion.

Limited notions of language as at once arbitrary and "fixed upon a rigid and authorized grid" may "linger in the average literate psyche," writes Kenner, but in the era of Pound and Joyce:

[8] Hugh Kenner, *The Pound Era* (Berkeley: University of California Press, 1971), 95.

Both were rendered obsolescent by the slow discovery of *language*, a complex coherent organism that is no more the sum of its constituent words than a rhinoceros is the sum of its constituent cells, an organism that can maintain its identity as it grows and evolves in time; that can remember, that can anticipate, that can mutate. . . . We are to think not of babelized language but of Language, a mesh of filaments uniting all human beings. . . . We are joined—this is the theme of Comparative Philology—as much to one another as to the dead by continuities of speech as of flesh. (95–96)

Language in this model is an ideal organism comprised of the productions of artists (such as Joyce and Pound) who are smarter than "the average literary psyche," and more modern precisely to the degree that they create "continuities of speech as of flesh" by shunning mere language and using Language instead. This model of humanity, much like the notion of "tradition" Eliot offers in his essay "Tradition and the Individual Talent" (1919), substitutes for the heterogeneous human community an organism called Language with its endlessly evolving "identity" and memory. Language itself is thus seen as autonomous, mutating according to the dictates of its own philological genes into some linguistic *übermensch*; conversely, all human beings (who are not "average") become mythically "one" in Language.

   In a Language unified to such a degree that everything human, finally, is part of it, and any expression that seems coherent is understood as being language, all reference is necessarily self-reference. Self-reference becomes the sine qua non of the high modernist text—and perhaps the necessary source of limits to an organicism that otherwise would deliquesce into the rest of the world. As Marjorie Perloff suggests, coherence is ultimately the rule even of those avant-garde works which take aim against what she calls "the coherency model of High Modernism."[9] In her "Ezra Pound and 'The Prose Tradition in Verse,'" she connects Pound-

[9] Marjorie Perloff, *The Futurist Moment: Avant-Garde, Avant Guerre, and the Language of Rupture* (Chicago: University of Chicago Press, 1986), 110.

speech "with its jagged lines, abrupt collage cuts and startling juxtapositions . . . to a source more immediate than
Flaubert's or even Joyce's prose: namely the *parole in libertà*
of the various Futurist performances that were the talk of
London in 1913–14" (171). The style of these performances
was improvisatory but deliberately designed to pretend to
leave room for "accident and surprise." Pound embraced the
"energy, force, dynamism," and "simultaneism" of futurist
art as described by Boccioni and his fellow painters but
included them within unitary constructs generally interpreted as symbolic. Russian formalism too depicted objects
"in fragmented or partial form, as they would appear from
multiple points of view," but "as only the first step toward
the desired 'higher consciousness' that Ouspensky associated with the fourth dimension" (127). Marinetti called for the
abolition of "the old syntax," "no adjectives, no adverbs, no
finite verbs . . . [and] no punctuation" in order better to render with "naked nouns" "the synthesis of a day in the
world's life" (57).

In an essay called "Modernity—An Incomplete Project,"
Jürgen Habermas discusses what he calls the "false negativity" of the avant-garde movements, those "hopeless surrealist
revolts" intent on "blowing up the continuum of history."[10]
Habermas describes the coherence of "aesthetic modernity"
as characterized by "a changed consciousness of time"(5). As
indicated by the cubists' and futurists' use of anti-narrative
symbolic "simultaneism"—a form of anti-historicism—as an
artistic convention in the service of anarchism, perhaps "aesthetic modernity" would be better characterized as a wish to
deny and thereby transcend time. What is interesting here is
that although the avant-garde used apparent incoherence as
an antihistorical strategy, it failed to "blow up history" or to
be really incoherent or anarchic. That the purported revolutionary anarchism of the avant-garde is so obviously of a
coherent piece with its modernist context suggests either

---

[10] Jürgen Habermas, "Modernity—An Incomplete Project," in *The Anti-
Aesthetic: Essays on Postmodern Culture,* ed. Hal Foster (Port Townsend,
Wash.: Bay Press, 1983), 13, 5.

that it depended upon, and existed in dialectical relation with, its contexts (how could it do otherwise?) or that we as critics create coherent narratives no matter what, even when the subject is anarchism.

Both of these are probably so; but it is nevertheless the case that the avant-garde defined itself as an act of negation, that is, of dialectical relation to existing trends. It is inevitable, then, that the avant-garde and whatever context against which it defined itself should seem to make a conceptual unit. The avant-garde was not so much a unified movement, however, as a concatenation of "isms," each of which claimed its autonomy, its independence of the others by virtue of how it negated their contemptible idealism or conceptual spinelessness. Vorticism, for example, the only indigenous British avant-garde art movement, claimed to owe nothing to the strategies of the Futurists or other innovators. Wyndham Lewis, defining vorticism for the catalog of an exhibition of vorticist works, wrote:

> By Vorticism we mean (a) *Activity* as opposed to the tasteful *Passivity* of Picasso; (b) SIGNIFICANCE as opposed to the dull or anecdotal character to which the Naturalist is condemned; (c) ESSENTIAL MOVEMENT and ACTIVITY (such as the energy of a mind) as opposed to the imitative cinematography, the fuss and hysterics of the Futurists.[11]

Pound described *BLAST 1* (1914) as "a new Futurist, Cubist, Imagiste Quarterly."[12] Lewis gave its address as "Rebel Art Centre," and used its oversized pages and bold type to trumpet the news that, aesthetically, politically, and temperamentally, vorticism was in "revolt against Formula," against "Nature [who] is just as sterile as a tyrant," and against "'Life' . . . [which] is a hospital for the weak and incompe-

[11] Wyndham Lewis, *Wyndham Lewis on Art: Collected Writings 1913–1956*, ed. Walter Michael and C. J. Fox (New York: Funk & Wagnalls, 1969), 96.
[12] Quoted in Reed Way Dasenbrock, *The Literary Vorticism of Ezra Pound and Wyndham Lewis: Towards the Condition of Painting* (Baltimore: Johns Hopkins University Press, 1985), 13.

tent."[13] This was his way of saying that vorticism was not to
be confused with futurism, which "is largely Impression-ism
up-to-date" (143). "The futurist," Lewis complained, "is a
sensational and sentimental mixture of the aesthete of 1890
and the realist of 1870" (8). Nevertheless, as Marjorie Perloff
points out, "whatever the protests lodged by Lewis, Pound,
and their artist friends, vorticism would not have come into
being without the Futurist model" (*The Futurist Moment*
171).

Just as Lewis announced vorticism as an original revolt
against formalist post-impressionism and sentimental futurism, both of which staked their own claims to a progressive
aesthetic radicalism, in "Dada Manifesto"(1918), Tristan
Tzara explained the birth of dada as a rejection of academic formalism: "DADA was born [in 1916 at the Cabaret
Voltaire in Zurich], out of a need for independence, out of
mistrust for the community. People who join us keep their
freedom. We don't accept any theories. We've had enough of
the cubist and futurist academies: laboratories of formal
ideas."[14] Tzara speaks in the name of a "we" who shared a
mistrust for community and for the very idea of "we," as
well as for theories and communities united by shared theories (what Stanley Fish has called "interpretive communities"). He spoke simultaneously for the negation of all we's,
as an anti-we, asserting instead the authority of an "I" identified as an absolute and absolutely internal subjectivity dedicated to negation, for "man" who is "the chaos that constitutes . . . infinite, formless variation" (5). No work of art can
be "beautiful, by decree, objectively, for everyone." And criticism is "therefore, useless; it only exists subjectively, for
every individual, and without the slightest general characteristic" (5). Criticism for Tzara makes the particular into the
general and thereby falsifies it.

The theoretically anti-theoretical independence of dada

---

[13] *BLAST 1* (1914), ed. Wyndham Lewis (facsimile edition; Santa Barbara,
Calif.: Black Sparrow Press, 1981), 129, 130.
[14] Tristan Tzara, *Seven Dada Manifestos and Lampisteries*, trans. Barbara
Wright (London: John Calder, 1977), 5.

depended on the autonomy of the isolated subjectivities of which it purported to be a representation. To establish dada as an independent movement required that Tzara simultaneously negate the authority of other competing avant-gardisms and claim an autonomy for his based on the prior authority of alienated consciousness—or rather, of the unconscious. The unconscious, and the fact that everyone has one and no one knows it, makes it possible to be part of a community and an "I" at once. The conceptual autonomy vaunted and flaunted by avant-garde movements in the early decades of this century is the aggressively desublimated version of the same fantasy, which, denied and displaced, animated modernist art in general, and characterizes the version of modernism we teach and write about and perpetuate in tamer ways. The idea of the unconscious both justified and naturalized the anarchism of the avant-garde, and the proliferation of symbolic art. Allegiance to its conception of the unconscious rendered avant-garde art "radical" and intentionally incomprehensible—in order to be "mimetic" of the supposedly cryptic unconscious. At the same time its allegiance to the idea of the unconscious historically "situated" avant-gardism, as both Breton and Tzara were well aware.

We may think at times that we (post)moderns are the first to appreciate the extent to which the idea of autonomous art was an illusion born of the wish to deny art's historicity, but situating art was part of the avant-garde program, even of surrealism. André Breton, for example, admittedly with the benefit of hindsight, defended the poetry and manifestos of Tristan Tzara in a lecture delivered in 1935 titled the "Political Position of Today's Art," as devoted both to "a process of *symbolization*" and to "the emancipation of man" in a political sense.[15] In the "Second Manifesto of Surrealism" (1930), Breton sought a reconciliation with Tzara, who, when dada was "liquidated" as a movement in 1922, "no longer saw eye to eye" with him, by announcing that he considered

---

[15] André Breton, *Manifestoes of Surrealism*, trans. Richard Seaver and Helen R. Lane (Ann Arbor: University of Michigan Press, 1972), 231; Breton's emphases.

Tzara's poetry, "apart from Surrealism, as the only really 'situated' poetry" (*Manifestoes of Surrealism* 171–72).

At its beginning surrealism emulated the "pantheistic
delirium" exemplified by Rimbaud's 1875 poem "Dream,"
aspiring to a post-decadent poetic, which was to be a "new
vice . . . like hashish . . . [like] opium images," thus embracing to a degree the reactionary sentimentalism Lewis had
criticized a decade earlier (264, 36). It also indulged in that
famous "psychic automatism" and in the use of dream
images, which, as they did not arouse sustained interest,
were criticized as being "'virtuoso pieces'" (157). Indeed,
Breton bragged in the second manifesto that "Surrealism is
not interested in giving very serious consideration to anything that happens outside of itself, under the guise of art, or
even anti-art, of philosophy or anti-philosophy" (124). But as
it developed, as Breton relates in the second manifesto, surrealism, which like symbolism, futurism, vorticism, and
dada, considered itself both revolutionary and self-sufficient,
had to deal with questions touching on things happening
"outside of itself," such as whether "to go along with
Marxism or not" (165). What Breton realized was that, if surrealism went "farther and farther beyond" its "strict framework," it did so "to avoid seeing it turn aside onto an apolitical plane where it would lose all its historical meaning, or
commit itself exclusively to the political plane, where it
would merely be redundant" (233). Breton felt that by making itself "hermetic and difficult" like the symbolist poetry
at the end of the previous century, surrealism paradoxically
guaranteed that it would one day matter historically as part
of the poetic narrative, that one day its works would begin
"to speak *for us*."

And, he thought, it would come to matter historically, to
be situated, through the work of interpretation. Although
this is to some extent a contradiction in terms, Breton represented the surrealist as consciously "situating" works that
would share "the same lot as all previous works that are *historically situated*" (233) because they give up "the personality that [the artist] was so jealous of" to an art that is "*is none*

other than the collective treasure" (232). Breton felt pres-
sured —under "orders"—"to count only upon the proletarian
Revolution for the liberation of mankind" but he could not
believe "in the present possibility of an art or literature
which expresses the aspirations of the working class" (153).
At least, since he himself was "a product of the bourgeoisie,"
he felt "incapable of translating these aspirations" (154). But,
as an artist in what he thought to be a "prerevolutionary period," his works demanded "to be *situated* in relationship to
certain other already existing works and must . . . open up
new paths" (155). These new paths were to be "the rediscov-
ery, at any price," the release, of the natural energy of art,
which formalism had quelled, from "the immense reservoir
from which symbols spring completely armed and spread to
collective life through the work of a few men" (231). The
unconscious as Freud had defined it was the location of a collectivity that knew no class distinctions: "It was a question
of foiling, foiling forever, the coalition of forces that seek to
make the unconscious incapable of any sort of violent erup-
tions; a society that feels itself threatened, as bourgeois society does, rightly thinks that such an eruption may be the
death of it" (232). From Breton's point of view, Marx was
unerringly accurate in his analysis of social problems, and
accordingly surrealism "deliberately opted for the Marxist
doctrine" (159); at the same time Freud offered "the first and
only" criticism "with a really solid basis" when it came to
"the evaluation of ideas"(160); and Rimbaud's poetry, so "full
of sap," embodied the unique ability of art "to study the
human problem in depth" (240).

To combine the concerns suggested by these three role
models into one aesthetic, prerevolutionary, avant-garde
praxis (or postrevolutionary; Breton wasn't sure which) was
the goal of surrealism as formulated by Breton: to liberate the
masses through the work of "a few men" capable of allowing
symbols to erupt from the unconscious. How could the erup-
tions of a few serve the many? Through the act of interpretation. Breton believed that "the automatic text and the Surrealist poem are no less interpretable than the dream narra-

tive, and that nothing must be neglected to carry through such interpretations" (232). "The activity of interpreting the world," he maintained, "must continue to be linked with the activity of changing the world" (240). This self-description is far from Habermas's of avant-gardism as expessing the anarchistic wish to "blow up the continuum of history." It asks us, on the contrary, in those manifestos which mediate between ostentatiously puzzling works of art and their puzzled public, to see its self-conscious anarchism as a strategic attempt to urge history toward the complication of its own narrative.

The efficacy of this strategy, or the lack of it, is not the issue here; I have not included this brief discussion of the questionable autonomy of avant-garde art so much to fit it into a historical narrative about autonomous art forms as to point out that even those varieties of modernist art which most asserted their autonomy from each other, as well as their absolutist devotion to the production of symbolic art, arrived upon the cultural scene fully equipped with their own critical narratives—upon which they depended. And they depended upon these narratives (as they do still) to explain that they were both symbolical and situated, symbolical-and-therefore-human, symbolical-and-therefore-real, to make accessible, interactive, and cultural what, as art, represented itself as spontaneous, automatic, and unconscious. The symbolic and the social could only *appear* antithetical.

From the point of view of the artist, the autonomy of art and its "situatedness" (or "historicity") were not mutually exclusive. When Breton proclaimed his allegiance to Marx, Freud, and Rimbaud, he was suggesting that they shared an anti-bourgeois faith in revolutionary eruption. Breton viewed the source of such salutary eruption as the unconscious. Paradoxically, the idea of autonomous art is conceptually inseparable from the kind of semiotic materialism we now call "construction": the belief that culture is the concrete enactment of our ideas, narratives, or fictions. But surrealism (which serves here as the "type" of autonomous art), as Breton wished to convince us, invoked the symbol-producing activities of the unconscious in order to reject ivory-tower formalism in the name of biologism, to ground representation in the body instead of something metaphysical, and thus assert the complex interdependence of ideas and the real. At least, this is how he expressed himself in the 1930s.

Karl Marx's *Capital* is, among other things, a remarkable analysis of how the capitalist economy requires that the material and the ideal support each other.[16] Marx's discussion of what he called "commodity fetishism" has recently attracted renewed critical interest (with the subject of fetishism in general), especially among those who have found psychoanalytic categories and concepts helpful, if not sufficient, in thinking about the cultural construction of identities, or about popular art forms like film. In the present context too a brief discussion of a passage or two from *Capital* will be useful, since I theorize fetishism as the idealization of representation in ways that touch, I hope, on questions of culture.

Marx begins *Capital* with a well-known analysis of "the individual commodity," the "elementary form" of "that immense collection of commodities" of which capitalist wealth consists. In this part of his discussion, Marx attributes to commodities aspects quantitative and qualitative. The quantitative aspects of a commodity have to do with its "use value" and its "exchange value," both of which derive from its physical, more or less quantifiable, properties. The use value of a thing "is conditioned by the physical properties of the commodity, and has no existence apart from [them]"; use values are "only realized in use or in consumption. They constitute the material content of wealth, whatever its social form may be" (126). The exchange value of a thing is the "quantitative relation, the proportion, in which use values of one kind exchange for use values of another kind" (126). Exchange value is therefore an "abstraction" from use value, and thus an abstraction from the physical to the convention-

[16] Karl Marx, *Capital: A Critique of Political Economy, Volume One*, trans. Ben Fowkes (New York: Vintage Books, 1976).

al, by means of substitutions that make possible the equating of diverse and diversely useful objects. In the process of abstraction and equation—a process as basic to the capitalist economy as marriage has been—the "sensuous characteristics" of objects are displaced by other kinds of quantifiable value, i.e. the human labor that went into them. Marx discusses labor as physical and quantifiable, part of the "quantitative" aspect of the commodity: "The useful kinds of labour, or productive activities" that go into production, "whatever may be its nature or its form, [comprise] essentially the expenditure of human brain, nerves, muscles, and sense organs" together with "the duration of that expenditure or the quantitity of labour" (164).

Marx describes labor as quantifiable in algebraic equations that express in symbolic terms its physical properties. But it is this same abstractability, he suggests, that makes possible the betrayal of materialism by idealism as the quantitative is co-opted by the qualitative thanks to the "metaphysical subtleties and theological niceties" of how we valorize physical objects (163). Physical objects express in physical form not only the amounts, but also the kinds, of labor that went into their production. Thus when commodities are evaluated in relation to one another, they "take on the form of . . . social relation[s]" (164). The "enigmatic," "mystical," or qualitative character of the commodity, Marx argues, derives from the hierarchical social relations of which it is the objectification. Commodities reflect "the social characteristics of men's own labour" as if they were "objective characteristics of the products of labour themselves, as the socionatural properties of these things" (164–65). In other words, the "mystery" of a commodity is the by-product of the "substitution" for "the physical relation between physical things" of "the fantastic form of a relation between things" (we might today say "fantasmatic" instead of "fantastic").

Instead of "the definite social relation between men themselves," instead of "the social relation of the producers to the sum total of labour," the commodity comes to represent a symbolic "relation which exists apart from and outside the producers," a relation through which the value of the commodity ceases to have "connection with the physical nature of the commodity and the material relations arising out of this." To find a suitable analogy for this displacement of material relations onto their products, Marx says, "we must take flight into the misty realm of religion" where "the products of the human brain appear as autonomous figures endowed with a life of their own, which enter into relations both with each other and with the human race. So it is in the world of commodities with the products of men's hands. I call this the fetishism which attaches itself to the products of labour as soon as they are produced as commodities, and is therefore inseparable from the production of commodities" (165).

Insofar as it has been and remains hierarchical rather than fully egalitarian, capitalism, which Marx describes as a set of equations solved by means of a series of pernicious substitutions, is perhaps more like a syntax that pretends to be an equation in which subject and object come to stand in for each other.

In capitalism as Marx describes it, thanks to these substitutions, ultimately "machinery . . . becomes the real master of living labour" and the means of production, or agency itself, comes to seem autonomous (983). "All material wealth confronts the worker as the property of the commodity possessors": "This money and this commodity, these means of production and these means of subsistence confront labour-power, stripped of all material wealth, as autonomous powers, personified in their owners. The objective conditions essential to the realization of labour are *alienated* from the worker and become manifest as *fetishes* endowed with a will and soul of their own. *Commodities* in short, appear as the purchasers of *persons*" (1003; Marx's emphasis). The ostensible autonomy of the commodity, furthermore, makes it possible for "the buyer of labour-power," who in reality "is nothing but the personification of *objectified* labour" to "cede a part of itself to the worker in the form of the means of subsistence in order to annex the living labour-power of the remaining portion so as to keep itself intact and even to grow beyond its original size by virtue of this annexation" (1003–4).

Even leaving aside the psychological implications of this annexation and incorporation of the worker by the voracious fetish, capitalism, the economic system virtually synonymous with the rise of modern Western civilization, appears in this description as an economy in which dollar amounts are attached to essentially religious values so that symbols can be bought and sold. In this economy, the more autonomous a commodity appears, the more it seems to embody a thoroughly objectified significance rather than merely to represent something "other" than itself, the more of this mysterious value it has. In any case Marx is describing a system based on a romanticization of the commodity by means of which any individual laborer, or buyer for that matter, who achieves substantial financial power as the corporate "we," which in a capitalist society replaces the royal "we," disappears as an agent into a system of mystified, seemingly autonomous, representation. The fetishism he describes "consists in regarding economic *categories,* such as being a commodity or productive labour, as *qualities inherent in the material incarnations of these formal determinations or categories"* (1046; my emphasis).

It is in particular this quality of the fetish as an apparently autonomous symbol, a symbol-in-itself, as a category that is at the same time a member of itself, which I want to emphasize before turning to psychoanalytic and other definitions of fetishism. For Marx fetishism is a species of *idealization* by means of which what ought to be merely a reference to something material masquerades instead as a something-in-itself, an autonomous signifier signifying itself as transcendent *because* autonomous. In the century or so since the publication of *Capital,* partly due to Freud's definition of "psychical reality," new notions of intentionality and history and related developments in philosophy, and de Saussure's invention of the science of semiotics, we have ceased to find meaningful the distinction between "subjects" and the symbolic economy in which they participate. This is arguably a definition of modernity. Marx, however, concerned with the material existence of particular persons, depended on this distinction, the erasure of which seemed to him part of the problem he sought to remedy.

Many of us who do literary criticism still do not want to take this distinction seriously (or to take Marx seriously). Still fascinated by what Frank Lentricchia calls "the language of fictionalism," for example, we still conventionally operate on the basis of only partly revised assumptions about what we used to call the "autonomy" of art and which we now refer to as the "constitutive" powers of representation (or discourse) in general.[17] Because of the extent to which we base our work on the idea of discourse as concretely "constitutive" (of the real) I want to re-problematize the modern notion of autonomous art *because* it is continuous with, and has lead us to, the very notion of (inter)textuality we invoke to free us from the confines of the autonomous and isolated work. The postmodern idea, for example, of intertextuality does not simply replace or rehabilitate that of the autonomous work, but activates it by granting it an agency that its creator and its perceiver supposedly lack, presumably in the interest of treating the work as a social rather than an aesthetic construct. In the process the work becomes not less "autonomous" than when it was considered a work of art for art's sake, but more so: it becomes not a static and isolated work of art, but a fetish, magically charged with its own imposable power, not the effect of complex psychological and social causes so much as itself a cause of other effects both private and public.

But discourse is constitutive not because it is agent-less and speaks us rather than being spoken by us, but rather *because* you and I are its agents, producers, and users. That language speaks us, rather than the other way around, is a fantasy, and a potentially pernicious one, like the fantasy that commodities purchase persons, rather than the reverse, which Marx describes as endemic to capitalism. The idea of constitutive discourse conceived as the speaker of persons seems as omi-

<hr>

[17] Frank Lentricchia, *After the New Criticism* (Chicago: University of Chicago Press, 1980), 30.

nously religious to me as the idea of fetishized commodities being the purchasers of laborers seemed to Marx. Furthermore, the two ideas seem two sides of one coin: the use of fetishized commodities in advertising to elicit psychosexual responses from carefully targeted purchasers shows this. Accordingly I present the somewhat hyperbolic argument that our cherished notion of discourse-as-constitutive is fetishistic, magical, and regressive, and needs to be thoroughly supplanted by the idea (gaining ground, for example, through renewed interest in social history) that discourse is "constructed" rather than constitutive. Marx's idea of fetishism as pernicious idealization offers a solid foundation for this argument because it shows the monumental and perdurable sociohistorical consequences of this perverse act: the excessive valuation of a category that masquerades as particularity

Psychoanalysis locates "inside" us the fetishism Marx described as inherent in capitalist society. But whether used to name the overvaluation of certain commodities, a type of primitive idolatry, a sexual perversion, or a disingenuous confidence in the materiality of language, "fetishism" describes an act of idealization by means of which some "other" is endowed with the transcendent wholeness, autonomy, and power the self presumably lacks. Fetishism reveals itself as more an inability to tolerate the necessary incompleteness of experience than a reduction of experience to a mere part. The appalling case history of an unhappy fetishist who lived and died about a century ago dramatizes some of these aspects of fetishism. Among the thirty-six pathological fetishists Krafft-Ebing describes in *Psychopathia Sexualis, L,* or "Case 97" is peculiarly emblematic of the kinds of self/other conflation that can make romance—even in the broadest cultural sense—dangerous.[18] The man referred to as *L* tried to make quite literal the disfeaturing symbolizations Mrs. Light enacted only metaphorically.

[18] Richard von Krafft-Ebing, *Psychopathia Sexualis: With Especial Reference to the Antipathic Sexual Instinct, a Medico-Forensic Study,* 12th ed., trans. Franklin S. Klaf (New York: Bell, 1965).

The case, as Krafft-Ebing recounts it, is that of a laborer who was arrested "because he had cut a large piece of skin from his left forearm with a pair of scissors in a public park" (156). From the age of thirteen, L was driven by the impulse to bite off and consume a piece of fine white flesh from the beautiful young girls he observed. He never had any desire for intercourse nor any interest in any part of the female body other than the skin. Hoping to satisfy this hunger he carried a pair of scissors with him for years, and was nearly successful on several occasions. At last, however, he grew unbearably frustrated by his failures and "decided upon a substitute"—himself. On those occasions when he had sighted and pursued unsuccessfully some fair-skinned maiden, "he would cut a piece of skin from his own arm, thigh, or abdomen and eat it. *Imagining that it was a piece of the skin of the girl whom he had pursued,* he would whilst masticating his own skin obtain orgasm and ejaculation" (57; Krafft-Ebing's emphasis). The logic of L's pleasure consisted of a series of substitutions by means of which L replaced what Krafft-Ebing called the "physiological" woman with an idea of a part of her. It would be even more appropriate, however, especially in L's case, to refer to this logic (in Lacan and Granoff's phrase) as "a metabolism of images," since for him images become the food of love; L quite literally is what he eats (as well as that which eats him).

From the sexologist's point of view, for the natural charms (those having a "direct relation to sex") of a whole woman L substituted a piece of her. For coital penetration L substitutes the puncture of skin with his teeth, and for sexual friction, mastication. Denied these pleasures, L replaces his teeth with a pair of scissors and, last but not least, the flesh of a (presumed) virgin with his own. Our understanding of him is reduced to what we can deduce from reading about him. For the once actual, living, and suffering person whose full name is now reduced to the letter L and the number "97," we substitute the few facts Krafft-Ebing gives us. Thus, for us as readers, L becomes a mere character in a narrative, an ideal case, an exemplar of the category "fetishism," whose mem-

bers have in common precisely a predilection for the substitution, the replacement of "the idea of certain portions of the
female person" or "certain articles of female attire" for the
real female person as a whole. For the physiological man who
once was L, we substitute our partial idea of him and his case
history. As exemplar and fetish, L becomes a substitute for,
embodiment of, and, one could say, a symbol, for all other
fetishists, or lustful substituters, in other words, all men, all
persons. Thus the syntax of substitution basic to reading
extends from L the onanistic cannibal to us readers who take
him in. If the substance of any text is the understanding of its
readers, the extent to which we understand and appreciate
what we read is the extent to which we dine on our own
imaginative flesh.

L is an ideal case of auto-symbolic subjectivity, primarily
because the logic of his pleasure appears reflexive, psychically hermaphroditic, self-contained and self-consuming, and,
after its fashion, neat. L consummates in his flesh the marriage of the fantasmatic with the physical and furthermore
here he is reduced to print, the representation of an idea of an
idea.[19] L is an icon of fetishism, an isolated case. When he
chews his own bloody flesh, imagining it to be that of the girl
he desired, he in the most literal way possible erases the distinction between subject and object and eats them both
simultaneously. At this moment of self-consumption he de-
forms and re-forms himself in the image of the desired other,
and yet both he and that other have been sacrificed for the
sake of a monstrous unitary conception. By a process of imaginative substitution L becomes the living symbol, the fetishistic embodiment, of the girl of his dreams.

And yet this imaginative self-substitution has physical
consequences: orgasm and ejaculation; mutilating self-canni-
balism; finally, suicide attempts in the asylum where special-

---

[19] I do mean to suggest that critical writing, and probably philosophical
writing, if not in fact any kind of writing or purposive intellection, has certain affinities with fetishism. Lustful idealization, in other words, is a
process basic to the mind/body unit (or "material-semiotic actor" as Donna
Haraway would say).

ists were unable to help him. *L* was not only an ideal case or a case history. He was a man for whom the fantasmatic became the literal instead of the symbolic, for whom *soma* and *seme* were inextricable. Or at least, that is how he must seem to us because this is all the information we have about him. How much does the presumably historical *L* have in common with Mrs. Light, James's invented fetishist? To what extent do they function as verbal fetishes by virtue of our attributing provisional reality to them? That fictional characters function in readers' minds as fetishes seems to be what Leo Bersani implies when he writes that "what we call character is also a partial self. Its appearance of completeness, of wholeness, may be nothing more than the illusion created by the *centralizing* of a partial self. Such centralization involves both the organization of our desires into psychic structure and the expulsion of nonstructurable desires. Character, in short, is also a piece of a person; it has the factititous coherence of all obsessions."[20] In the text you are constructing as you read it, *L* is an icon or type of the reader at his most receptive, that condition of temporary fusion with the text in which he loses himelf, particularly through identification with characters in novels. The idea of characters as "partial selves" is itself a kind of idealization but one that calls attention to the fetish-like illusory autonomy of the literary character.

When Bersani describes a character as "a piece of a person" with "the factitious coherence of all obsessions," he implies that characters function both as fetishes and obsessions as Freud has defined them. Accordingly I will turn at this point to some of Freud's hypotheses in order to see the degree to which such criticism might be a response to the modernist overvaluation of the symbol. In his article on the subject published in 1927, a piece that has since proven an irresistible target for theorists of gender, Freud describes fetishism as concerned with one loss, one absence, namely that of a mater-

---

[20] Leo Bersani, *A Future for Astyanax: Character and Desire in Literature* (New York: Columbia University Press, 1984), 313; Bersani's emphasis.

nal phallus.[21] "Probably no male human being is spared the
fright of castration at the sight of a female genital," wrote
Freud (*SE* 21:154). Most overcome this fright. Some become
homosexual, Freud asserted, but others "fend off" this horror
by creating a fetish. The fetish is meant to substitute for the
mother's penis, according to Freud, even though, as he has
grown up, he has both "retained" and given up his belief that
women have a phallus. Creating a fetish is "a very energetic
action . . . undertaken to maintain the disavowal" of the
woman's castration (*SE* 21:154).

In the mind of the fetishist, "the woman has got a penis, in
spite of everything; but this penis is no longer the same as it
was before. Something else has taken its place, has been
appointed its substitute, as it were, and now inherits the
interest which was formerly directed to its predecessor. But
this interest suffers an extraordinary increase as well, because *the horror of castration has set up a memorial to itself*
in the creation of this substitute" (*SE* 21:154; my emphasis).
Despite Freud's somewhat hysterical assertions that all
males experience the horror of what he elsewhere calls the
"fact" of maternal castration, and that all fetishes replace
this lost penis, we can expand Freud's notion of fetishism to
cover more semiotic ground. Michael Balint, in his "Contribution on Fetishism," published seven years after Freud's
paper, claimed that the fetish symbolizes not only the penis,
but the vagina as well, and that furthermore it conflates the
two by symbolizing as well their psychic precursors, the parents' feces, giving the fetish "a close connection with the
anal theory of birth and coitus."[22] Balint bases these conclu-
sions on the observation that a fetish is almost always "a
worthless object" that has been raised to excessive sexual
"dignity."

The sexual fetish—and herein lies what Marx referred to in
the economic context as the mystery of the fetish—must

[21] Sigmund Freud, "Fetishism," in *SE* 21:147–58.
[22] Michael Balint, "A Contribution on Fetishism" (1934), in *Problems of
Human Pleasure and Behavior* (New York: Liveright, 1956), 172.

show signs of use, of wear, of possession, and more often than not have the right (wrong) sort of smell to fulfill its function of symbolic substitute. In other words the symbolism enacted by the fetish must be perceptible to the senses and seem palpably to embody the person or part of the person for which it is the equivalent. It must be a living image. When the fetish is adequate, the fetishist is content; he (or, much less often, she) does not need a living partner to reach orgasm, only this living image. As Freud wryly points out, the psychoanalyst tends not to see many fetishists as patients because they don't feel they need help.

In their article "Fetishism: The Symbolic, the Imaginary, and the Real," Jacques Lacan and Wladimir Granoff speak of fetishism as *"a metabolism of images."*[23] Fetishism, they tell us, may seem like "a primitive perversion completely beyond the reach of analysis," but, on the contrary, it is analyzable through language because it is itself a language. Lacan and Granoff associate fetishism (as I shall in discussing D. H. Lawrence in the next chapter) with the cryptic language of dreams:

> Freud introduced us to the study of the fetish by indicating that it has to be deciphered, and deciphered like a symptom or a message. He tells us even in what language it has to be deciphered. . . . From the beginning, such an approach places the problem explicitly in the realm of the search for meaning in language rather than in that of vague analogies in the visual field. (Such as, for example, hollow forms recalling the vagina, furs the pubic hair, etc.) From "Glanz auf der Nase" to the female penis, passing through "Glance on the Nose," the passage is strictly incomprehensible unless one has stuck to the path which Freud indicated. (267)

The "path which Freud indicated" is the study of fetishism as an "idealization of the sexual tendency" manifested in the

---

[23] Jacques Lacan and Wladimir Granoff, "Fetishism: The Symbolic, the Imaginary, and the Real," in *Perversions: Psychodynamics and Therapy*, ed. Sandor Lorand and Michael Balint (New York: Gramercy, 1956), 267, 268; my emphasis.

realm of language by a syntax of displacement designed to deny and asseverate, memorialize and denegate, the fear of castration.

Another way to articulate the denial fetishism enacts would be to say, Lacan and Granoff imply, that the fetish exists in order to deny that there is any difference between the sexes (273). One could extend this idea further to suggest that the fetish embodies the denial not just of sexual difference, but of the very possibility of difference, the possibility of the existence of the uncategorizable, in other words of the particular, the individual, the me and the you who may not form a we. This is more fruitful than thinking of the fetish simply as a penis-substitute, for example when we are thinking of our capitalist culture as massively fetishistic. Understanding fetishism as an erotic mystification that conceals the fear of difference helps to explain how our culture can be individualistic, democratic, and capitalistic on the one hand, and severely classist, homophobic, misogynist, and racist on the other. To give this idea another turn, we could consider fetishism, even in the work of Freud, to be itself the fetishistic apotheosis of the penis into the symbolic category "phallus," a glorification of the penis into what Lacan calls the "logical copula." As such fetishism becomes the erotic metaphysic not just of capitalism, but of patriarchy generally, a capitalistic system that has not yet become fully democratic and egalitarian. Marx and Freud both, without perhaps putting it in quite these terms, were diagnosing patriarchy's hypervaluation of its own masculinist authority as fetishistic.

It is Freud's reflexive definition of fetishism, then, that is itself fetishistic, or rather that demonstrates what fetishism is all about, since it insists that the penis is the source and real referent of all value systems, all languages, and that fear of its loss is constitutive of personality, perversion, character, culture, and history. Concerning this horror it couldn't hurt to say again that, although castration anxiety seems to be an *idée fixe* of Freudian psychoanalysis, it is by no means the constitutive fright for both sexes; but it is not surprising that men are the fetishists in a patriarchal culture where power is equated with possession of the phallus. The illogic, even the absurdity, of Freud's conception of penis envy, and the self-confessed inadequacy of his understanding of female psychosexual development, have been definitively demonstrated by Karen Horney, Jane Gallop, Luce Irigaray, Sarah Kofman, and others. Their arguments need not be repeated here. Their main point, however, remains relevant to this study, namely, that, as Sarah Kofman put it, for psychoanalysis "the penis is always the leading erogenous zone" for both sexes.[24] When Robert C. Bak called fetishism "the basic perversion" because of how it epitomizes "the reinvestment of the fantasy of the phallic woman," he was agreeing with Freud that "the regressive revival of the maternal or female phallus" serves to deny the "fact" of castration, which distinguishes mother from father, female from male.[25] Through the "dramatized or ritualized denial of castration" the subject supposedly restores the ideal perfection of his bisexual self-image, and finds it possible temporarily to believe that only one sex exists. That there is no distinction between the sexes may or may not be a "primal fantasy"; who knows? It does appear, however, to be a fantasy inseparable from the hegemonic authority of patriarchy, which depends not only on compensating fantasmatically for what woman does not have, but also, and more important, on denying what woman does have. The metabolism of images, which fuels patriarchy, gobbles up other, rival images and image systems.

In her essay "The Denial of the Vagina" (1933) Karen Horney argued that the account of human sexual development offered by psychoanalysis depended illogically on "a denial of [the] existence of the vagina."[26] As she pointed out, and as we

[24] Sarah Kofman, *The Enigma of Woman: Woman in Freud's Writing*, trans. Catherine Porter (Ithaca: Cornell University Press, 1985), 134.

[25] See Chapter 1 for a fuller discussion of the implications of the subject of Robert C. Bak, "The Phallic Woman: The Ubiquitous Fantasy in Perversions," in *The Psychoanalytic Study of the Child*, ed. Ruth S. Eissler et al., 25 vols. (New York: International Universities Press, 1968), 23:15–36.

[26] Karen Horney, "The Denial of the Vagina" (1933), reprinted in *Feminine Psychology*, ed. Howard Kelman (New York: Norton, 1967), 160.

have become all too aware, Freud calls "the period of blossoming of childish sexuality, the period of infantile genital primacy in girls as well as boys . . . the *phallic phase*" (147). Horney concluded, based on personal experience, therapeutic practice, and research, that, contrary to what Freud maintained about the vagina remaining "undiscovered" as a locus for sensations separate from motherhood, even baby girls "discover" their vaginas as the source of female sexual excitation in general "from the very beginning." Her discovery of the primacy of the vagina in female sexual experience leads Horney to conclude that "behind the 'failure to discover' the vagina is a denial of its existence" by Freudian psychoanalysis (160). This failure on the part of the psychoanalysis then current, one might add, is symptomatic of the modern era generally, and remains in effect to the extent that, as a theoretical discourse, psychoanalysis fails to accord a constitutive conceptual authority to the vagina equal to that of the penis. We still do not have, for example, a term analogous to "phallus" to denote the vagina as generative symbolic construct, as *copula*. Nor do we have any kind of cultural event that reaffirms ritualistically and publicly the community of women the way Superbowl Sunday, to take just one spectacular example, celebrates that of men.

To some extent this is because we have not accorded the vagina such a status in our discourse (although I am not sure I want us to); it cannot exist as a concept, let alone operate as a signifier capable of proliferating meanings, in a discourse that offers it virtually no representation. Furthermore, Horney found that, for a variety of reasons, many of her female analysands denied the existence of their own vaginas by repressing its representations even in their fantasies. The problem with this state of affairs is that if we do not represent objects mentally they do not exist for us. According to psychoanalysis, in other words, symbols possess a unique ontology. As Melanie Klein (1929) explained, one cannot have feelings or thoughts about that which we are unable to symbolize, unable, in other words, to allow into consciousness.[27]

---

[27] Melanie Klein, "Personification in the Play of Children" (1929), in *Love, Guilt, and Reparation and Other Works* (New York: Free Press, 1984).

Without symbols we cannot recognize our fantasies in order to narrativize them. And if we cannot narrativize them, they cannot become part of the historical record (and history remains *his* story). "Fetishists habitually treat the vagina as an unknown and dangerous territory" even after years of experiencing intercourse, writes Phyllis Greenacre, and yet their fetishism magically reconfers upon woman a potency believed to be hers by virtue of her motherhood.[28] What is missing from the psychosexual repertory of the unbalanced symbolic imagination in both sexes, then, tends to be the adequate symbolization of female genitality or, as I would prefer to think of it, the individuality of females.[29] Besides, while it may be fun, finding the proper anatomical referent for the fetish is quite beside the point. The problem of the fetish is that it represents the valorization of valorization itelf, that it idealizes idealization by conflating it with what seems to be its embodiment. No matter which, or whose, body part one idealizes, the result is still idealization. To undo the "denial of the vagina" to the point where we think of the two sexes as complementary halves fitting together yin-yang style to form a unity would merely maintain their status as Platonic categories. The contemporary dramatistic psychoanalyst Joyce McDougall exemplifies this strategy of unification when she says, for example, that

the paternal penis, an idealized and coveted object for all children, plays a different role depending not only on the anatomical sex of the [subject] but also on the extent to which it has or has not become the symbol of sexual complementarity. This fundamental signifier . . . also determines the way in which the female genitals are represented in the unconscious. . . . As long as the representation of the vagina has not benefited in imagination from its phallic significance (that is, the penis is a genital organ that requires the female genital to complete it and give it

---

[28] Phyllis Greenacre, "The Fetish and the Transitional Object" (1964), in Eissler et al., *The Psychoanalytic Study of the Child*, 24:150.
[29] See Noël Montgrain, "On the Vicissitudes of Female Sexuality," *International Journal of Psychoanalysis* 64 (1983): 169–86.

its sexual significance, and vice versa), then not only does it run the risk of becoming a detached representation but also a limitless and potentially dangerous one. . . . When there is no psychic scenario capable of uniting the two sexes in the love act, in which each sex becomes the reason for the existence of the other, then the autonomous penis risks being an object that tears and lacerates in the psychic repertory, while the unlimited vagina separated from its function as a loving and desiring container for the penis becomes an organ that may crush, strangle, and castrate all that it encounters.[30]

Apparently, despite our increasing awareness of the degree to which the meanings of "gender" are culturally determined, we still idealize the body, particularly the genitals, as if they were prior to and safe from such determinations. But, as Christine Delphy points out, those who want to deconstruct patriarchal ideology must reject even those of its suppositions "which appear not to be such, but rather to be categories furnished by reality itself, e.g. the categories 'women' and 'men.'"[31] Anatomical difference in itself, Delphy says, is "devoid of social implications" but becomes significant insofar as the oppression that divides humanity hierarchically in two creates gender, transforming anatomical difference into "a relevant distinction for social practice. Social practice, and social practice alone, transforms a physical fact (which is itself devoid of meaning, like all physical facts) into a category of thought" (144).

With these words Delphy returns us to language as "the realm of the search for meaning," to language for a possible solution to the problem of categories. We turn necessarily to language even for those meanings that seem most, to use Bersani's word, "nonstructurable," especially since we have always queasily equated the "nonstructurable" with the vaginal, and kept both out of language; they are both by defini-

---

[30] Joyce McDougall, *Theaters of the Mind: Illusion and Truth on the Psychoanalytic Stage* (New York: Basic Books, 1985), 44–45, in response to Jacques Lacan, *Écrits* (Paris: Seuil, 1966).

[31] Christine Delphy, *Close to Home: A Materialist Analysis of Women's Oppression* (Amherst: University of Massachusetts Press, 1984), 144.

tion what is outside-of-language. And yet these nonstructurable feminine meanings paradoxically find their representation precisely in that mode that most pretends to be wholly masculine and phallic: the fetish, or masculine masquerade. To appropriate and redirect McDougall's words, the fetish embodies that "psychic scenario capable of uniting the two sexes" by seeming to embody at once "the autonomous penis" and "the unlimited vagina." In the economy of the fetish the lost continuity between the me and the not-me is magically retrieved. The fetish is both content and container, writes Janine Chasseguet-Smirgel, both McDougall's "loving container" and the loved contents.[32] The former has lace-up boot and corset fetishists in mind here; but the definition might apply as well to formalist critics old and new enamored of the well-wrought (well-constructed?) urn and its seemingly seamless unity of form and content.

[32] Janine Chasseguet-Smirgel, *Creativity and Perversion* (New York: Norton, 1984), 87.

Living Words: Character and
the Romance of Gender

> "When I read a novel my imagination starts off at a gallop and
> leaves the narrator hidden in a cloud of dust; I have to come jogging
> twenty miles back to the dénouement. . . . I mean to write a novel
> about a priest who falls in love with a pretty Mahometan and swears
> by Allah to win her."
>
> "O Hubert!" cried Nora, "would you like a clergy-man to love a
> pretty Mahometan better than the truth?"
>
> "The truth? A pretty Mahometan may be the truth. If you can get it
> in the concrete. . . ."
>
> —Henry James, *Watch and Ward*

$\mathbf{B}$y present-day standards the above passage from Henry
James's first published novel sounds overwrought and even
campy,[1] but the fictional Hubert's conviction that a fictional
character could be "truth . . . in the concrete" represents, in a
nutshell, modern thinking about fictional character and literary language. In this chapter I explore the fantasmatic concreteness of character; in the next I examine the modernist
conception of poetic language as "sensuous thought," another abstraction made concrete. In short, it is the paradoxical
idea of language as "truth in the concrete" that most interests me, along with its related manifestations and postmodern corollaries, some of which I consider in the final two

[1] Henry James, *Watch and Ward* (1871), with introduction by Leon Edel
(1959; New York: Grove Press, 1979), 160.

chapters. The social problems of race and gender, which Hubert inadvertently raises by suggesting that the embodiment of truth be a "pretty Mahometan," are inextricable from the general problem of modern idealism, which repressively "essentializes" dualistic distinctions, and from the more specific problem of what could be described as the postmodern essentialization of language.[2]

The novelists to be discussed in this chapter all exploit female characters and the idea of the feminine to embody the truth of masculinity *for* the male characters. The logical consequences of this idealization of the other are, as usual, racism and sexism. I am not trying to prove that modern literary norms are stereotyped as "masculine" and "feminine," although clearly they are. These categories masculine and feminine are the sort of formal, binary opposition that we always invent. We create these pairs *ad nauseam*, these oppositions which Gilles Deleuze and Felix Guattari call "bi-univocal relations" composed of codependent terms, whose reflexivity can prevent us from seeing "where the system is coming from and going to, how it becomes, and what element is going to play the role of heterogeneity" to break up its symbolic structure, its ordinary hermeneutic, and its imaginary archetype.[3] Anyway, "who could tell," ask Deleuze and Guattari, "what the difference is . . . between a structural, differential opposition and an imaginary archetype whose role is to differentiate itself?" (7)

That characters in novels possess a peculiarly intractable psychological realism is fairly obvious, but that this realism masks its own function as a kind of idealization is not. It is this idealization I wish to examine in certain "moments" in the writing of James, Forster, Joyce, Genet, and Lawrence, all of whom were intensely aware of the virtual fleshliness of fictional characters. As heirs to both the naturalist and the sym-

[2] For a provocative discussion of the problem of "essentialism" in and for feminist theory, see Diana Fuss, *Essentially Speaking: Feminism, Nature, and Difference* (New York: Routledge, 1989).

[3] Gilles Deleuze and Félix Guattari, *Kafka: Toward a Minor Literature*, trans. Dana Polan (Minneapolis: University of Minnesota Press, 1986), 7.

bolist traditions, each of these modernists experimented with the novel's unique capacity to enact a symbolist poetics of embodiment, which happens to be what makes literary modernism and psychoanalysis two horns of one dilemma. Both literary modernism and psychoanalysis idealize the body as language, and language as material, by conflating language with the body. Both idealize the body as a kind of wild card, as if the "wild body" (to quote Wyndham Lewis) and its unpredictable instincts could "play the role of heterogeneity" and disrupt "the system." Far from accomplishing such a disruption, however, "the body" as trans-historical category simply replaces God.

Aesthetic modernism inherited a romantic belief in the symbol as the mirror in which the immanent subject could "half-perceive, half-create" (Wordsworth) the transcendence to which it felt entitled. Psychoanalysis, meanwhile, took six thousand years of Western cultural history with its myriad symbols and reduced them all to one, namely, "the phallus"—specifically, the maternal phallus. These twinned moves leave us with the postmodern, post-psychoanalytic conception of ourselves as our mother's missing phallus, which would be laughable if it were not so oppressive. In turn, the *Norton Anthology's* beatification of the symbolic *as* the human now belongs, as Jean-Joseph Goux put it apropos of Freudian art interpretation, with psychoanalysis "to the science of sociohistorically anachronistic modes of signifying which nevertheless continue to effect the economy of the individual."[4]

Experiencing fictional worlds and characters remains one of the great pleasures of novel reading, a pleasure definitely not limited to the reading of modern novels. The moderns, however, were uniquely conscious that the psychological realism of character constituted a fascinating problem of reference rather than a natural "given." Characters, after all, are no less verbal, and no more substantial, than other verbal constructs. How is it that they can seem so alive, so "con-

---

[4] Jean-Joseph Goux, *Symbolic Economies: After Marx and Freud*, trans. Jennifer Curtiss Gage (Ithaca: Cornell University Press, 1990), 190.

crete"? Why, as the passage from *Watch and Ward* suggests, is there something licentious, even erotic, about the pleasure they can offer us? Within the worlds they inhabit, characters could be described (to borrow another elegant phrase from Goux from a different context) as a novel's "biotic anchoring point" (193), both because they represent embodied humans who live, act, interact, and even die, and also because they connect the novel to the body of the reading subject. We experience the virtual reality of characters in our bodies, by responding to them emotionally, physically, even sexually.

At the same time, can we say in any simple, unvexed, uncontestable way, what it means to be alive, individual, or sexual, or what it means to experience something "in our bodies?" I think not, although this has not stopped us from writing as if, unlike gender, "the body" were beyond question. We may all agree that we are uncertain what it means to be a man or a woman, but we still accept that something we call "the body" as both the "ground" of our personal experience and the discursive intersection of history, psychology, politics, and semiotics. This is in part due to the enormous and timely influence of Michel Foucault on our thinking about "the body" in and *as* history. Michel Foucault's vision, as he put it in *The History of Sexuality*, was to supplant "a 'history of mentalities' that would take account of bodies only through the manner in which they have been perceived and given meaning and value" with "a 'history of bodies' and the manner in which what is most material and most vital in them has been invested."[5] In a sense we have taken advantage of Foucault's understanding of the body as the most material, heterogeneous, and vital of signifiers in order to leave "the body" itself unquestioned as a category, in order not to think of the body as a signifier rather than as the signified, and thus as open to question as any other referent.

The idea of the body, especially when we write or speak about it, is as much an idealization as any other "abstract equivalent," to use Marx's phrase, and one unexamined in

[5] Michel Foucault, *The History of Sexuality, Volume I: An Introduction*, trans. Robert Hurley (New York: Vintage, 1980), 152.

much contemporary critical discourse. One could think of fictional characters as "abstract equivalents" for "the body," and, as such, as fetishized abstractions with irresistible appeal (at least, until video has taken over completely). After all, what reader, no matter how sophisticated, has never rooted for a fictional hero or heroine, only to cry over his or her cruel fate; what reader has never felt anger at a fictional villain or villainess, or contempt for a coward or cad made of words? What reader, in short, has never experienced the "truth" of a fictional character as if it were human? Furthermore, what literature professor must not sometimes struggle to convince her students to look askance at their own subjective responses to characters, in order to look at them more objectively, that is, structurally, historically, poetically, or politically? In so doing we ask our students to think about what Goux calls (to adopt one more felicitous phrase) the "form of form," which, as he says, "is conceivable not in any figurative terms but only as a tissue of relations" (*Symbolic Economies* 186). That these relations are in some sense always fundamentally material and social we tend (as Marx pointed out) to forget at the "highest" levels of abstraction where "what was form to a certain matter becomes in turn, at a higher level, matter to a more abstract form" (186).

To return briefly to the passage from *Watch and Ward* at the head of this chapter, a brief discussion of which is in order here, Hubert and Nora typify the undiscriminating novel reader whose various passions, from the sanctimonious to the sentimental, from the inquisitive to the acquisitive, spill into each other. Indeed, the passage does parody itself. Hubert is a foppish clergyman who lacks the "odour of sanctity" and who is two-timing his fiancée by wooing Nora, the novel's heroine (158). Nora, meanwhile, is the protegée or "ward" of a man named Roger who has raised her from girlhood to be his, keeping "watch" over her until such time as her "diminutive timepiece" should have grown to fit his manly "key" (109). Her function in the novel is to choose Roger more or less freely in the end and make a virtuous man out of him. But when the conversation quoted above takes place, Hubert, not yet out of the picture, has come upon Nora, who has just been reading a "very silly" novel in which a young clergyman, in love with a Roman Catholic, almost leaves his faith to marry her, but in the nick of time converts her instead. Scandalized by this "hotch-potch," Hubert proclaims that the proper order of events would be to "marry her first and convert her afterwards." "Isn't a clergyman after all, before all, a man?" he protests (163).

Determined to outdo the author of this silly novel, whom he apparently imagines as a rival for the heart of the generic female reader, Hubert vows to write a novel in which "a priest falls in love with a pretty Mahometan and swears by Allah to win her." This valiant priest would be a man "before all," one who could recognize "truth" even in the shape of a pretty Mohemetan. He would not prefer abstract orthodoxy to immanent truth prettily embodied "in the concrete." Hubert's hero is even more fetishistic than the hero of Nora's silly novel, who was not satisfied with the concrete "object" but wants his bride sanctified "in the cold abstract" of his Protestant faith. Hubert, on the other hand, knows the fetish-in-itself when he sees it, proclaiming, "I stand up for passion! If a thing can take the shape of passion, that's a fact in its favour" (163). By "thing," the reader is not certain whether Hubert refers to the story, the woman in the story or, more slyly, the duplicity he is currently practicing and may be trying to justify. Most likely he means the story line he can imagine taking "the shape of passion," rather than the woman; but either way for Hubert "the shape of passion" equals truth "in the concrete," and both may be embodied by a pretty woman.

Hubert is not alone in thinking this way. Even though *Watch and Ward* is James's first novel, the plot of Hubert's would-be clerical (pastoral?) romance foreshadows, or more aptly caricatures, what becomes the typical Jamesian plot. In virtually every James novel principal characters find themselves "interested" in each other to the extent that they appear "in the concrete" to personify beauty, agency, sensibility, or even that mysterious Jamesian essence "felt life."

These characters first hit upon their objects of interest, then either fail to get or to appreciate what they thought they wanted, and finally spend the rest of the plot disengaging themselves, learning instead either to be nobly disinterested or extravagantly self-interested.[6] Hubert is simply the crudest of James's interested parties, and Roger the most awkward. In the case of Mrs. Light in *Roderick Hudson,* James recognized and diagnosed the clandestine fetishist in the guise of the devoted mother, whereas in the case of, say, Maggie Verver in *The Golden Bowl,* the relation of desire to possession—the question of cupidity, in short—is more ambiguous, but no less self-conscious. Furthermore, if every James novel is about "interest" in every sense of the term, every one of James's famous New York prefaces tells the story of his own interested disinterest in the interests of his characters. Richard Poirier pointed out in *The Comic Sense of Henry James* that the often manipulative interest James's characters take in each other reflects James's concern that he in turn could be exploiting them.[7]

Logically, of course, an author can't "exploit" a character in the ethical sense. Nevertheless, logical or not, just as Poirier claims, "the question is felt on every page" of a James novel: "Who is exploiting the life of another human being? . . . 'Am I guilty,' James seems always to be asking, 'of violating the dramatic freedom of this character in order to place him in some system of meaning?'" (9). Even Henry James, perhaps the most cerebral of novelists, harbors the fantasy countless authors have shared with friends, colleagues, and diverse audiences,

---

[6] In the present context I can only suggest some examples of what I mean, but even this is difficult since as James evolves into his "late style" the interplay among literal and figurative kinds of "interest" and "disinterest" becomes increasingly complex. In any case, one could consider the financial, aesthetic, erotic, and spiritual value of Claire de Cintré for Christopher Newman in *The American;* Isabel Archer for Ralph Touchett, for Gilbert Osmond, and for her own imagination in *The Portrait of a Lady;* Miriam Rooth for her admirers in *The Tragic Muse;* Milly Theale and Merton Densher for each other in *The Wings of the Dove;* her father, her husband, her son, and her own power for Maggie Verver in *The Golden Bowl.*

[7] Richard Poirier, *The Comic Sense of Henry James* (London: Chatto and Windus, 1960).

that their characters are autonomous beings. I don't mean by this that, once created, characters live in the minds of readers and fans, but rather that the characters, not the authors, "write" the story, follow their own paths, interact with each other, and even supply their creators with some surprise ending. On television not long ago, Alice Walker told Oprah Winfrey that she felt novel writing to be magical, that she "recorded" rather than created what is going on in her characters' lives once they came to conception "inside" her. This is an experience I have heard many fiction writers describe.

E. M. Forster thinks of plot, not character, as the fetish-aspect of fiction because its artifice is obvious to him. In his *Aspects of the Novel*, the published version of some lectures delivered in the spring of 1927 at Trinity College, Cambridge, and one of the classic studies of the novel, Forster describes characters as oversexed "word-masses."[8] He does not find the realism of characters, on the other hand, to be problematic, although describing them as "word-masses" might have alerted him. He complains, for example, of a section of one of Meredith's plots that is too closely knit, that "there is an attempt to elevate the plot to Aristotelian symmetry, to turn the novel into a temple wherein dwells interpretation and peace" (91). Such an attempt to fashion plot into an enclosed form moves Forster to ask: "Plot is exciting and may be beautiful, yet is it not a fetish, borrowed from the drama, from the spatial limitations of the stage?" (97). He calls his chapter on literary characters "People," however, and distinguishes between "those two allied species, *homo sapiens* and *homo fictus*" (55) by saying we know more about the latter than the former since in novels unlike life "the secret life is visible" (63). Novels deal with five main facts of human life, he says, of which we can report little about the most important, namely birth and death. These are "strange because they are at the same time experiences and not experiences"; "we [real people] move between darknesses" (48). The novelist, however, is able to "know" these things about characters. Forster

[8] E. M. Forster, *Aspects of the Novel* (New York: Harcourt, Brace, and World, 1954), 44.

says that "the novelist is allowed to remember and understand everything, if it suits him," even these two unknowable facts. Otherwise we start life "with an experience [we]
forget" and end it with "one which [we] anticipate but cannot
understand."

Characters come to life within the temporal space afforded
them by these two unknowable boundaries. They come to
possess a factitious substantiality because "the novelist is
himself a human being," so that "there is an affinity between
him and his subject-matter which is absent in many other
forms of art." Forster is unrepentant about what is to him the
delightful reflexivity of characters that partake of their
author's actuality. He calls characters *word-masses,* a perfect
description of the paradoxical psychological concreteness
characters possess for us: "The novelist, unlike many of his
colleagues, makes up a number of word-masses roughly
describing himself (roughly: niceties shall come later), gives
them names and sex, assigns them plausible gestures, and
causes them to speak by the use of inverted commas, and perhaps to behave consistently. These word-masses are his characters" (44). And although it seems to Forster that love
"bulks" too "enormously" in novels, making them "monotonous," still bulk it does, even more than it does in life. In
novels, love "in its sex form" appears everywhere as "a man
and woman who want to be united and perhaps succeed,"
whereas in real lives love leaves "a very different and a more
complex impression" (54). Forster believes that this dispro-
portionate representation of love as an impulse to sexual
unity has more to do with "the novelist's own state of mind
while he composes" than the force of that impulse in people's lives (55).[9]

Although Forster uses the word "fetish" to denote unnatu-
rally symmetrical plots, it is characters which he describes as
fetishes in our terms. For Forster characters are verbal facsim-

---

[9] In the last chapter of *A Room of One's Own* (New York: Harcourt Brace
Jovanovich, 1957), Virginia Woolf draws an analogy between the tranquility
she feels watching a man and a woman get into a taxi together and the ideally balanced creativity of mind at work.

iles of their authors with a certain extra something, an x, that ordinary people don't have: "A novel is based on evidence + or - x" (45). This x is precisely the mysterious "autonomy" that enables characters in novels to seem real. "The character escapes from its author, becoming its own singular being," writes Jean Genet in *Querelle*.[10] "Thus we have to admit that the author is able to reveal certain traits of this character only after the fact" (251). The creation of character is a process of embodiment, writes James in his preface to the New York edition of *The Portrait of a Lady*. Isabel Archer, for James, begins as a "vivid individual," a "constituted, animated figure or form" of which the imagination is at the start in "complete possession." This figure, "placed in the imagination that detains it, preserves, protects, enjoys it" grows there by a "process of logical accretion" from "the mere slim shade of an intelligent but presumptuous girl, to find itelf endowed with the high attributes of a Subject."[11]

Novels may function as idealized worlds. Characters function as fetishes, which are "accretions" of idealizations. Together they comprise an idealized psychological interiority extended through a makeshift duration. Effective characters resist even the most strenuous efforts to deconstruct them entirely because we cling more stubbornly to characters than to any other verbal constructs. No doubt this is because we still see ourselves as selves. Even the Russian formalist critics, high moderns in their own way, as interested as they were in showing that "art has no mainstay" and that fiction is on the contrary best described as unique arrangements of conventional motifs, did not entirely reduce character to plot functions or word masses.[12] Boris Tomashevsky writes that "experienced readers" "need realistic illusion" and "demand . . . . lifelikeness": "Although firmly aware of the fictitious

[10] Jean Genet, *Querelle* (Paris: 1953), trans. Anselm Hollo (New York: Grove Press, 1974),250–51.

[11] Henry James, *The Art of the Novel*, ed. Richard P. Blackmur (New York: Charles Scribner's Sons, 1934), 48–49.

[12] Victor Shklovsky, "Sterne's *Tristram Shandy:* Stylistic Commentary," in *Russian Formalist Criticism: Four Essays*, trans. Lee T. Lemon and Marion J. Reis (Lincoln: University of Nebraska Press, 1965), 43.

nature of the work, the experienced reader nevertheless demands some kind of conformity to reality, and finds the
value of the work in this conformity. Even readers fully
aware of the laws of aesthetic structure may not be psychologically free from the need for such illusion."[13] To satisfy
the psychological need for realistic illusion from which even
readers "fully aware of the laws of aesthetic structure" may
not be free, the author of a novel "must arouse the attention
of the reader, hold it, and interest him in the fates of the
characters." To accomplish this "the basic way is to arouse
sympathy for the characters, who are usually presented with
some emotional coloring" (89).

The Russian formalists were able to concede (albeit with a
certain distaste) that even aesthetically sophisticated authors
might have to provide "emotional coloring" for their characters to arouse the reader's sympathetic interest; Freud, on the
other hand, perceived a certain metapsychological lawfulness
about the work of art. A work of art, insofar as it constitutes
a kind of memorial to itself enshrining its own mystified
integrity, may seem, Freud writes in "Obsessive Actions and
Religious Practices," like some "travesty, half-comic and
half-tragic, of a private religion."[14] He is not the first, he
admits, "to be struck by the resemblance between what are
called obsessive acts in neurotics and those religious obser-
vances by means of which the faithful give expressions to
their piety" (*SE* 9:117). As a form of piety obsessional neurosis is like fetishism, only less pleasurable, in that it denies
itself the pleasure of perfect "embodiment" and devotes its
energy instead to the continual defense against the allure
of that perfection. "Fresh mental efforts are continually
required" to counterbalance the impulse it seeks to deflect.
Yet at the same time, just as in fetishism, the obsessive act
"represents the sum of the conditions subject to which something that is not yet absolutely forbidden is permitted, just as
the Church's marriage ceremony signifies for the believer a

[13] Boris Tomashevsky, "Thematics," in *Russian Formalist Criticism*, 81.
[14] Sigmund Freud, "Obsessive Actions and Religious Practices," in *SE*
9:119.

sanctioning of sexual enjoyment, which would otherwise be sinful." (*SE* 9:124–5). Obsessional neurosis always effects "a compromise between the opposing forces in the mind," always producing "something of the identical pleasure they were designed to prevent." The factitious coherence of the literary characters, then, which partakes as Bersani says of the factitious coherence of all obsessions, exists ritualistically to "represent the sum of all the conditions under which something not yet absolutely forbidden becomes permissible." Through them we may experience "not yet absolutely forbidden" conjunctions that would make us uncomfortable in other contexts. These conjunctions are both sexual and linguistic, since the search for the meaning of the fetish takes place in the realm of language, and characters are uniquely "sexed" or gendered bits of language.

The work of D. H. Lawrence taken as a whole constitutes an extended literary meditation upon the psychosocial conjunctions of class conflict, psychology, and religion. He took the battle between the sexes to be the enactment par excellence of conflict among these meaning systems. Also, and conversely, Lawrence criticized Christianity for how it elevated what he regarded as an anti-individualistic effeminacy into a religion that thrived on conformity and reviled the leadership of real men (see, for example, *Apocalypse* [1931]). Logical consistency was never one of Lawrence's hobgoblins: ultimately he homophobically rejected logic and analytic thinking, which he associated with the mystical, the romantic, the ideal, and the feminine, in favor of a unity of the symbolic, the sensuous, and the phallic (designed to bolster his belief in the immanent manliness of men). The product of Lawrence's idiosyncratic "metabolism of images" is a fetishistic masculinism, which enacts in *The Plumed Serpent* (1926) a patriarchy reduced to the absurdity of phallus worship and a fearful attraction for the anal.[15] At the same time

---

[15] D. H. Lawrence, *The Plumed Serpent* (New York: Vintage, 1959). Lawrence implies, in *Women in Love* (1920) and *Lady Chatterley's Lover* (1928), that anal penetration—of female by male—is implicitly a means to enlightenment (or endarkment), to transcendence of bourgeois morality.

the heroine of *The Plumed Serpent* occupies the central,
mediating position, triangulating and safeguarding the
fetishized mutual identifications of the two male characters.
For these reasons I shall discuss Lawrence's work, in particular *The Plumed Serpent*, and its relation to some of Freud's
notions about the unconscious.

The most accessible example of these combined conflicts
in Lawrence's work is probably the marital strife between
Will and Anna Brangwen in *The Rainbow* (1915).[16] Rever-
sing, as do most of Lawrence's characters, the usual stereotyped characterization of gendered styles of knowing, Will's
way of experiencing the world could be described as emblematic, iconic, religious, self-effacing, and affective, whereas
Anna's is analytic, materialistic, logical, critical, and ironical.
The two clash continually in small spats but confront each
other in deadly earnest in the chapter titled "The Cathedral."
In this chapter Anna "spoil[s] his passionate intercourse with
the cathedral" he has loved for years and shatters with her
"pouf!" of woman's laughter Will's illusion that the cathedral
can remain "his absolute, containing all heaven and earth."
Anna forces Will to accept that it is merely the "church
building he cared for" and through which he had hoped to
possess the feminine, whereas there remained "something
unformed in his very being . . . some folded centres of darkness which would never develop and unfold whilst he was
alive in the body." She at once seems to castrate him by
demystifying his passion and to deprive him of access to his
own femininity, which she claims utterly for herself by tor-
menting him with her fecundity, producing baby after baby
in the years to come.

The plot of Lawrence's least accessible and perhaps most
infuriating (although not the least beautiful) novel *The
Plumed Serpent* (1926) involves a visionary Mexican named
don Ramon who organizes a rebellion against Christianity,
which has sapped his people's native strength and dignity, to

[16] D. H. Lawrence, *The Rainbow* (1915), ed. Mark Kinkead-Weekes
(Cambridge: Cambridge University Press, 1989), chap. 7, "The Cathedral."

reinstate a supposedly indigenous form of ritualized phallus worship dedicated to the phoenix god Quetzalcoatl. In *The Prisoner of Sex* (1971), Norman Mailer defended *The Plumed Serpent* against its detractors, who claimed variously that the novel was proto-fascist, misogynist, and by turns both crude and mystical.[17] Mailer claimed that, at his worst, Lawrence was only a "Hitler in a teapot," but at his best he was "the blessed breast of tender love." Surely the novel fits all too well Freud's comparison of obscurely symbolic art to obsessional neurosis, that "travesty, half-comic and half-tragic, of a private religion" (*SE* 9:119). But the private religion celebrated by the novel is of interest to us because of its familiarity: it celebrates the holy order of the signifier. *The Plumed Serpent* is a fantasia of the unconscious that indulges the fantasy that literary character, if not representation more generally, can be a kind of embodiment. The religion of Quetzalcoatl is one in which characters solemnly ritualize their own symbolic embodiment *as* the phallus, in which the horror of phalluslessness, which Freud says underlies fetishism, is celebrated as the momentary unity of signified and signifier.

The heroine of *The Plumed Serpent* is an Anglo-Irish woman named Kate Leslie, an attractive and independent widow, forty years old. She is tired of England and has come to Mexico, where she becomes fascinated by two dark handsome men determined to reinstitute the worship of Quetzalcoatl, an ancient phoenix god (the phoenix being one of Lawrence's favorite images). At first it seems to Kate that Mexico has little to recommend it, but her mood is black from the start. She has, Lawrence implies, come to Mexico to die, if not physically, then spiritually. And Mexico is not even a good place to die, she thinks. Once Mexico had "an elaborate ritual of death," but, it seems to Kate, the place had lost even that to Christianity, "even the passion of its own mystery" (51). Clearly, however, it is Kate and not Mexico who has lost the passion of her own mystery, and this is precisely what she must find through the ministrations of the

[17] Norman Mailer, *The Prisoner of Sex* (New York: Signet, 1971), 100.

two "big, handsome, male-looking" men.

It is important to emphasize Kate's sense of incompleteness because of how don Ramon and don Cipriano will eventually complete her (as the novel would have it). They will return to her "the passion of her own mystery." Kate feels she has lost love, faith, and hope:

> She was forty: the first half of her life was over. The bright page with its flowers and its love and its stations of the Cross ended with a grave. Now she must turn over, and the page was black, black and empty.
>
> The first half of her life had been written on the bright, smooth vellum of hope, with initial letters all gorgeous upon a field of gold. But the glamour had gone from station to station of the Cross, and the last illumination was the tomb. (52)

Kate likes to be alone: she admires the Mexican women, who seem to be individuals contented and complete in themselves. But when such individuals must come into relation with each other (to use a Jamesian expression), they lose their sense of completeness, as if they cannot help rending each other, or perhaps sacrificing parts of themselves to each other: "With the family there was always a kind of bleeding of incompleteness" (160). It would not be going too far to say that to Lawrence human life *is* this bleeding.

Lawrence proposes various psychobiological unities to staunch the bleeding and heal the wound. One is his Bergsonian assertion in "Psychoanalysis and the Unconscious" that life, consciousness, and the unconscious are incarnated simultaneously at the moment of conception, "in the very first fused nucleus of the fertilized ovule."[18] Another is the idea of marriage as genital dialectics propounded in *Apropos of Lady Chatterley's Lover* in which "the phallus is a column of blood that fills the valley of blood of a woman."[19] In words that are

[18] D. H. Lawrence, "Psychoanalysis and the Unconscious" (1921), in *Psychoanalysis and the Unconscious and Fantasia of the Unconscious,* ed. Philip Rieff (New York: Viking, 1960), 19.

[19] D. H. Lawrence, *Apropos of Lady Chatterley's Lover* (1930; London: Martin Secker, 1931), 67.

just as relevant to *The Plumed Serpent,* Lawrence asserts that "if England is to be regenerated . . . it will be by the arising of a new blood-contact, a new touch, and a new marriage. It will be a phallic rather than a sexual regeneration. For the phallus is only the great old symbol of godly vitality in a man, and of immediate contact" (77). In *The Plumed Serpent,* the incompleteness of Kate Leslie is healed by means of a phallic regeneration, which gives her the vitality of "a new touch," "a new blood-contact"—in short a verbal phallus when she is renamed by the two men who admit her into their pantheon.

But Lawrence does not conceive of the feminine and the masculine, the phallic and the vaginal (or, better, the uterine) as two complementary attributes of each individual (nor does Freud). Instead he characterizes, even caricatures, gender difference by creating characters who are either extremely masculine or extremely feminine, sometimes absurdly so. He further polarizes the two sexes by making their interactions, even their intimacies, hopelessly antinomial: sexual difference itself becomes the subject of endless heated debate between characters, who all the while struggle to achieve an ideal distance from each other (Lawrence's so-called star equilibrium). How Lawrence conceives of character "denies and asseverates" the difference between the sexes.

On the one hand, Lawrence's characters are alarmingly gender determined. Don Ramon is not merely a sexy man; he is the tumescence of the universe. He worships and is the vehicle for a cosmic sexuality of which man's body is the penis rising from the belly of the earth. This sexuality is both ideal and mindless. In its grip Ramon experiences a kind of spiritual orgasm, which rigidifies and releases his body as if he were a phallus. In the darkness of his room he "thrust his clenched fists upwards above his head, in a terrible tension of stretched, upright prayer. In his eyes was only darkness, and slowly the darkness revolved in his brain too, till he was mindless. Only a powerful will stretched itself and quivered from his spine in an immense tension of prayer. Stretched the invisible bow of the body in the darkness with inhuman tension, erect, till the arrows of the soul, mindless, shot to the mark, and the prayer reached its goal" (186). If man is a phallus, he is animated by Quetzalcoatl; and don Ramon becomes through the activity of his religion this eerily "living Quetzalcoatl," at once the embodiment and the disembodiment of the phallus.

In one of the first hymns Ramon writes for the new religion, Quetzalcoatl announces his return to Mexico: "I am the wind that whirls from the heart of the earth, the little winds that whirl like snakes round your feet and your legs and your thighs, lifting up the head of the snake of your body, in whom is your power. When the snake of your body lifts its head, beware! It is I, Quetzalcoatl, rearing up in you, rearing up and reaching beyond the bright day" (134). Ramon and Cipriano offer themselves as fetishes capable of restoring a natural potency to a people they believe emasculated by Christianity. Mexican men, Lawrence seems to think, are prodigies of manhood unaware of their sleeping sexuality. Ramon and Cipriano will save them by becoming "living words," Ramon tells his appalled wife. "All I want them to do," he explains, "is to find the beginnings of the way to their manhood, their own woman-hood." If manhood means being phallic from top to toe, womanhood means submitting completely to "the ancient god Pan," that "phallic wind rushing through the dark." Ramon and Cipriano invite Kate to join their pantheon when she at last learns to be "perfect in her proneness" beneath the phallic wind of Cipriano's Pan-like love. If Ramon is the snakey tumescence of the universe, the "living Quetzalcoatl," then Cipriano comes closer to representing the phallus itself. Cipriano is known both as the "living" Huitzilopochtli, and the "red" Huitzilopochtli. It is he who makes Kate understand what Ramon means when he says, "man is a column of blood, with a voice in it." Kate experiences with Cipriano, her "demon-lover," a new kind of ecstasy, not the "seething electrical female ecstasy" (433) of the usual peak orgasm, but something soft, heavy, hot, and mindless (perhaps Tantric), "with no personal or spiritual intimacy whatever. A mindless communion of the blood" (464).

Kate is attracted to Cipriano because he represents the end of her own activity. The "power of his blood is

> like a whirlwind that rises suddenly in the twilight and raises a great pliant column, swaying and leaning with power, clear between heaven and earth.
>
> Ah! what a marriage! How terrible! and how complete! With the finality of death, and yet more than death . . . the sheer solid mystery of passivity. Ah, what an abandon, what an abandon, what an abandon! of so many things she wanted to abandon. (342)

The "passion of her own mystery" has become "the sheer solid mystery of passivity." She is to lie still, dwarfed by this "great pliant column, swaying and leaning with power, clear between heaven and earth." (Surely this column between heaven and earth is Lawrence's old rainbow with an erection.) She is pleased to abandon the British bourgeois woman she has known as "Kate Leslie" for the sake of "mindless blood communion" with a man whom she cannot know, with whom she cannot be intimate. She abandons Kate Leslie in order to become "Malintzi." In the final ceremony of the novel, the living Quetzalcoatl (otherwise known as don Ramon) and the red Huitzilopochtli (otherwise known as don Cipriano) rename Kate Leslie "Malintzi" (not the "living"). In the process Ramon in his capacity of priest marries Cipriano to Kate, in effect giving away the groom to whom he has been a kind of father.

In *The Plumed Serpent* Lawrence has rewritten the oedipal drama from several angles at once. But Kate does not play the role of mother, nor is she the object of male desire. Instead she admires and desires the "horribly handsome" Ramon, along with Cipriano and all the "red indians" Lawrence describes with their powerful thighs and burning mindless glances, men who are the focus of sexual interest in the novel, who are gazed at lustfully through the "itching, prurient, knowing, imagining eye" of Kate and received also through her. She lies perfectly prone beneath the phallic wind, and serves as benefactor and beneficiary in a circuit of imaginary penetration and reception, deprivation and reconstitution in which Cipriano, the living, the red, is the medium of exchange, the "logical copula." If, as Lacan wished, the phallus were the sign of all desire, it could like a magic wand transform absence into presence and vice versa, inexhaustibly. It would be, as Lacan did not wish, the mother of us all.

According to the official oedipal personality profile, every child, having been disconnected from mother at birth, unconsciously conceives of himself or herself as mother's missing penis. Consequently to some extent he or she would conceive of life's purpose as the fulfillment and completion of the mother. And if, as André Green suggested in a passage quoted earlier, the child "can only achieve his status as subject" by imagining a reunion with the mother's body in order thus to complete her, then that child's psychological health would depend upon the ability to identify with the mother as well as with the father. The boy must be willing imaginatively to feminize himself in order to remasculate her. Why in *The Plumed Serpent* does this identification take place in a fetishistic swoon in which the subject becomes the grandiose copula connecting "heaven" and "earth"? Ramon, Cipriano, and Kate are happiest when falling out of selfhood into a kind of mindlessness in which they are both undifferentiated and more themselves than ever. For Lawrence getting beyond the personal means not only the end of discrimination or differentiation but also the end of desire. Watching a symbolic Mexican festive dance one evening, Kate feels herself "gone into her greater self, her womanhood consummated in the greater womanhood"; "she was not herself, she was gone"; "her own desires were gone in the ocean of the great desire"; "her personal eyes had gone blind" (243). Later in the novel Lawrence associates this impersonality with "the blood" ("the blood is one blood"), as if these characters were being reborn at last into that "true unconscious" Lawrence claims is in the blood. Assuming, as we probably should, that it is not in the blood, where is this place of desire beyond desires?

It is in a womb beyond the womb. One consequence of the multiform copulation of *The Plumed Serpent* is that it produces out of the folds of the text a new female character, Malintzi, simply by changing the name of an old one. Ramon reconceives himself and produces the living Quetzalcoatl; he then makes Cipriano the next "living word," Huitzilopochtli; then they add the third, Malintzi. In syntactical terms, they form a complete simple sentence: subject, verb, object, respectively. But symbolically it is as if two men have given birth to a woman; as Ramon puts it, "She will be a mother among the gods." How could two men give birth to their own mother? In two interestingly confused ways: first as a father/son pair who together supply the mother with a phallus and thus complete her; and second, by imagining the rectum as a womb. These ideas are not far-fetched, in Freud's terms, given what he has said about fetishism and also about childish theories of coitus and childbearing. Nor are they far-fetched in Lawrence's terms, given *Women in Love* (1920) in which Birkin wished to get "beyond the phallic principle" to a place behind the "mystic loins," or Lady Chatterley's particular sexual enlightenment in *Lady Chatterley's Lover* (1928).

Understood literally this is a sterile fantasy; babies cannot be born rectally, but in at least one sense it is a fertile notion that generates meanings capable of carrying us out of what one of Lawrence's contemporaries described as the "monstrous wilderness of phallicism" characteristic of his work.[20] Psychoanalysis conventionally assumed that every child begins with a "bisexual identification," which meant that he or she identifies to some degree with both parents, not just the one of his or her own sex. According to a best-case scenario, a boy in the oedipal phase would not only wish to make love to his mother like his father, but would imagine as well being his mother in order to be loved by his father. We must assume that a girl child would experience an analogous-

[20] Robert Lynd in *The Daily News* (1915), quoted by Harry T. Moore in *The Priest of Love: A Life of D. H. Lawrence* (1954; Harmondsworth: Penguin, 1974), 306.

ly double sexual identification. She would not only wish to be possessed by her father, but to be her father in order to make love to her mother. It seems entirely possible that the vehement cultural denial of this latter identification with the father could engender the girl's so-called penis envy (insofar as any girl experiences any) rather than some presumable recognition of the superiority of the male organ. Penis envy would then be the sign of a presence, of desire and sexual aggression (toward her mother) rather than an absence. Analogously a boy would probably experience womb or perhaps breast envy, envy for the nurturing faculties of woman, yearnings that have been long repressed by "civilization," but which in our time are demanding expression. The lake in *The Plumed Serpent*, which is the novel's poetic center, is described as double: it is both a lake of sperm, and a "frail milk of thunder."

If womb envy is analogous to penis envy, then the fantasy of anal birthing should be taken to be the "objective correlative" for the naming of Kate by Ramon and Cipriano. If it is fair (and I'm not saying it is) to think of the clitoris as a little phallus, then it is fair to consider the male rectum as a little womb. In this light Lawrence's habitual oscillation between male and female points of view becomes neither simply homoerotic nor homophobic, neither misogynist nor feminist, so much as a literary way of halting "the bleeding of incompleteness" to which fetishism emerges as a hysterical masculinist response. *The Plumed Serpent* is a fetishistic text that memorializes not only the horror of castration, but also that of hysterectomy, in other words, of the loss of generativity and referentiality itself. As compensation for these horrors Lawrence claims that language is a cultural ritual capable of making ideas concrete; the text can embody, materialize, constitute the thing named. Literary characters—word-masses that take the form of a man and woman who want to unite—unite signified and signifier in such a way that they may never be put asunder, since it is the estrangement of signified and signifier that represents human sterility, the inefficacy of humans at work in their world.

For Lawrence, like Forster and others, fictional characters are different, more real, than other kinds of words. Characters embody "the voices of the honourable beasts that call in the dark paths of the veins . . . the lowing of the inner-most beasts, the feelings, that roam in the forest of the blood."[21] Again, this asks to be taken literally, as if characters were textual platelets we could absorb like a transfusion from the body of the author to heal our own "bleeding." Such characters know more than we do about what is real; if we don't recognize our own feelings, "if we can't hear the cries far down in our own forest of dark veins, we can look in the real novels, and there listen-in . . . to the low, calling cries of the characters, as they wander in the dark woods of their destiny" (759). Characters in "real novels" subject *our* feelings to *their* destinies. This naive idea of character expresses the wish that representation be more than a system of cognizable signs—that it be, indeed, capable of embodiment in the form of "living images," a notion, right out of Freud's *Interpretation of Dreams*.

The nonliterary image construct most like literary character is the over determined dream image. In *The Interpretation of Dreams* Freud tells us that some elements of our dreams are more vivid and intense than others. These especially vivid elements are determined "by two independent factors. In the first place, it is easy to see that the elements by which the wish-fulfillment is expressed are represented with special intensity. And in the second place, analysis shows that the most vivid elements of a dream are the starting-point of the most numerous trains of thought—that the most vivid elements are also those with the most numerous determinants."[22] These overdetermined elements of a dream most directly representative of a wish-fulfillment come as close to being "embodiments" as any representations Freud describes. In the dream of coherence represented by the discourse of

[21] D. H. Lawrence, "The Novel and the Feelings" (1936), in *Phoenix: The Posthumous Papers of D. H. Lawrence*, ed. Edward D. McDonald (Harmondsworth: Penguin, 1978), 759.
[22] Freud, *The Interpretation of Dreams*, in *SE* 4:330.

psychoanalysis taken as a whole, the overdetermined living image or so-called switch-word functions much as the living words of *The Plumed Serpent*. Both express a belief in the brain as the natural producer of reflexive, self-referential, internally coherent, representation.

For both Freud and Lawrence, healing the "psyche," whether defined as mind or soul, meant acknowledging that consciousness is continuous with the unconscious, and that both are somatic entities. This is so despite the seeming dichotomy between Lawrence's fervent irrationalism and Freud's indefatigable rationalism; both were motivated by an anti-idealism based on the de-transcendentalizing notion that consciousness is a function of physiology. Consciousness for both, in other words, a by-product of the brain rather than a phenomenon of mind, is dominated by the unconscious, while the unconscious, in turn, appears as the voice of the body. It would not be going too far to say, then, that for Freud and Lawrence the source for what we think of as the "I" is the body, and that the body becomes by implication the ultimate referent of all representation, all discourse, all signification. By this logic, representation begins and ends inside us, and would be, finally, merely reflexive, or at most expressive, *if* Freud and Lawrence had it right. This model is analogous to "la langue" rather than "la parole," to language rather than discourse; it accords no place to culture, interaction, or the public sphere. This identification of representation with the body constitutes at once a mystification and a reduction of meaning: and the question Freud and Lawrence raise by implication is to what extent do we continue to think of language as embodiment, as symbol, as fetish by, on the one hand, viewing the body as the product of cultural technologies and, on the other, their material substratum? And my answer would be, precisely to the degree that we think of language as speaking us, rather than the reverse.

Paul Ricoeur has said that for Freud psychoanalysis is pre-eminently "the great work of 'becoming conscious.'"[23] For

---

[23] Paul Ricoeur, *Freud and Philosophy*, trans. Denis Savage (New Haven: Yale University Press, 1970), 412.

Lawrence, on the other hand, as for the artists of the modern avant-garde, art, and by extension life, is the great work of becoming *unconscious*. *Sum, ergo non cogito,* writes Lawrence (1929) in a late poem.[24] Freud suggested that there exists in us what I shall call a "drive to representation" as basic and organic as our other instincts. The unconscious cannot help expressing itself all the time, or at least, it cannot stop trying. (Where there's life, there's art.) Expression is an act of which we may become conscious through interpretation: interpretation interrupts the flow of expression and makes consciousness possible. We become conscious insofar as we are able to reflect upon and interpret the expressions of the unconscious. For Freud consciousness is desirable, even therapeutic, because it frees us to some degree from the willful unconscious and its importunate self-expression.

For Lawrence the road to freedom runs in exactly the opposite direction, away from consciousness and interpretation back to expression. Lawrence seems enamored of the drive-to-representation itself—that is, he idealizes, sexualizes, and fetishizes it—and wants consciousness to surrender to it. He exhorts us, thirsty from the unnatural heats of post-Enlightenment consciousness, to plunge instead into the Bergsonian life of the "blood" whose expressions alone are real. Lawrence's idea of good literary language is therefore like Freud's definition of "dream-work," that rich symbolic discourse we produce while we sleep. (This helps explain the unapologetically uneven and spontaneous feel of Lawrence's language.) For Lawrence art is experienced with the feelings; art is to be taken literally, not literarily, as if it could embody meaning, not merely express or represent it, as if literary language were not a representation of something, but a something-in-itself. As we have seen in works from *Capital* to *The Plumed Serpent,* the "drive to representation" when fetishized seems to offer a magical cure for our "bleeding of incompleteness," for our painful knowledge that experience is never whole, but

---

[24] D. H. Lawrence, "The Spiral Flame," in *The Complete Poems,* ed. Vivian de Sola Pinto and Warren Roberts (Harmondsworth: Penguin, 1977), 439.

always only in part(s). This fetishization appears in turn to fetishize us, who in our daily lives as members of a self-concerned patriarchal culture are asked to fulfill hyperbolic categorical definitions of gender that institutionalize difference as varieties of one untranscended materiality.

The idea of a biological "drive to representation" is implicit almost everywhere in Freud's work but is relatively explicit in *The Interpetation of Dreams*. As is often the case with definitions of the so-called natural, this one serves as the justification for certain metaphysical assumptions. Based on the assumption that the brain is "always already" engaged in representation, and that there is no mental act prior to representation, however unconscious, Freud argues that the mind is by nature formal, far more formal than psychoanalysis can begin to suggest (*SE* 4:329). Freud thus suggests that the mind itself is the prototype for autonomous art (even though humans themselves are not autonomous, but forever psychologically dependent) and implies at the same time that autonomous art is, conversely, the natural expression of biologically immanent embodied beings. One might think that this innate drive to representation would, like other instincts such as hunger or self-preservation, be spared gender labeling.[25] Apparently, however, this drive too, like the sexual "instincts" with their teleological heterosexuality, comes to have "psychological meaning" only when its vicissitudes "coalesce . . . with the antithesis masculine/feminine."[26]

According to psychoanalysis, the polymorphous infantile libido must ultimately come under the rule of heterosexual genitality. Even so, and in an analogous way, the polymorphous mind of the writer, Forster told us, creates word masses which, despite the complexity and variety of love in real life, in "monotonous" fashion behave like "a man and woman who want to be united." Even in twentieth-century novels, then, (just as in classical comedy) the operation of

[25] Scientific attempts to prove that the brain is always already gendered persist. See, for example, the singularly unconvincing Anne Moir and David Jessel, *Brain Sex: The Real Difference between Men and Women* (Secaucus, N.J.: Carol Publishing Group, 1991).
[26] Freud, "Instincts and Their Vicissitudes," in *SE* 14:134.

Hymen can guarantee a work aesthetic unity and psychosocial palatability. More to the point, in the modern novel the
two come to "mean" each other reflexively, as Forster's
weary tone indicates. Nevertheless, the thematic ubiquity of
man/woman love in the novel needed some explaining, just
as Freud felt obliged to explain somehow the predominance
of heterosexuality among adults who had all once been thoroughly polymorphously perverse. Neither Forster nor Freud
nor any of the other moderns, however, explained the ubiquity of heterosexual love and marriage in primarily social or
cultural terms, but rather as the normal progress of bodies
ruled by reproductive instinct, or as an image of the creative
mind at its work of manufacturing unity.

At least this was so publicly. In *Maurice,* Forster's novel
about men desiring men written in 1913–14 but not published until 1971, the title character learns to accept that his
unconventional desires "have arisen inside his own body."[27]
He was born with what his doctor calls "congenital homosexuality"; and, despite the doctor's best efforts to redirect his
libido, Maurice apparently can't change what came naturally
(180). Forster represents heterosexuality, by contrast, as a
social construct, a product of the educational system, and a
function of the propertied classes' will to propagate themselves. Forster represents Maurice's desire for men as originating in his unconscious. We know of it first (before he does)
from Maurice's boyhood dreams, memories, desires, and
fears. Heterosexuality, on the other hand, Forster portrays as
a cultural institution maintained by weak women and the
men who feel obliged to support them. A case in point is the
character Clive, Maurice's first lover, who one day involuntarily rejects his homosexuality, gets married, and becomes a
"pillar of society." The novel ends with Maurice and his new,
sexy, working-class lover eloping together away from England
to another land where, they hope, men can "share" without
fear of prosecution. In imagining same-sex desire as a utopian
alternative to class-ridden British domesticity, *Maurice* was,
to say the least, unusual.

[27] E. M. Forster, *Maurice* (New York: Norton, 1987), 192.

But, on the other hand, Forster's "project" in *Maurice* is typically modern because he both defines Maurice's sexuality as congenital, as in the "blood," and criticizes the institution of marriage even as he relies on the usual gender stereotypes to rationalize differences that are hard to explain as innate (239). Biologism, it should be stressed, is not inconsistent with hierarchical sexism. Whether or not they seem logically compatible, historically they are of a piece. Biologism, or scientific individualism, which began to take hold in the middle of the nineteenth century, did not dislodge patriarchy but merely provided it with its modern incarnation, namely the body/sex system. Characters in novels represent biological immanence; they mimic the "form of the form" of the individual. Although made out of words— letters and characters—they are almost invariably "male or "female."[28] Characters thus are verbal constructs which, to apply Delphy's words here concerning the meaning of sex in patriarchal culture, more than any others "appear not to be such, but rather to be categories furnished by reality itself, e.g. the categories 'women' and 'men.'" Like the categories women and men, which become categories of thought through "social practice alone," the genders of literary characters become "relevant distinctions" in the social worlds of their novels. Animated by the idealized energies we project into them, as we imaginatively introject them, they appear to be autonomous, to desire each other, to have ambitions, selves, psychologies, identities, "interiors." They function both as fetishes in a "metabolism of images," which offers us as readers the sensation of plenitude and continuity, and as mysterious commodities, which seem at once to create and satisfy some need for which we are not responsible.

A novel offers itself to us as a utopian sphere, utopian because it appears to be an object of whose self-sufficiency

---

[28] One exception to this convention, or rather an experiment with it, is Beckett's novel *How It Is* (1961), in which characters with names such as Bem, Bom, and Pim, and couples designated by single letters and numbers, seem barely human, barely gendered, but because they are "barely" so, the reader is forced to realize what minimal cues are needed to provoke the anthropomorphic projection of character and gender onto verbal fragments.

we can paradoxically partake. Pornographic and formulaic romance novels capitalize on the undifferentiated sexual, emotional, and mental responses they evoke regardless of whether or not some of those readers also analyze their texts. The pleasure such fictions offer—an experience of fusion and escape, of sensory *under*-load—is for many small compensation for what Georg Lukács describes as the inner emptiness of work, no matter how well written, which lacks "idea."[29] Any work, of course, can have "idea" if a reader has an idea about it. Even so, one could argue that interiority is the fetish-idea of the modern novel, with characters its most stubbornly psychologistic embodiment; insofar as characters appear to be at the center of the "sphere" of the novel, they are instrumental in maintaining the illusion of interiority. This interiority is actually composed of a set of isomorphic interiorities nestled inside each other like Chinese boxes: characters are inside the book; the book is inside my head; the characters have their own insides, and live in houses, in towns, in nations, all of which fit inside my head. These interiorities pretend to belong to the novel; but really they belong to me.

If from a contemporary perspective we would describe reading as intersubjective and interactive rather than private, the modern novel resists that analysis at every turn.[30] In her essay "Mr. Bennett and Mrs. Brown" (1924) comparing Edwardian fiction with more recent work, Virginia Woolf criticized Edwardians such as Wells, Bennett, and Galsworthy for writing books not complete in themselves. Their novels, it seemed to Woolf, were not enough interested in themselves or their own characters' impressions of things but rather forced the reader to "complete them," a phrase she didn't explain.[31]

---

[29] Georg Lukács, *The Theory of the Novel*, trans. Anna Bostock (Cambridge: MIT Press, 1971), 115.

[30] For a psychoanalytic, yet not psychologistic, account of meaning in Henry James's *The Turn of the Screw* as intersubjective, see Shoshana Felman, "Turning the Screw of Interpretation," in *Literature and Psychoanalysis: The Question of Reading: Otherwise*, ed. Shoshana Felman (Baltimore: Johns Hopkins University Press, 1982), 94–207.

[31] Virginia Woolf, "Mr. Bennett and Mrs. Brown" (1924), in *Collected Essays* (New York: Harcourt, Brace, World, 1967), 1:326–27.

Woolf admired modern novels that were self-contained worlds but felt they had a new and different limitation. The novelist of her generation lacked a "convention" for proceeding from common ground to intimacy with the unknown reader, a maneuver a skillful hostess might manage, for example, by discussing the weather, or a gentleman his property (331). Modern novelists, Woolf thought, lacked a social copula. (Woolf's characters suffer from the same affliction; it is excruciating for Lily Briscoe in *To the Lighthouse*, for example, to get out of her head and speak to someone.) As representation and the interiority it constituted became themselves valued aesthetic commodities, their referentiality, their commonsensical conventional relation to a social world with a material substratum not made of language became more tenuous.

The novel may be, as Lukács has put it, "the epic of a world that has been abandoned by God" (88), the epic story of the "great battle of interiority against the prosaic vulgarity of outward life" (104). But as even this formulation makes clear, in the novel "interiority" stands in for God, for the experience of transcendence as immanent, a substitution fraught with all the attendant problems of idealized subjectivity, leaving the novel in the same problematic relation to stuff "outside" the autonomous world it comprises as any other ideal. For Lukács, "the hierarchical question of whether inner reality is superior to outer reality or vice versa" becomes an ethical one to the degree that he considers art as autonomous and the novel as a vessel for the (fetishized) idea of some unborn world. Lukács wonders how to get from the interior world to the world of action, whether the novel, "this rounded correction of reality [can] be translated into actions which, regardless of outward failure or success, prove the individual's right to self-sufficiency. To create, by purely artistic means, a reality which corresponds to this dream world, or at least is more adequate to it than the existing one, is only an illusory solution" (115). The modern novelists we have come to revere, and teach most often as quintessentially modern, were not looking for "solutions" but substitutions, "rounded correction[s] of reality."

As the architect Christian Norberg-Schulz has written concerning buildings that appear too self-sufficient because they are too rounded, the sphere is "the most forbidding . . . of the elementary stereometrical forms."[32] Spheres, having "no directions," rest in themselves. "The closed curve . . . returns to its starting point" and suggests "closure," defying the perceiver's "participation" in a form too forbidding to be desirable in architecture, a form of ostensibly material and public art when it is intended for other than religious purposes (136). I mention this passage because in it Norberg-Schulz suggests that closure is in aesthetic effect religious. To put this another way, one could say that religion is —or that God is—the form of inclusive closure, of closed inclusiveness, the unitary signifier, the form of self-sufficiency, rounded, resistant. For many readers, Woolf's novels, complete in themselves, have proven to be public art as forbidding to "participation" as a dome. As a unitary signifier, the reflexive novel, which fetishizes its own interiority, could be said to play upon the reader what Donna Haraway calls (in a different context) "the god-trick." God is One, one circle whose center is everywhere and whose circumference is nowhere; unity is God; one is God; God is one. Here are some other God-tricks we play on ourselves:

(male) body = One
fetishist + fetish = One
you + what you eat = One
man + woman = One
mother + baby = One
lover + lover = One
Father + Son + Holy Ghost = One
mother + father + baby = One

The reader has probably noticed that the fantasmatic psycho-geometries of religion, of romance, and of oedipality are

[32] Christian Norberg-Schulz, *Intentions in Architecture* (Cambridge: MIT Press, 1979), 134.

suspiciously similar. This explains why "the fetish" is such a useful term.

In *The Heresy of Self-Love*, Paul Zweig discusses literary works that seem to conflate the experience of self-sufficient subjectivity with God, or rather substitute the former for the latter.[33] In Rousseau, for example, "the correspondence between Macrocosm and Microcosm, exploded by seventeenth-century science and skepticism is re-established in the emotional experience of the *Reveries*":

> During such periods of reverie, the mind becomes like crystal, emptied of all disturbing images. The boundaries of the self expanded, until the entire world became a delicate rhythm, a gentle interpretation of thought and object, seer and seen: "What do we enjoy at such a moment? Nothing outside us, nothing if not ourselves and our own existence; as long as this feeling continues, we are self-sufficient, like God." Self and world were so profoundly intermingled as to have become synonymous. (164)

The pretense of this interiority, however, is that it represents:

> . . . a world that has once again been shaped with and by humanity; a world that is neither hostile nor formal and hierarchical. It is an "ego-morphic" world, shaped by the pleasures and the character of a single imagination. (165)

Zweig distinguishes between two routes writers take to achieve the transcendent synonymity of self and God, which he calls the way "up" and the way "down."

The goal of poets on the way up, such as Wordsworth and Shelley, was, according to Zweig, a "regeneration of the ego" in the service of some greater good by means of which the love of self comes to approximate selflesslessness, poets who like Stephen Dedalus in *A Portrait of the Artist as a Young Man* through "inner work" give birth to God. The individual merges with the general when he feels personal will and

---

[33] Paul Zweig, *The Heresy of Self-Love: A Study of Subversive Individualism* (Princeton: Princeton University Press, 1968).

impersonal desire have become synonymous. A writer on the way down, one who takes what has been called "the negative way," a writer like Baudelaire, Kierkegaard, Nietzsche, or Dostoevski, through a "terrible concentration of self" changes "himself into what he already was" (257). Aggressive individuation and personalization is such a writer's response to isolation in a world "abandoned by God." Georges Bataille offered a more exciting, less theistic but still sacral version of this formulation, one even more relevant to the romantic epistemologies of modernism. Bataille contrasted the "Icarian revolt" with its opposite, "base" revolt or what he called "excremental vision."[34] In Bataille's terms, many modernists, including André Breton, were "fucking idealists", engaged in "Icarian revolt," and doomed to fall from the heights of their own egoism.[35] Base revolt, Bataille's chosen route, took the low road; instead of the homogeneous ego-morphisms of idealism, base revolt cultivated (at least in theory) community, heterogeneity, excess, and sacrifice.

Bataille thought that everyone's deepest and truest desire was to break out of what he called "discontinuous" being, to escape that painful "nostalgia felt by discontinuous beings for the continuity lost at birth" and become indistinguishably continuous with everyone and everything else instead. At the same time, because "continuity" means death, it is what we most fear: "Two things are inevitable; we cannot avoid dying nor can we avoid bursting through our barriers, and they are one and the same."[36] "Discontinuous" being is synonymous with individuality and survival: ". . . while we desire a return to the continuity of being which death promises, our fear of the loss, of the disappearance of our discontinuous self, is embodied by the anguish and fascination felt before the spectacle of death in sacrifice, which permits us to identify with the victim's return to continuity without having actually to

[34] Georges Bataille, *Visions of Excess: Selected Writings, 1927–1939*, ed. and trans. Allan Stoekl (Minneapolis: University of Minnesota Press, 1985).
[35] Quoted in Maurice Nadeau, *The History of Surrealism*, trans. Richard Howard (Cambridge: Harvard University Press, 1989), 156.
[36] Georges Bataille, *Death and Sensuality: A Study of Eroticism and the Taboo* (New York: Walker, 1984), 140.

undergo our own dissolution."[37] Icarian revolt, which Bataille
associates with idealism, would be a quest for eternal discontinuity, to be, to the greatest extent possible, eternally but
the spectator at the sacrifice of others. Base revolt, on the
other hand, would mean to bring into this discontinuous
existence, the greatest degree of continuity possible.

The ideas of Zweig and Bataille mentioned here referred, in
their original contexts, mainly to authors, artists, and political
subjects rather than to characters in novels, novels as whole
constructs, or readers, my topics in this chapter. Nevertheless,
I return to the novel in order to suggest that the verisimilitude
of its virtual psychologism arises from a disavowal analogous
to the disavowal operative in fetishism. The fetishist, to paraphrase Freud, both believes in the maternal phallus and dis-
avows that belief. The fetish is the "memorial" standing in
the place of the lost object, proving it is irrevocably lost while
at the same time replacing it. The fetish accretes in the liminal space in which the subject oscillates between his individuation and his annihilation and is therefore the switch-point in
the machine language of the binary subject as he moves from
"one" to "zero." The algorithm of one and zero symbolized by
the fetish only seems to refer to the woman: as if either she
has the penis or she doesn't. It would be more accurate, more
truthful, however, to say that this algorithm defines the subject in his presence or absence to himself, for himself; the subject, insofar as he (or she) is the virtual other in a fantasmatic
dyad, either is or isn't. It is the horrible mistake made seemingly since the beginning of history to think that this algorithm represents sex difference, rather than individuation versus relation per se.

In Krafft-Ebing's Case 97 (discussed in Chapter 2), no one
could help the self-cannibalizing fetishist escape the hunger
of an unconscious metabolism that insisted on taking the
images of his desire literally. He could only fetishize and idealize; he could not individualize, intentionalize, or narrativize. That is, he could not step outside the story into which

[37] Georges Bataille, *Inner Experience*, trans. and intro. Leslie Anne Boldt
(Albany: State University of New York Press, 1988), xii–xiii.

he had disappeared. Could he have saved himself if he could have been the "reader" as well as the author and subject of his history, if, in other words, he could have maintained some point of view outside the text from which to recognize the self-consuming subject/object reflexivity that destroyed him? If a reader is while reading the audience and spectator at a symbolic drama of his own making, is he then more than the other half of a dyad consisting of the implied author and the reader (as Georges Poulet suggests ecstatically in "The Phenomenology of Reading") whose romantic fusion comprises the regressive aspect of reading? Is he a third party observing and conscious of the suspicious doings of the other two? Would this third party, phenomenologically speaking, be able to triangulate the self/other pair that is otherwise always in danger of deliquescing into mere subject/object reflexivity? Is this spectator in psychoanalytic terms, analogous to the child who turns the oedipal couple into an eternal triangle by becoming the interested spectator at the primal scene?[38]

This spectator, this reader, this child, this subject, occupies a far more ambiguous position, even or perhaps especially within psychoanalysis, than even psychoanalysis has been willing to suggest. If we "read" the position of the interested spectator of the primal scene in terms of the algorithms of fetishism, the subject is limited to being a "one" or a "zero" whether he feels vicariously included in the scene or excluded from it. If included, he becomes in effect the "copula" uniting the two lovers (the parents, in Freudian terms) and thus becomes "zero" as himself but "one" with them. If excluded, he sees the other two as "one" while he is an excluded one and thus a zero who must find another with whom to become one. A dualistic model offering the choice of "two" versus "three" is congruent with the one/zero model. Neither allows for either individuality or heterogene-

[38] I would suggest that Lacan's entire theory of psychoanalysis, including how he trains novice analysts, can be read as stemming from his dominant sense of himself as this third party, intruding on the intimate interactions of couples of which he is not a part (for example, the analyst-in-training and the analysand).

ity. Both are bi-univocal relations that oscillate between the two psychometric poles defining modernism, poles Deleuze and Guattari call "schizo Eros and Oedipal Thanatos" (36).

But psychoanalysis, with its investment in oedipality, privileges the so-called third position as if it were the essence of maturity and genitality. Psychoanalysis equates the subject position of the epistemophilic child with that of the detached and sublimating individual. Wondering, as did Lukács, how one escapes from interiority to action, from reflexivity to referentiality, from fetishism to object relations, Julia Kristeva found the solution to be this "third position: father, form, schema." Assuming, she writes, that feeling or affect is the "most archaic inscription of internal and external events, how does one get from there to signs?" How do archaic inscriptions, in other words, become what we call "representations"? As a result of our triumph over our sorrow at discovering that we are individuals:

> By following one hypothesis, the infant, prompted by separation (note the necessity of a 'lack' if the sign is to arise) at first produces or utilizes objects or vocalizations that are the symbolic equivalents of that lacking. . . . Subsequently, and from the so-called depressive position, he tries to signify the sorrow that submerges him by producing in his own ego elements that while alien to the exterior world, are to correspond to that lost or displaced exteriority: we are, then, no longer in the presence of equivalences but of symbols in the proper sense of the word. . . . [S]uch a triumph over sorrow is rendered possible by the ego's capacity to now identify no longer with the lost object but with a third position: father, form, schema. This identification with a third position, that may be called phallic or symbolic identification, ensures the subject's entry into the universe of signs and of creation.[39]

Calling this third position in the symbolic order (as opposed to the order of the fetish) "phallic" is a dead giveaway that

---

[39] Julia Kristeva, "On Melancholic Imagination," in *Postmodernism and Continental Philosophy*, ed. Hugh J. Silverman and Donn Welton (Albany: State University of New York Press, 1988), 15.

Kristeva's symbolic order is nothing more than patriarchy. Equating the female with the phallic, and the phallic with form, structure, or schema, reconstitutes the very syntax of displacement and equivalence by means of which the economy of fetishism erases difference and creates autonomous ideals out of signs and symbols. Triangulation, oedipalization, is merely dyadic oscillation stricken into stability. The oedipalization of everyday life, after all, remains the most commodifiable legacy of psychoanalysis.

The novel flourishes in the space between our psychological credulity that one, two, and three are different subject positions, and our fetishistic insistence than one, two, and three add up to one. Both beliefs are forms of romance for which the novel is perfectly suited. The novel's realism, in other words, is profoundly and disingenuously domestic. Reading is a religious experience represented as the drama of sex and gender. Even Jean Genet, the facts of whose own life and whose ironical attitude toward that life reveal a singular rejection of the bourgeois domestic social world, represents the author and reader as a nondiffering couple, more like co-parents than like, for example, the sado-masochistic author-reader pair constituted by Beckett's fiction. As the asocial or antisocial co-creators of a sinful spectacle that unfolds within us as we read, as a psychologically primitive and fused pair, and because we form this pair, reader and writer share special sins and a possibility of redemption. That is, within the womb-like work —here a male womb identified with an antisocial rectal space like that "beyond the phallic principle" in D. H. Lawrence—within the social world, a parallel religious universe reconstitutes itself.

Genet's exquisite novel *Querelle* is at the same time an exercise in triangulation, or perhaps trinitization, a prolonged meditation upon what two-ness and three-ness—the order of the fetish versus the order of the story—look like from the hypothetical vantage point occupied by the narrator, who tells us in different ways about a man who watches another man being loved by others. For him writing is alternately the occupation and resignation of the problematic "third position," occupations and resignations seen as erotic, spiritual, and moral:

> It is not our design to disengage two or several characters—or heroes, as they have been extracted from a fabulous domain, that is to say, they have their origin in fable, fable and limbo— and describe them, methodically, as odious. One should rather consider it to be ourselves, pursuing an adventure unfolding in ourselves, in the deepest, most asocial region of our soul; it is indeed, because he breathes life into his creatures—and voluntarily assumes the burden of sin of this world he has given birth to—that the creator delivers and saves his creature, and at the same time places himself beyond or above sin. May the reader, too, escape from sin, while he, reading our words, discovers in himself these heroes, who have been in hiding until this time. (94)

The narrator is beyond sin at the same time that he is up to his neck in it; he "voluntarily assumes the burden of sin" because he does not fear feeling feminized by it. Genet welcomes the role of the feminized patriarch and like the mothery Son takes the world into himself to carry its burden of sin: "I shall not know peace until he makes love to me, but only when he enters me and then lets me stretch out on my side across his thighs, holding me the way the dead Jesus is held in a Pietà" (275). The one who holds the spent body is the one who while entering that body does so "with seemingly the same passion a female animal shows when holding the dead body of her young offspring—the attitude by which we comprehend what love is: consciousness of the division of what previously was one, of what it is to be thus divided, while you yourself are watching yourself" (75). This passage suggests a mythical prehistory for itself in which what is now divided "previously was one," a oneness figured by a pregnant animal. The passage refers to at least four separate couples: two who are unnamed except as "they," Norbert and Querelle (who are for the moment in the background), and the female animal with its dead offspring (to which they are compared); the "we" comprised by the narrator and the reader who together "comprehend what love is"; and the pair made up of the "you yourself" watching "yourself," who seem to comprise all three other couples at once.

Genet thus opens the novel to the competing metanarratives of unity he has inherited—Christianity, sexology, naturalism, aestheticism—and sounds them together. By striking them in unison he causes them to amplify and intensify each other, so that they resonate together in rich chords of ironic, aching desire. Genet's is anti-autonomous art aware of its own dependencies, and of ours. In Genet the long abjected Mother/Son relations of Christianity emerge as the truth of a soiled and delicious oedipal drama any number can play, and must play as long as this drama remains the constitutive romance of the modern era. It could be argued, on the other hand, that, as E. Ann Kaplan has suggested in discussing the poetics of MTV, following Baudrillard, that we are now living not only in the postmodern era, but in the post-oedipal era as well.[40] The oedipal narrative, in other words, may no longer be adequate to describe our various family romances, let alone the interactions among individuals, families, and larger social systems. If this is true, then the oedipal narrative, continually replotted as the story of a man and woman striving to become one, thus becomes as much a period piece as "significant form," autonomous art, or automobilism.

[40] See E. Ann Kaplan, *Rocking around the Clock: Music Television, Postmodernism, and Consumer Culture* (New York: Routledge, 1987).

[4]

Sensuous Thought and the Autosymbol: Modernism and the Subjective Correlative

People these days no longer write with their race, but with their blood
(what a platitude!)
— Tristan Tzara, "Open Letter to Jacques Rivière"

Based on the arguments made in the preceding chapters, the omnipresence of romantic love and heterosexual marriage as structural themes in the novel can be seen as a kind of literary repetition compulsion, an obsessive domestic ritual enacted in public by generations of novelists. This obsession does not represent an absolute human psychology, however, but rather the long social, cultural, and economic history of masculinist oedipality we have inherited. Of our own time, the most we can say for sure is that this history continues, even as it fragments, reproduces, and wars against itself. As far as the history of the novel is concerned, it was the modern novelist who foregrounded an awareness that the endless romantic travails of seemingly male and female characters, made, after all, only of words, needed explaining and who explained them as symbolic epiphenomena.

Some modern novelists, such as James, Forster, Woolf, and Joyce, who conceived of the imagination as a collector of impressions, a conjoiner of forms, or a racial conscience, explained their romantic preoccupations as by-products of the mind at work. Others, such as Lawrence or Genet, explained these preoccupations as expressions of the soul in its somatic experience. Either way the peculiar vivacity that animates literary characters reflected both the paradoxically natural immanence of language and, conversely, the symbolic nature of human experience as understood by the modernists. Psychoanalysis, the science of the imagination in its instinctual drive for meaningful coherence, institutionalized these very assumptions even as it tried to free them from their religious and moralist determinants. In this chapter I attempt to locate similar themes in the poetry we most frequently teach as "modern."

By "similar themes," I do not mean romantic love, heterosexual marriage, or the gender identity of character, but rather the complementary phenomena of idealization and abjection, which keep them alive. In modern poetry these two problems manifest themselves in the idealization of language as material and the abjection of the subject as immaterial. Together they effect the would-be feminization of representation—that is, divorcing it from an external "world" to make it seem a self-sufficient embodiment of meaning, a phallic mother, a repressive feminization to which postmodernism could then be read as a playful, and often despairing, response. Even without going that far, however, literary high modernism can be interpreted as a kind of self-conscious epistemophilia by means of which the modernists valorized representation in ways that develop logically into our nearly global conflation of image with information, and identity with meaning.

T. S. Eliot long ago noticed and praised as characteristically poetic what I diagnose as characteristically modern. He named the epistemophilic idealization of language and the epistemophobic abjection of the subject, respectively, "sensuous thought" and the "objective correlative." These perfectly expressive, and now perhaps too familiar, neologisms, and what they signify, add an ascetic twist to the theme of fetishism. The technical coherence of high modernism is derived from how it represents the incoherence of consciousness in flux because our canon of formalist modernist texts present consciousness simultaneously as real and as that which defines and constitutes what is real. Modern consciousness associated itself, however, not with transcendental but with linguistic concepts of "being" or "soul," with language as nonmetaphysical, even antimetaphysical and antitheological, language that was its own religion and thus made certain creationist claims on its own behalf, language that, by embodying meaning, as it were, "outside" the body, made us both the creators of, and creatures in, the world.

Fetishism is the ironic concretization of godlessness, one form of which was the romantic belief in "art for art's sake" valorized aesthetically by the New Criticism and socioculturally by structuralism. In the modern era the side of the moon we could not see, and which we still choose not to see, is the "subject" in his or her particularity.[1] If the erasure of the subject seems to the reader an old problem not worthy of resurrection, I would respond that feminist critique as well as those forms of politicized historicism practiced by what David Simpson has called "the history party" have begun to show what we collectively lose by erasing the subject without having any radically politicized individualism with which to replace it.[2] That modernism did not particularize the subject was so despite the seemingly single-minded interest of psychoanalysis in that very subject, and despite our conventional understanding of English literary high modernism as the climax of a trend toward artistic subjectivity originating in both English and Continental romanticism.

In a formulation designed to burst the balloon of linguistic "presence" inflated by such accounts and simultaneously to

---

[1] Donna Haraway's recent theorization of "agency" as always particular and interactive, although not necessarily human or even animal, suggests exciting new ways to de-center the subject without abandoning the idea of agency. See, for example, her essay "The Promises of Monsters: A Regenerative Politics for Inappropriate/d Others," in *Cultural Studies*, ed. Lawrence Grossberg, Cary Nelson, and Paula A. Treichler (New York: Routledge, 1992), 295–337.

[2] David Simpson, "Literary Criticism and the Return to 'History,'" *Critical Inquiry* 14 (Summer 1988): 4. For related contemporary issues in feminist theory and practice, see Marianne Hirsch and Evelyn Fox Keller, eds., *Conflicts in Feminism* (New York: Routledge, 1990).

express the poignancy of having to do so, Stanley Fish wrote that "the insight of God's omnipresence is violated by the very act of predication (This or that 'is')." With these words Fish suggests the possibility that our experience of the God/us as purely continuous Being would be intact, if it and we were not "violated" by "the very act of predication."[3] It is language, he suggests, that "prevents us everywhere" and discomposes, while it desanctifies, the subject. For T. S. Eliot, however, language with its limitations performed a valuable service in preventing us from mistaking ourselves for God, or our subjectivity for his omniscience. For Eliot, because impersonality was next to godliness, objectivity was the proper goal of the human subject. In his famous and amusingly obtuse essay on "Hamlet and His Problems" (1919), T. S. Eliot said that the only good emotion in art is "objective" emotion; that is, emotion in the form of what he called an "objective correlative." Eliot claimed that *Hamlet* was not one of "Shakespeare's more successful tragedies" because "Hamlet (the man) is dominated by an emotion which is inexpressible, because it is in *excess* of the facts as they appear, [and that the] only way of expressing emotion in the form of art is by finding an 'objective correlative'; in other words, a set of objects, a situation, a chain of events which shall be the formula of that *particular* emotion; such that when the external facts, which must terminate in sensory experience, are given, the emotion is immediately evoked."[4] In Shakespeare's better tragedies we find "this exact equivalence" among the emotion the creator wants to express, the "formula of that *particular* emotion," the "sensory experience" in which the "facts . . . must terminate," and the emo-

---

[3] Although I wrote down Fish's words when I first read them and posted them in a place of honor on my bulletin board which they held for years, I neglected to write down their source and have been unable to find them since. Even Fish doesn't remember the source, although he doesn't disown the lines.

[4] T. S. Eliot, "Hamlet and His Problems" (1919), in *Selected Essays* (1932; New York: Harcourt, Brace, and World, 1964), 125. The term was apparently first coined by the American artist Washington Allston, as Eliot discovered and as Frank Kermode reminds us in his *Selected Prose of T. S. Eliot* (New York: Farrar, Straus, Giroux, 1975), 16–17.

tion all this evokes. In *Hamlet* Shakespeare does not effect this equivalence, Eliot claims, because he was too close to "Hamlet (the man)"; because of "the supposed identity of Hamlet with his author" the problem of Hamlet "proved too much for him." We in turn cannot understand Hamlet's problem because Shakespeare "did not understand [it] himself."

Although in retrospect even Eliot came to find this essay relatively embarrassing, we routinely refer to Eliot's notion of the objective correlative as a significant artifact of modernism. Nevertheless these statements of Eliot's remain puzzling—did he really think that every successful work of art is the product of lucid self-consciousness? Did he suffer from such an extreme case of the "intentionalist fallacy" that he believed authors know exactly and completely what they intend? Based on his statements in this essay, apparently so, partly because he was both creator and critic and thus perhaps experienced their unity in himself. Even more puzzling than his remarkable self-confidence, however, is the notion that separable distinguishable "particular emotion[s]" exist inside us like single shoes in a closet for which the exact mates may be found outside us in words and that, furthermore, like the dirty Cinderella and her transmogrified self, the reader and the author are identical because they wear the same size shoe. (If the shoe fits, you'll feel it.) Behind Eliot's implausibly impersonal description of the "objective correlative," in other words, a whole lot of identification is going on, as it were, in the shoe closet, behind the mask of Eliot's objectivity. The objective correlative, far from bestowing upon emotions and their representation the status of objects in the world accessible to sensory experience, names what is for Eliot the exaggerated mirror image of a subjective experience that dare not speak its name, and dare not appear as such in the mirror. It is this which makes the objective correlative a significant artifact of modernism.

The objective correlative is Eliot's name for the modern fetish, that is, an idealized impersonality animated by our own displaced and devalued subjectivity. (To an atheist this sounds like the definition of God.) Eliot's critical writing gen-

erally is one body of work in which it is easy to see how, as
Regis Durand says, modernism posits the disappearance of
that "old-fashioned subject," which narrative theory has
since tried "to recapture"—if not *the* subject, then *a* subject—"through ever more complex categories."[5] Literary
modernism replaced that "old-fashioned subject" with a newfangled object, namely, its objective correlative, representation (or language or the signifier or discourse) to which was
attributed an agency formerly reserved, in theory, to God, or
to persons (men) believed to be created in God's image and
thus having access to the logos (phallus). As the course of
Eliot's poetic career shows, a metaphysic that begins by effacing the personal subject in favor of an objectified equivalent
is already on the road to its reactionary displacement into the
form of the Church and/or State.

Another suggestive name for Eliot's newfangled object,
taken like the "objective correlative" from his critical writing, is "sensuous thought," which he defines in "The Metaphysical Poets" as the unity of thought and feeling. Just as
the objective correlative is a formula for feeling that adds up
to our having sensory experience in response to art, sensuous
thought is what we experience when we read the work of a
poet whose "mind is perfectly equipped for its work" of "con-
stantly amalgamating disparate experience." Whereas "the
ordinary man's experience is chaotic, irregular, fragmentary,"
because he is unable to bring together the experience, say, of
falling in love with that of reading Spinoza, because he cannot see how "the noise of the typewriter or the smell of cook-
ing" have anything to do with each other, "in the mind of the
poet these experiences are always forming new wholes."[6] In
the work of a poet such as Chapman or Donne "there is a
direct sensuous apprehension of thought, or a recreation of
thought into feeling," Eliot writes in these oft-quoted, vaguely passive lines (246). "There is a direct sensuous apprehen-

[5] Regis Durand, "On *Aphanisis:* A Note on the Dramaturgy of the Subject
in Narrative Analysis," in *Lacan and Narration,* ed. Robert Con Davis
(Baltimore: Johns Hopkins University Press, 1983), 862.
[6] Eliot, "The Metaphysical Poets" (1921), in *Selected Essays,* 247.

sion," he says—where exactly is "there"? In the poet? the reader? the work? To say that the good poet turns his interests into poetry "by transmuting ideas into sensations" and "observation into a state of mind" is to suggest that art comes to mimetic life in the form of an autonomous being in which thinking and feeling find the ideal and enduring unity they found too briefly (or too infrequently) in us.

In time Eliot came to disapprove of his own belief in the vitality of language. In effect he recognized the extent to which language as he had believed in it rivaled the Anglican faith he had embraced. In addition he realized that the "unified sensibility" of the poetry he had once eulogized implied a smugly intact self, which he could not, as a believer in God, sanction. In the essay "For Lancelot Andrewes" Eliot reevaluated Donne's language and the "sensory experience" it induces. Donne's sermons, he then writes, are the work of a "flesh-creeper": "About Donne there hangs the shadow of the impure motive; and impure motives lend their aid to a facile success. He is a little of the religious spellbinder, the Reverend Billy Sunday of his time, the flesh-creeper, the sorcerer of emotional orgy. We emphasize this aspect to the point of the grotesque. Donne had a trained mind; but without belittling the intensity or the profundity of his experience, we can suggest that this experience was not perfectly controlled, and that he lacked spiritual discipline."[7] In "The Metaphysical Poets" Eliot had praised Donne's "perfectly equipped" mind as being "unsullied by Milton's and Dryden's dazzling disregard for the soul" (248). But sensuous thought now has something impure, even grotesque, about it for Eliot. Why the change of heart?

I won't resurrect here the argument of Eliot's doctoral thesis, *Knowledge and Experience in the Philosophy of F. H. Bradley*, except to point out that in this early attempt to "amalgamat[e] disparate experience" into monadic moments of subject/object fusion, Eliot argues that there are only practical, provisional distinctions to be made between those aspects of experience we conventionally call "real" and "ideal,"

---

[7] Eliot, "Lancelot Andrewes" (1926), in *Selected Essays*, 302.

"immanent" and "transcendent," "object" and "subject," and so on.[8] Nevertheless, even here Eliot's terms are never altogether amalgamated; from each description of unified experience-in-flux, the idea of a knowing, experiencing subject persistently detaches itself, to confront him anew with the logical necessity of naming or explaining away the subject. An idealized monism, in other words, inevitably reemerges as a disguised dualism. Although it seems fair to suggest, as George A. Knox did, that, at least metaphorically, "the discipline in the Quartets is an integration of the spiritual discipline with the poetical," it is not the case that the *Four Quartets,* or Eliot's poetry as a whole, offers itself as the sacramental union of logos with Logos.[9] On the contrary, his later poetry, like his critical writing, roundly rejects such a union as impossible, the vain wish of the excessively "personal" poet (the early Yeats, for example).

Eliot's inability to rid himself of his selfhood, subjectivity, and personality, indicated to him that a union of logos with Logos was impossible, and that to wish for it was vain. Because he, unlike other modernists, learns this lesson, he feels he is different from them. They are (to his way of thinking) hopelessly "secular"; they "have no real belief in a supernatural order," only a makeshift belief in the holy order of the signifier.[10] Eliot's "real belief" is a side effect of his failed monism, the alienation of the thinking and feeling subject from its own experience, which he comes to observe from a distance with punctilious acuity. In the wake of *Knowledge and Experience* the subject seems abandoned on one side of a shifting tumid river across which it glimpses its self-knowledge, its salvation, its own body, with mistrust, uncertainty, even a fine disgust.

Such subjects are "The Hollow Men" (1925), the stuffed men, "Leaning together / Headpiece filled with straw. Alas!" The hollow men are the eyeless former habitations of dis-

---

[8] T. S. Eliot, *Knowledge and Experience in the Philosophy of F. H. Bradley* (London: Faber and Faber, 1964).
[9] George A. Knox, "Quest for the Word in Eliot's *Four Quartets,*" *English Literary History* 18 (December 1951): 310–21.
[10] Eliot, "Religion and Literature" (1935), in *Selected Essays,* 353.

placed subjectivities, "shape without form, shade without colour, / Paralysed force, gesture without motion." Offering "the supplication of a dead man's hand / Under the twinkle of a fading star," they appear like comically animated objects to the wearily psalming and estranged speaker of the poem.[11] In this unsatisfactory condition the estrangement of the self from its own vitality is so complete that the body is thought of as already dead, unfamiliar, although vilely animated by its own perverse negativity. Fidelity to the impotently monizing metaphysics of *Knowledge and Experience* transformed the world into a charnel house and consciousness into psychopannychy (that death after death, that sleep in the grave between death and resurrection). Eliot seems to find grotesque Nietzsche's thought that the body may be a "social structure composed of many souls." And yet orthodoxy, for Eliot, means maintaining "a consensus between the living and the dead" known as tradition.[12] But which is which in this definition of culture as flesh-creeping—which the living, which the dead?

In *Four Quartets* the poet seems to reach the limit of the estrangement of subject and object to arrive at a point where he finds they are again interdependent, "where past and future are gathered," "at the still point of the turning world. Neither flesh nor fleshless."[13] Having officiated at the death of his merely personal self (to paraphrase Lawrence), Eliot takes refuge in a transcendental subjectivity, which he takes to be the soul newly impersonalized through the agency of God. He finds that the resulting state of being is not hollowness or darkness or light or silence, but a state in which "the mind is conscious but conscious of nothing":

I said to my soul, be still, and wait without hope
For hope would be hope for the wrong thing; wait without love
For love would be love of the wrong thing; there is yet faith

[11] T. S. Eliot, "The Hollow Men" (1925), in *Collected Poems 1909–1962* (New York: Harcourt, Brace, and World, 1970).
[12] John D. Margolis, *T. S. Eliot's Intellectual Development* (Chicago: University of Chicago Press, 1972), 172.
[13] Eliot, "Burnt Norton" (1935), in *Collected Poems.*

But the faith and love and the hope are all in the waiting.
Wait without thought, for you are not ready for thought.[14]

Here the spiritual discipline is a lesson in objectlessness, not subjectlessness. In proportion to the self-sufficient beauty of *Four Quartets* are Eliot's acceptance in the poem of his own delimiting point of view and detachment from his ongoing "wrestle / With words and meanings." Having rehearsed painstakingly his self-divestiture in search of "a condition of complete simplicity / (Costing not less than everything)," Eliot includes in the "everything" to be given up words themselves, together with the plenitude of meaning toward which the earlier poetry struggled in spite of itself like a "patient acolyte of pain."[15]

What is supposed to be left once everything including words is given up is the impersonal Subject, as closely approximate to God as is possible in Christian terms—and yet it is to be as purged of its objects, attributes, and desires as the "objective correlative" was to be free of all but the hypostasized "sensuous thought." Eliot's poetry evolved from fetishism to deism, from a critique of the subject to a critique of the object, which despite the so-called primitivism of fetishism described a slow dance of reaction backward through intellectual history. In a sense Eliot dropped off the face of modernism when he converted to Anglicanism, much as we tend still to view the fascist sentiments of Ezra Pound and Wyndham Lewis as aberrations that justify our handling them with a kind of ten-foot pole.[16] In practice we often

---

[14] Eliot, "East Coker" (1940), in *Collected Poems.*

[15] Eliot, "Little Gidding" (1942), in *Collected Poems,* and "The Burnt Dancer," dated June 1914 [by hand], Berg Papers, CP & P folder [p. 46], New York Public Library.

[16] Jerome J. McGann, in "The *Cantos* of Ezra Pound, the Truth in Contradiction," *Critical Inquiry* 15 (Autumn 1988):1–25, is willing to integrate Pound's fascism into a discussion of his poetics. On Lewis, see Fredric Jameson, *Fables of Aggression: Wyndham Lewis, the Modernist as Fascist* (Berkeley: University of California Press, 1979). Jameson defines fetishism as a "pathological personalization," the opposite of my definition. The recent discovery of Paul de Man's anti-Semitic writings has raised this problem again.

regard such sentiments in those whose work we admire as embarrassments and treat them as beside the point, despite the lucid and disturbing connections that have been drawn among, for example, German idealism, romanticism, and fascism. This avoidance is part and parcel of how we still preserve the impersonality and "autonomy" of modern literature, that autonomy derived from modernism's self-understanding as the embodiment of "sensuous thought."

Sensuous thought was the newfangled object of modernity, the mythological key to its mythologies. In *Beyond Good and Evil* Nietzsche bragged that intellectual curiosity is his "vice" and pleasurable for its own sake; in *Three Essays on the Theory of Sexuality* Freud informed us that every intellectual act has its sexual component; in "The Metaphysical Poets" Eliot claimed we must respond to poetry with our senses. "We only believe," wrote Yeats in "Certain Noble Plays of Japan" (1916), "in those thoughts which have been conceived not in the brain but in the whole body."[17] Indeed, Yeats at times describes the artist's special mission as the task of becoming the objective correlative of himself. In "Personality and the Intellectual Essences" (1906), he writes that the "exciting person, whether the hero of a play or the maker of poems, will display the greatest volume of personal energy, and this energy must seem to come out of the body as out of the mind."[18] Similarly, literature and art seem "wrought about a mood, or a community of moods, as the body is wrought about an invisible soul," which is why Rossetti can paint a moment of intensity on a woman's face by listening "to the cry of the flesh till it becomes proud and passes beyond the world where some immense desire that the intellect cannot understand mixes with the desire for a body's warmth and softness."[19]

This is sensuous thought with a vengeance, at once the

[17] W. B. Yeats, "Certain Noble Plays of Japan" (1916), in *Essays and Introductions* (New York: Macmillan, 1961), 235.

[18] Yeats, "Personality and the Intellectual Essences" (1906), in *Essays and Introductions*, 266.

[19] Yeats, "The Moods" (1895), in *Essays and Introductions*, 195, and "The Happiest of the Poets" (1902), in *Essays and Introductions*, 53.

inheritor of the sentimental intellectual onanism of romanticism, and the initiator of the nonreferential symbolism of modernism. In "The Symbolism of Poetry" (1900), Yeats asks, "How can the arts overcome the slow dying of men's hearts that we call the progress of the world, and lay their hands upon men's heart-strings again, without becoming the garment of religion as in old times?"[20] What he recommends, again, amounts to remaking himself as artist into an animated symbol that the world could use to effect its own revitalization, to reunify sense, intellect, emotion, and style. "The last two decades of the nineteenth century, which Yeats preferred to call "the autumn of the body," "lie dreaming of things to come," ready "to take upon their shoulders the burdens that have fallen from the shoulders of priests."[21] Ready to react against the "despotism of fact"—rejecting both the rationalism of the eighteenth century and the materialism of the nineteenth, Yeats in his early writings embraces a Shelleyesque Platonism that perversely insists on using the body as an image for poetry rather than the reverse:

> We should come to understand that the beryl stone was enchanted by our fathers that it might unfold the pictures in its heart, and not to mirror our own excited faces, or the boughs waving outside the window. With this change of substance, this return to imagination, this understanding that the laws of art, which are the hidden laws of the world, can alone bind the imagination, would come a change of style, and we would cast out of serious poetry those energetic rhythms as of a man running, which are the invention of the will with its eyes always on something to be done or undone; and we would seek out those wavering meditative, organic rhythms, which are the embodiment of the imagination. ("The Symbolism of Poetry" 163)

Oscar Wilde, that charming personification of sensuous thought, put it this way seven years earlier: "Scientifically

[20] Yeats, "The Symbolism of Poetry" (1900), in *Essays and Introductions,* 162–63.
[21] Yeats, "The Autumn of the Body" (1898), in *Essays and Introductions,* 191, 193.

speaking, the basis of life—the energy of life, as Aristotle would call it—is simply the desire for expression, and Art is always presenting various forms through which the expressions can be attained."[22]

Wilde's description of art as a biological impulse, coming almost a decade before Freud in *The Interpretation of Dreams* formulated the inexorable activity in humans of a drive-to-representation, shows again the general dispersion in the cultural mainstream around the turn of the century of the germ idea of "sensuous thought." Art, like a fine lie, is "simply that which is its own evidence."[23] But, because art is its own evidence, it is also like a fact, not controvertible: "A Truth in art is that whose contradictory is also true."[24] The synthetic facticity of art in Wilde is inseparable from its nonreferentiality: "Art never expresses anything but itself" ("The Decay of Lying" 80). Wilde reminds us that "Know thyself!" an imperative that implies the unquestioned existence of knower and known, subject and object, "was written over the portal of the antique world." But "over the portal of the new world 'Be thyself' shall be written," indicating that in the new world the subject/object dialectic of classical epistemology collapses into the lyrically fetishistic self-referentiality of "Be thyself" ("The Soul of Man under Socialism" 29). (In the 1960s this became "Do your own thing," which in turn produced the "Me generation.")

The words "Be thyself," adds Wilde, are "the message of Christ to man." Thus, according to our most famously idiosyncratic aesthete, the order of the signifier coexists happily with "the secret of Christ"—reminding us that Jesus Christ was the original proponent of the holy order of the signifier. Christ, however, does not have as flexible, nor so ironclad, a notion of Truth as does Wilde. Wilde's notion, as we have seen, has to do with the willed identity, or perhaps the mas-

<hr/>

[22] Oscar Wilde, "The Soul of Man under Socialism" (1891), in *De Profundis and Other Writings*, ed. Hesketh Pearson (Harmondsworth: Penguin, 1954), 78.
[23] Wilde, "The Decay of Lying" (1889), in *De Profundis*, 59.
[24] Quoted in Peter Raby, *Oscar Wilde* (Cambridge: Cambridge University Press, 1988), 3.

querade of identity, of the artist with his art. Ideally the psychological payoff of so firm a faith in the romantic myth of the artist would be that autonomy William Kerrigan has defined as "the feeling that the self is given to the self."[25]

Charles Baudelaire, whose oeuvre is often cited as the beginning of modernism, was, as T. S. Eliot wrote in the introduction to the English translation of *Intimes*, "inevitably the offspring of romanticism, and by his nature the first counter-romantic in poetry."[26] To be described as both the inevitable "offspring of" something or someone, and its prime opponent, is to be pegged, as if by a parent or psychologist, as a rebellious adolescent. It is also to be valorized, however, as the embodiment of the aesthetic dialectic. One could point out in condescending retrospect that the modernist interest in autonomous art resembles in more than one way the psychological profile of the adolescent, who often forgets the reality of other people as he or she struggles toward autonomy. It is perhaps enough to say that adolescent and autonomous artist resemble each other because of the importance to both of "the feeling that the self is given to the self."

Baudelaire describes those moments in which this myth seems real as follows: "In certain semi-supernatural conditions of the spirit, the whole depths of life are revealed within the scene—no matter how commonplace—which one has before one's eyes. This becomes its symbol."[27] If taking the romantic view means seeing the world as symbol of the "spirit," defined as man's total and totalizing perceptual apparatus, then taking the modern view means seeing the world as a symbol of itself. Insofar as Baudelaire is the offspring of romanticism, he sees the world as symbolizing spirit in moments like those described in prose above and in poems such as "Correspondences" (1857) in which the presumed divinity of nature is both eclipsed and represented by the transcendent glory of the human senses.

[25] William Kerrigan, in *Introduction to Interpreting Lacan*, ed. Joseph H. Smith and William Kerrigan (New Haven: Yale University Press, 1983), 139.

[26] Eliot, "Baudelaire" (1930), in *Selected Essays*, 376.

[27] Charles Baudelaire, *Intimate Journals*, trans. Christopher Isherwood (San Francisco: City Lights, 1983), 35.

But insofar as Baudelaire is the first counter-romantic, and thereby, as Eliot likes to think, helps define what modern poetry should be, Baudelaire views epiphanic "conditions of the spirit [in which] the whole depths of life are revealed" as "Auto-Idolatry. Poetic harmony of character. Eurhythmic of the character and the faculties. To preserve all the faculties. To augment all the faculties" (*Intimes* 34). The temple of nature described in "Correspondences" is not the Nature of Wordsworth but its synesthetic appropriation by the desublimated imagination, the evil twin of romanticism, and its memorialization in the fetish object of the modern era, sensuous thought. In "Nature's temple"

> There are odors succulent as young flesh,
> sweet as flutes, and green as any grass,
> while others—rich, corrupt and masterful—
>
> possess the power of such infinite things
> as incense, amber, benjamin and musk,
> to praise the senses' raptures and the mind's.
>   ("Correspondences")[28]

To praise at once "the senses' raptures and the mind's" is to celebrate in poetry aspiring to perverseness that unity of thought and feeling Eliot in his early writing described in more sober terms as the sensuous thought of the unified sensibility. But Baudelaire was more honest when he called that epiphanic fusion, in the symbol, of the poet with his experience "auto-idolatry."

In his *Proust* (1931), Samuel Beckett reduces the equation further, eschewing the spirit, the scene, and even the poet's eyes, to leave the symbol which is only the symbol of itself: "For Proust the object may be a living symbol, but a symbol of itself. The symbolism of Baudelaire has become the autosymbolism of Proust."[29] Autosymbolism is the poetic realization of an autonomy that, as in the case of Joyce, repre-

---

[28] Charles Baudelaire, *Les Fleurs du Mal*, trans. Richard Howard (Boston: David R. Godine, 1982).

[29] Samuel Beckett, *Proust* (New York: Grove Press, 1957), 60.

sents itself in the form of literature that, as Beckett says in discussing *Ulysses* (in an essay suggested by Joyce), "is not written at all. . . . His writing is not about something; it is that something itself."[30] Joyce is thus for Beckett a consummate poet who, like "Vico, asserts the spontaneity of language and denies the dualism of poetry and language" (25). In Beckett's description of the work of Proust and Joyce, both are poets who produce autosymbolic writing, language that is not a representation of something, but a something-in-itself.

This description of poetic language as noumenal phenomenon—contradictory and therefore incontrovertible, to paraphrase Adorno on Hegel—is both romantic and counterromantic. The autosymbol may embody the idea that the symbol is given to itself, but in a form that denies the fact that this idea is ours to begin with. As such the autosymbol is like a dream image meant both to "asseverate and deny" (Freud) our wish for autonomy and integrity in a world that necessarily denies us both. Jacques Lacan with his "mirror stage" has made us aware of the extent to which the subject is itself an autosymbol, the fictive protagonist of that waking dream we call desire. An almost magically animated language, composed of "living symbols" (Beckett), "living images" (Freud), or "living words" (D. H. Lawrence), is the constitutive romance of (bourgeois patriarchal) modernity, at once the subject and object of our displaced desire for self-presence.

If modernism defines language as the real, as that which defines and constitutes what is real, this definition depends on an idea of language as the natural expression of a romanticized subjectivity or "self" that, like language, is thought to be immanent in the individual unconscious. Through the autosymbolic self-referentiality of modernist art and literature, language becomes at once its own subject and object. The fetishism, that perverse fantasy of the *causa sui* (or self-caused), which Nietzsche, Marx, and Freud had diagnosed as

---

[30] Samuel Beckett, "Dante . . . Bruno . Vico . . Joyce" (1929), in *Disjecta: Miscellaneous Writings and a Dramatic Fragment* (New York: Grove Press, 1984), 27.

the ubiquitous fantasy of the bourgeoisie, comes to seem in
the modern era more than ever a quality pertaining to language per se in its vaunted constitutiveness.

In modernism, the symbolic is the real, even in dadaist
works, in which a purposive incoherence, taken to be mimetic of a fragmented modern world, was designed to critique the
"organic" unity of form and content that had come to seem
aesthetic old hat; significance could accrue safely and seemingly without bad faith to those works which seemed symbolic-and-therefore-real. It is here that we become enamored
of the idea of fictionality as such. In the Kantian philosophy
of Hans Vaihinger, "'fiction' becomes . . . the whole conceptual structure by which man constructs a cultural world."[31]
Language is then the partial object par excellence, capable of
replacing the world by constituting it. But to believe that this
is so requires the fetishism of the signifier as if it were a
something-in-itself, a presumption that, as any student of
philosophy knows, constitutes the most simple-minded idealism. Fetishism values things "as if" [they are] "as and for
themselves," all the while denying the force of this "as if," a
willed naiveté basic not only to fetishism but also to both our
waking life and our dreams. "Common sense" as well as
"dream logic" depend upon denial, and the denial of denial.
From this point of view, all knowledge is knowledge "as if."[32]

Thanks to what we call common sense, it is as if what we
know about the world is real. In daily life this kind of knowledge seems to suffice. Yet this pragmatic denial of skepticism
is basic to our dream life as well. Erich Fromm writes in *The
Forgotten Language* that, from the point of view of the dreamer, there is no "as if" in dreams; yet we experience dreams "as
if" they were sensations.[33] In other words, we experience our

[31] Hazard Adams, *Philosophy of the Literary Symbolic* (Tallahassee:
Florida State University Press, 1983), 191.
[32] In *The Philosophy of "As If,"* trans. C. K. Ogden (New York: Harcourt
Brace, 1925), Vaihinger attempts to systematize this insight into a metaphysics.
[33] Erich Fromm, *The Forgotten Language: An Introduction to the Understanding of Dreams, Fairy Tales, and Myths* (New York: Rinehart,
1951), 5.

dreams as if they were not dreams. This is what, in retro-spect, makes them seem so odd. What makes dreams seem real to us is our denial that they are really denials. The sensa-tion that our dreams are sensations enables us to experience them. Thus both when we are conscious and rational and when we are asleep, when we feel in control and when we are psychically out of control, we inevitably conflate the "physi-ological" or material with the imaginary and allow our imagi-nations to dictate what our senses perceive. We live in a world of sensuous thoughts—or at least, this is what psycho-analysis implies. Worse yet, as Fromm implies, perception sometimes *is* its denial because we must deny that the boundary between the real and the ideal is anything but self-evident in order simply to get through the day.

Valorizing the idealistic notion that man constructs a world by conceiving of it (an idea we often accept with an air of knowing cynicism) is what put the "significance" in "sig-nificant form." Significant form is that version of sensuous thought that gave off the headiest scents for the New Criticism to follow with its intellectual nostril.[34] Significant form, long part of the conceptual stock-in-trade of critics and teachers of literature, is what Bloomsbury formalists Roger Fry and Clive Bell considered to be left intact after a work was pried loose from its sociohistorical contexts. The aes-thetic theories of Fry and Bell, as Lisa Tickner points out, helped to identify "art" with principles, "those formal values that were held to have survived the contingent circum-stances of a work's original production and reception."[35] The concept of significant form, although not synonymous with fictionality in its present wider multidisciplinary cultural meanings, is nevertheless its precursor in that acceptance of the former led logically to the now general theoretical accep-tance of the latter.

As we have come to realize, this ahistorical notion of sig-

[34] "The nostril of intellect" is one of Henry James's most pleasingly bizarre fetishistic abstract concretions. See his preface to *What Maisie Knew*, in which this conceit rules.

[35] Lisa Tickner, "Feminism, Art History, and Sexual Difference," *Genders* 3 (November 1988): 94.

nificant form, meant as a reverential appreciation of particular works, at the same time elevated them into categories of absolute value. In an attempt to give historical validity to this idealization, Dorothy Van Ghent stated in *The English Novel: Form and Function* (1953), a book on significant form intended for "the general reader and the student," that "one of the oldest themes in the novel is that language is a creator of reality."[36] And Van Ghent offers as an example *Don Quixote*, whose hero "is supremely a man animated by 'the word.'" But she says this to introduce her chapter on James Joyce's modern "classic," *A Portrait of the Artist as a Young Man*, the final chapter in "a rereading of eighteen classical novels," all English novels (she notes apologetically) except *Don Quixote*. This exception she explains by quoting Lionel Trilling, who claimed "that all prose fiction is a variation on the theme of *Don Quixote*" (viii)—an idea shared by Lukács.

This theme, again, particularly poignant since it expresses as a pedagogical maxim the beliefs of academics who came of age during the great wars and who must have noticed a certain incongruity between the "reality" of belles lettres and the world beyond its precincts, is "that language is a creator of reality."[37] It has survived as a kind of institutional vision in our English departments long after its revolutionary heyday.[38] It is also the subtext of our new culturally conscious theoretical projects, seeming to lend new promise to historical narratives—maybe we can, we think, help shape history after all. For, after all, to us "fiction" means "the whole conceptual structure by which man constructs a cultural world." It was partly out of a lack of faith in this doctrine, particularly as canonized by academic formalism, and

[36] Dorothy Van Ghent, *The English Novel: Form and Function* (New York: Harper and Row, 1953), 264.
[37] Hourik Zakarian spoke eloquently and ironically on the inexpressibility of such horror in relation to the earthquakes in Armenia at the conference "Feminism and Representation" (Rhode Island College, Providence, April 1989).
[38] See Gerald Graff, *Professing Literature: An Institutional History* (Chicago: University of Chicago Press, 1987).

partly out of utter devotion to it, that avant-garde artists felt impelled to act.

Tristan Tzara, speaking in "Monsieur Antipyrine's Manifesto" (1916) of the new dada "intensity" acknowledges that although dada "remains within the framework of European weaknesses" and thus is "still shit," dadaists want "to shit in different colors so as to adorn the zoo of art" (1).[39] In "note on poetry" (1919) he asserts that the new poetry, the real poetry, offers "vigour and thirst, emotion faced with a form that can neither be seen nor explained" (75). "The rest," however, merely fenced in by principles, "called literature, is a dossier of human imbecility for the guidance of future professors" (77). The following bit of text from Tzara's "Unpretentious Proclamation" (1919) is an example of a "form that can neither be seen nor explained," a synthesis of form and content playfully representing an onomatopoetic anarchy that is itself the text, a piece of shit in different colors:

We are looking for a **straightforward pure sober**

unique force we are looking for **NOTHING**

we affirm the VITALITY of every **instant** the

the anti-philosophy of **spontaneous acrobatics** (16)

The dada manifesto, with its "coterie address, its complex network of concrete but ambivalent images, and its complex word play and structuring," is symptomatic of the "technopoetics of the twentieth century," occupying a space "between lyric and narrative, or lyric and theatre, or lyric and political statement."[40]

Dada tries in a variety of ways, to be in "between." It attempts to hover in a space at once negative and positive, both vital and nothing, sober and spontaneous, brazenly self-refer-

---

[39] All citations in this paragraph to Tristan Tzara are from *Seven Dada Manifestos and Lampisteries,* trans. Barbara Wright (London: John Calder, 1977).

[40] Marjorie Perloff, *The Futurist Moment: Avant-Garde, Avant Guerre, and the Language of Rupture* (Chicago: University of Chicago Press, 1986), 114–15.

ential, insisting simultaneously upon its noninstrumentali-
ty and its irresistible allure. Dada looks backward to the
seductive vogue of "Art for Art's Sake" inspired in England
as on the Continent by the work of Théophile Gautier—
although, according to Eliot, the only two real practitioners
of art for art's sake were Henry James and Gustav Flaubert
(*Selected Essays* 393)—and forward to an antiliterary future.
"The true Dadaists were against Dada," writes Tzara in
"Memoirs of Dadaism," reprinted in an appendix to *Axel's
Castle* (1931).[41] Their literary journals "developed the absolutely anti-literary point of view which will be the rela-
tivist point of view of future generations." Thus did Tzara
narrativize how "the virgin microbe" of dada paradoxically
propagated itself (307).

"The spirit and discipline of aesthetic modernity" may
have "assumed clear contours in the work of Baudelaire," and
continued to "unfold in various avant-garde movements" to
reach "its climax in the Café Voltaire of the dadaists and in
surrealism," but it possessed along with its revolutionary
playfulness a reactionary impulse disguised as "anti-philosophy."[42] Wilson worried in *Axel's Castle* about the relativism
Tzara predicted as being our cultural future. It seemed to
Wilson that writers "such as W. B. Yeats, James Joyce, T. S.
Eliot, Gertrude Stein, Marcel Proust, and Paul Valéry represent[ed] the culmination of a self-conscious and very important literary movement" whose work was "largely a continu-
ance or extension of Symbolism" (24). But he could not
approve of an art that, he says, quoting Valéry, "has become
'an art which is based on the abuse of language—that is, it is
based on language as a creator of illusions, and not on language as a means of transmitting realities.'" If this trend were
to continue, Wilson says, again quoting Valéry, "literature
will survive as a game—as a series of specialized experiments
in the domain of 'symbolic expression and imaginative values

[41] Edmund Wilson, *Axel's Castle: A Study in the Imaginative Literature of
1870–1930* (New York: Charles Scribner's Sons, 1931).
[42] Jürgen Habermas, "Modernity—An Incomplete Project," in *The Anti-
Aesthetic: Essays on Postmodern Culture*, ed. Hal Foster (Port Townsend,
Wash.: Bay Press, 1983), 12.

attained through the free combination of the elements of language'" (284–85). The avant-garde did not so much desire to blow up the continuum of history as to see itself as an integral part of a cultural history in which language continued to devolve from being a repository of formalist principles, "a dossier of human imbecility for the guidance of future professors," to a utopian space in which "free combination" was possible. Of course, the irony is that there has come to seem so little difference between these two formulations, precisely because they both posit a magically constitutive language, rather than a politically dynamic interaction among professors and persons and institutions outside the university.

Yeats claimed that we enjoy poetry like Shakespeare's for certain "semi-supernatural" moments it induces, moments in which "style" frees the mind by giving it "sensible impressions." Style like "the free mind" "arise[s] out of a deliberate shaping of all things." In these moments the mind experiences "the freedom of self-delight: it is, as it were, the foam upon the cup, the long pheasant's feather on the horse's head, the spread peacock over the pasty."[43] The equation of freedom with self-delight, on behalf of which Oscar Wilde argued stirringly in "The Soul of Man under Socialism" and which, from the opposite point of view, Paul Zweig has called "the heresy of self-love," becomes increasingly problematic, although no less tempting, in the postmodern world. For Samuel Beckett such freedom means despair, incommunicable pain, not self-delight. Our autonomy proves we have been abandoned by God. "The suffering of being: that is, the free play of every faculty" (*Proust* 9). If the symbolic mode affirms the myth of creation, the autosymbolic mode dissipates it. I will hazard a further generalization: the symbolic mode, characteristic of romanticism and early forms of symbolist modernism, enjoyed and depended upon a relation with a stable concept of the feminine (until recently mistakenly equated with the female), which makes its self-delight possible. The autosymbolic mode, however, characteristic of high modernism and its postmodern descendants, depends upon that

---

[43] Yeats, "Poetry and Tradition," in *Essays and Introductions*, 254.

thoroughgoing idealization and denial of the feminine known as fetishism.[44]

To help clarify these remarks concerning the symbol and the autosymbol, even at the risk of seeming to digress wildly, I include here a brief discussion of some lines from Wordsworth. In the poem "Lines Composed a Few Miles Above Tintern Abbey" (1798), Wordsworth describes

> . . . —that serene and blessed mood,
> In which the affections gently lead us on,—
> Until, the breath of this corporeal frame
> And even the motion of our human blood
> Almost suspended, we are laid asleep
> In body, and become a living soul.[45]

The poet becomes "a living soul" as he contemplates anew the ruins of Tintern Abbey and the Wye valley, which he had first visited five years earlier, at the age of twenty-three. He does this by meditating simultaneously on his own past and future as they are contained in, but not by, the present.

Gazing upon the landscape before him, with its hedgerows, pastoral farms, and beauteous forms, he feels at once saddened by "many recognitions dim and faint" (line 59) and full of "the sense / Of present pleasure, but with pleasing thoughts / That in this moment there is life and food / For future years" (lines 62–65). He achieves a sensation of moral and psychological plenitude by compressing the ordinary sequence of life's events into virtual simultaneity and seeing this enlarged vision of himself reflected in his sister's "wild eyes." Perceiving his present, past, and future all at once as God might, Wordsworth rejects the narrative mode, with its inevitable course to closure and death, in favor of the iconic,

---

[44] This remains the case despite the advances of feminism both in the wider world of popular culture and in the narrower world of English departments, in which the "feminine" continues to be redefined and reassigned, and ghettoized. See Susan Sage Heinzelman, "Two Turns of the Screw: Feminism and the Humanities," *ADE Bulletin* 91 (Winter 1988): 14–20.

[45] William Wordsworth, "Lines Composed a Few Miles Above Tintern Abbey . . ." (1798; lines 40–46), in *William Wordsworth: Selected Poems and Prefaces,* ed. Jack Stillinger (Boston: Houghton Mifflin, 1965), 108–11.

that mode in which "spots of time" offer refuge from time itself like a paradisal island of mythic selfhood. This may not seem significant here, given the fact that the iconic (as opposed to the narrative) is the usual poetic mode (except in epics) and "Tintern Abbey" is a poem. Yet this poem, like others of Wordsworth's—"We are Seven," "Resolution and Independence," "Michael," even "The Prelude"—dramatizes as a kind of submerged narrative, the triumph of the iconic over the narrative, the power of iconic timelessness to "redeem the time," as T. S. Eliot would later say, and to bestow upon the poet intimations, if not hallucinations, of his own immortality.

To achieve that "serene and blessed mood" in which the poet can not only see his entire life at once, but also "see into the life of things" and hear "the still, sad music of humanity," requires that he lay to sleep his sight and his hearing, his body and his blood and cultivate the kind of "firm mind" he attributes to the old leech gatherer in "Resolution and Independence." In this state of suspended animation it is as if the poet's mind is in direct contact with the world, that is, with nature. That the poet sees his body with its lively responsive senses as an impediment to, rather than a requirement for, the direct experience of nature may seem less odd if we consider that for him the "passion," the "appetite," the "feeling and [the] love" the landscape aroused in him called forth dizzy raptures and thoughtlessness rather than "the picture of the mind" in which he is most interested. The senses, according to this logic, are part and parcel of the narrative mode with its inexorable and depressing chronology, and thus are rejected and sublimated, whereas the mind remains the agent of the symbolic, the iconic, the lyrical. The imagination is itself idealized; it is the romantic ego ideal, with the body viewed as an impediment to self-delight.

The poet freed from the disturbances of the body (How [gnostic] Christian the egotistical sublime turns out to be!) may experience his imagination as both the product and the producer of what it perceives, rather than the mere interpreter of what the body senses, but to do so is to sexualize the mind. When Wordsworth writes, on the other hand, that he must lay the body asleep to free the soul, he is espousing a Cartesian manichaeism central to the very Enlightenment repression from which he seeks to liberate human imagination. But to sexualize the mind, on the other hand, is to make possible our current view that, just as the imagination is our primary sexual organ, mind and body are not ontologically separate categories, any more than are knower and known.

In "Tintern Abbey" the mind (or imagination) becomes an aggrandized and exalted object as much as a valued aspect of the subject when the poet perceives "the mind of man" as part of the physical landscape. He senses the presence of something sublime "deeply interfused" with "the light of setting suns, / And the round ocean and the living air, / And the blue sky, and in the mind of man" (lines 96, 97–99). In "Tintern Abbey" the poet enjoys an expanded selfhood and immanent godhead, both of which he identifies with the creativity of universal mind: "A motion and a spirit, that impels / All thinking things, all objects of all thought, / And rolls through all things" (100–102). This universal mind, to which his own mind gives him access, is the poet's ego ideal, insofar as the ego ideal is the name not of a "model that the person is attempting to emulate," but of the fusion of the subject with his own mirror image (that image of one's own impossible perfection one sees in the Lacanian "mirror stage").[46] One cannot think of the ego ideal as merely a model to emulate if, "along with Freud, one considers it as 'the substitute for the lost narcissism of his childhood.'" The models one chooses to emulate are the secondary expression of the desire "to bridge the gap between the ego as it is and as it would like to be (which in the last analysis always refers to the time when 'it was its own ideal')" (7). "The desire to bridge the gap between the ego as it is and as it would like to be" is, from the point of view of psychoanalytic theory, which converts romantic myth into science, "a specific anthropological phenomenon (in the broadest sense

[46] Janine Chasseguet-Smirgel, *The Ego Ideal: A Psychoanalytic Essay on the Malady of the Ideal*, trans. Paul Barrows (New York: Norton, 1985), 7.

of the term) which takes man beyond the simple quest for instinctual satisfaction"(6–7), but which is at the same time the very definition of a human instinct that is inseparable from its representations. This gap, analogous to what Kristeva calls "the thetic break," is also proof that we are in the symbolic order, and which makes possible "the classic terms 'subject' and 'predicate,'" identifiable "as the two faces . . . of the thetic break."[47] It is across this gap that mimesis takes place, the "construction of an object, not according to truth but to verisimilitude," in other words, reproducing grammaticality itself, the "constitutive rules" of the symbolic order. The reader might recall, from Chapter 2, how the fetish (as opposed to the symbol) replaces the rules of syntax with a metabolism of equivalence.

The ego ideal, the symbolism of self-delight, in other words, turns part of the "I" into a "me" and grants it a magical autonomy without, however, sacrificing belief in the agency of the "I." This is the difference between the ego ideal and the fetish: the fetish attains full symbolic potency only at the expense of the "I." Romantic poetry is symbolic, but not autosymbolic; it un-self-consciously "refers" to and conceives of itself as expressing, as well as representing, certain human absolutes. The peculiar faith of romanticism is in the idea that the human, in an impersonal, pre-Arnoldian social sense, is the absolute. The lines that best represent how this is so are these from "Tintern Abbey" in which the poet affirms that he is "still"

> A lover of nature, of the meadows and the woods,
> And mountains; and of all that we behold
> From this green earth; of all the mighty world
> Of eye, and ear—both what they half create,
> And what perceive.
>
> (104–7)

The rhythm and syntax of these lines encourage the reader to

---

[47] Julia Kristeva, *Revolution in Poetic Language*, trans. Margaret Waller (New York: Columbia University Press, 1984), 55.

equate the phrases "all that we behold" and "all the mighty world" as if to suggest that we "behold" and therefore "love" the whole mighty world. Yet no sooner does the reader's mind settle on this equation than it is led in turn to reduce "all the mighty world" to the compass "of eye, and ear." To put this another way, first the poet expands the compass of "all that we behold" to include the whole world; and then reinscribes the mighty world within the compass of eye and ear. In this instant the private dialectic of the mind with its own interior objects replaces that between mind and nature or poet and world as we used to think of these terms. Furthermore, because the world is conceived as being half-created by the senses, which paradoxically must be put to sleep in order for this conception to take place, the world becomes an intentional object, the product of symbolic process, a formulation that, a hundred years after the writing of this poem, psychoanalysis will make the phenomenological basis of a science of the imagination.

The romantic poets were astonished and pleased to discover "mind" out in the landscape as well as inside their "living souls"; but for them there was considerable distance between these two locations or points of view, a distance exactly equal to the strength of eighteenth-century sanctions against abolishing the distance between God and man, mind and nature, "perceiving" and "half-creating." (Coleridge's poetry expresses the guilt and dread he feels when this distance between the self and its objects seemed to disappear.) Still, perceiving was *half* creating; and since Wordsworth the two—perceiving and creating—have, as epistemological categories, steadily yet asymptotically approached each other. They can merge completely only at the expense of the subject, who must disappear (like God behind his handiwork) in order for his creation to take on autonomous status. Perception and creation merge completely only in the fetish, that symbolic object born of the wish to deny any distance at all between representation and its referent. Ultimately, to deny this distance, and claim that a representation is its own referent, is to claim that it has no referent, that it is self-sufficient.

Although I argue that formal modern literature in effect rejects the symbolic, it has been more usual to argue that modernism canonizes the symbolic and that postmodernism rejects it in favor of the narrative. It seems to me rather that we have emphasized narrative to such an extent that we grant it iconic powers: we fetishize narrative. We deny its referentiality even as we overendow it with constitutive powers: we network in the void. In modern novels the iconic mode is characterized by the breakdown of narrative conventions and their replacement by simultaneism and epiphany. Yet simultaneism, as Janine Chasseguet-Smirgel points out, is another form of denial, in this case, the denial of the passage of time. It manifests psychologically as the denial of difference between generations or sexes. In the mind of a boy, for example, such a denial could take the form of the fantasy that he could be an adequate love-partner for his mother, and thus replace his father.[48] In the autosymbolic fiction of Samuel Beckett, for whom "art is the apotheosis of solitude" (*Proust* 47) one encounters characters like Molloy, who is interchangeable, sexually and otherwise, with his mother. Literary criticism has followed the same trajectory, replacing the old-fashioned subject with a newfangled object, namely, sensuous thought, or subjectivity without a subject.[49] I can think of no better essay to discuss as an exemplar, if not an effigy, of this tendency than Georges Poulet's "Phenomenology of Reading."[50] As Frank Lentricchia points out, in Poulet "the presiding image of the open and generous critic in Poulet is blatantly sexual," occupying both masculine

---

[48] Janine Chasseguet-Smirgel, *Creativity and Perversion* (New York: Norton, 1984), see chapter 3, "Narcissism and Perversion," especially 29, and chapter 8, "Reflections on Fetishism," especially 79. This disturbing argument is central to Chasseguet-Smirgel's work.

[49] For a history of the dialectical relation of the literary subject to its own disappearance, see Michael Levenson, *A Genealogy of Modernism: A Study of English Literary Doctrine 1908–1922* (Cambridge: Cambridge University Press, 1984).

[50] See Georges Poulet, "The Phenomenology of Reading," *New Literary History* 1 (October 1969): 55, for a fascinating account of how we make ourselves the "prey of language."

and feminine subject positions.[51] Poulet points out in this
essay that when we read, with "astonishing facility" we
"not only understand but even *feel* what we read" (57). What
Poulet means by "feel" is not emotional, but sensuous.
Poulet asserts that we experience with our bodies what we
read, that we think with our bodies as well as with our
minds. This notion of sensuous thought, the product and
expression of (to use Yeats's term) the "thinking body," may
well be the tastiest morsel the life of mind has to offer. It is
also, in a nutshell, the aesthetic principle that there be no
principles—the conflation of *soma* and *seme*—of literary
modernism.

Poulet's description of what he calls "The Phenomenology
of Reading" enacts the fetishization of subject-object fusion by
idealizing alternately the triumph of the literary text over the
consciousness it replaces, and the (perhaps retaliatory) triumph of the subject over all its objects. This derealization of
being can occur in two ways (and it is symptomatic that
Poulet conceives of "two" ways): either through excessive
identification with the text, so that the reader loses consciousness of himself and also "of that other consciousness which
lives within the work"; or else through excessive "objective"
distance from the text so that it "assumes the aspect of a
being with whom I may never establish any relationship whatever" (63). In the former case the critic indulges too much in
"the sensuous themes" of the text, whereas in the latter he
prefers solely to exercise his "cognitive power." Thus critical
consciousness can lose itself either in "a union without comprehension" or "a comprehension without union" (63).

Thus does the literary critic help perpetuate the life of
mind; thus does phenomenology metaphorize biology and
feminize the mind. If reading is the mental act that realizes
within me the being of a work of literature otherwise unreal,
then criticism is the act that realizes this being outside of

[51] Frank Lentricchia, *After the New Criticism* (Chicago: University of
Chicago Press, 1980), 79.

me. Just as reading makes of literature "a sort of human being . . . conscious of itself and constituting itself in me," criticism gives it a kind of "intentional consciousness" outside me, "a certain power of organization inherent in the work itself," so that it seems to stand apart from and outside of me. What stands apart from me is a peculiar hybridization of "object and mind," a nonphysical homunculus, a character, a fetish.

Poulet's essay represents the apotheosis of close reading, a purposive conflation of realization and derealization into the unity of significant form, the collapse of a dialectic fetishism whose halves were only mirror images of each other to begin with. The brainchild born of this conflation incarnates the denial of our own incarnation, even as it pretends to celebrate the particularities of physical existence. It represents the attempt to embody in an ideal, "sublime body" pure intentionality with no representation: as Poulet puts it, "subjectivity without objects," the critical instrument for perceiving art that is reciprocally made to appear as an object in itself.

Idealized subjectivity, like idealized language, is a fetish when it devalues realization in favor of the derealization that replaces it. Psychoanalysis tells us that an irrational belief in that psychosexual hybrid, the "phallic woman," is our first response to what we perceive as sexual indeterminacy. This response is essentially a denial, a reconstruction, of the facts, and yet one that is basic to mental life at this time. Psychoanalysis tells us that the "re-investment," the restoration to wholeness, of the phallic woman is the ubiquitous fantasy in perversion, and that perversion, in turn, is a ubiquitous component of mental life. In fact, Freud suggests, the more "mental" we are, the more perverse we are. There is no such thing as intellectual activity without its physical component, no such thing as subjectivity without objects, no such thing as intentions without representations; we have only written about such things "as if" they did exist. To speak reverentially of a subjectivity without objects or a discourse without referents is not only illogical but delusional. To idealize language is to idealize a potential for becoming that need not become anything, a desirousness afraid to be embodied, a form of suicide masquerading as a *causa sui*. One way for a theoretical system—whether structuralism or pragmatism or psychoanalysis—to pretend that it (unlike phenomenology) is not naive enough to believe in anything as vacantly metaphysical as a "subjectivity without objects" is to overvalue its own abstractions, symbolic objects such as "discourse." This of course misses the point: idealization is itself the problem; no matter *what* or *whom* we idealize.

Fetishism, in its psychoanalytic definition, is the pathological belief that Mother really does have a penis and that there is, after all, no difference between the sexes. But, as I have been arguing, although feminist theorists have by now made this definition of fetishism infamous, "fetishism" was the name of choice in diverse circles for a variety of romantic idealizations. Furthermore, in retrospect, fetishism appears as the pandemic affliction of a modern patriarchal order narcissistically concerned with the erosion of its own hegemony and which, as a kind of symbolic stopgap, replaced its superannuated god-concepts with a hyperbolic belief in logos itself. Friedrich Nietzsche, the ur-radical of the modern period, was aware that philosophical positivism disingenuously concealed and denied its own self-interest. He argued in *Beyond Good and Evil* (1885), for example, that "as soon as any philosophy begins to believe in itself" it necessarily "creates the world its own image."[52] He criticized philosophies materialistic, absolutistic, and psychologistic, because they all represent (or misrepresent) as disinterested and autonomous truth what are at bottom the "personal confession[s]," the "involuntary and unconscious memoir[s]" of their authors (12). Nietszche argued on behalf of an avowedly conditioned philosophy against what could only pretend to be "unconditional and self-identical"; philosophies which pretend to seek impersonally after "truth" end up guilty of "a sort of rape and perversion of logic," that "self-contradiction: known as *"the causa sui"* (28). And yet this argument, which sounds like a

[52] Friedrich Nietzsche, *Beyond Good and Evil: Prelude to a Philosophy of the Future*, trans. Walter Kaufmann (New York: Vintage, 1966), 16.

critique of fetishism insofar as it demystifies and personalizes the categorical in order to liberate the particular, shows symptoms of the same ailment when it holds the individual "subject," which Nietzsche seemed to view as the real fetish object of the modern intellectual, accountable for these excesses. This is because fetishism is at bottom the wish to deny the limitations of subjectivity by overrating—externalizing, objectifying, exaggerating—its importance.

There is *no* strictly individual subject, Nietzsche implied: "indeed, our body is but a social structure composed of many souls" (26). He writes, "Why couldn't the world *that concerns us*—be a fiction?": "And if somebody asked, 'but to a fiction there surely belongs an author?'—couldn't one answer simply: *why*? Doesn't this 'belongs' perhaps belong to the fiction, too? Is it not permitted to be a bit ironical about the subject no less than the predicate and object? Shouldn't philosophers be permitted to rise above faith in grammar?" (47). These ideas—of the individual as composite social structure, of the author as simply part of the textual apparatus, and of the human world as a fiction indistinguishable from the grammar which constitutes it—have become the ungrounding ground assumptions of postmodern critical practice. As such they represent the logical endpoint of Western culture (increasingly supplanted by a nascent global politics and economy) seen as a prolonged critique of object and subject by Platonism and Christianity, respectively. As of the turn of this century, it was as if all that was left of our syntax, from which both subject and object had been subtracted, was the "logical copula," that universal signifier of desire per se, the disembodied phallus (in search of a Mother to be its body). The overdetermination of this phallus as both connector and signifier, as bearer of meanings political, psychological, and historical, constitutes fetishism.

By and large the consequences of Nietzschean demythification have been liberating for textual studies. "We know now," for example, as Roland Barthes put it in "The Death of the Author," "that a text is not a line of words releasing a single 'theological' meaning (the 'message' of the Author-

God) but a multi-dimensional space in which a variety of writings, none of them original, blend and clash. The text is a tissue of quotations drawn from the innumerable centres of culture."⁵³ As a result of this once new conception of the text, culture, seen as myth, has "become a *different object*" to be studied by "a science of the signifier" which takes as its province not any one society but "historically and geographically, the whole of Western civilization (Graeco-Judaeo-Islamo-Christian), unified under the one theology (Essence, monotheism and identified by the regime of meaning it practices)" (166–167).

These lines from Barthes indicate not only what is exciting about postmodern textual studies, but also the fundamental problematic of fetishism—the problematic that makes postmodernity continuous with modernity—and the "down-side" of deconstructionism: the empire of the signifier, as it has been mapped out so far, extends its "regime of meaning" only in precise proportion to the shrinking of the subject. This complementary waxing and waning of subject and object (taking the signifier, in its widest sense, to be our new object) changes nothing. In effect it conserves the same totality, the same old unity, the same "One," in much the same way that the laws of conservation of matter and energy, as a physicist told me recently, far from supporting the world view known as "relativism," preserve the same old cosmos-wide unity professed by Christian theology and classical physics. To privilege one side or the other of a totalizing dialectic does not change that dialectic, although it may cause one side to drop temporarily out of sight. Nor does it show us the way out of that "philosophy of opposites" Nietzsche warned us against, and which D. H. Lawrence in *Women in Love* (1920) called wearily "tic tac—the dance of opposites."

⁵³ Roland Barthes, "The Death of the Author," in *Image, Music, Text,* trans. Stephen Heath (New York: Hill and Wang, 1977), 146.

[5]

Language as the Real:
Psychoanalytic Modernism

In "pure" psychoanalytic criticism, indeed, the social phenomenon
with which the private materials of case history, of individual fantasy
or childhood experience, must initially be confronted is simply language itself.

—Fredric Jameson

On the other hand, the symbolic knife represents no practical danger
at all, but as it is employed in a multitude of imaginary inner lives, it
becomes a sure sign of its owner's acceptance of crime.

—Jean Genet

The two passages quoted above present two contrary
definitions of language: one of language as quintessentially
social, and therefore the opposite of private; one of language
as fundamentally psychological, and therefore the "sure sign"
of the inner life. These two views in various guises have
probably always been with us, and there is no reason to
expect their reconciliation in the foreseeable future, although
there are perhaps indications in contemporary theory that
they may yet be brought fruitfully together. Perhaps the conflict of these two views may be aptly called, following Jean-
François Lyotard, a "differend," that is, a conflict "that cannot be equitably resolved for lack of a rule of judgement
applicable to both arguments. One side's legitimacy does not
imply the other's lack of legitimacy."[1] During the period of

---

[1] Jean-François Lyotard, *The Differend: Phrases in Dispute,* trans. Georges
Van Den Abbeele (Minneapolis: University of Minnesota Press, 1988), xi.

aesthetic modernity, nonrealistic and avant-garde art and literature tried to sidestep this "differend" by producing art supposedly for its own sake in the form of so-called autonomous works, art that was expressive, antisocial, and self-justifying. Modernist aestheticism, in a sense, exacerbated what was perceived as the antithetical relation between society and the individual.

If, as I have argued, the period of aesthetic modernity can be defined as that in which language, or, more generally, "representation," came to be valorized for being its own subject, object, and instrument—as that period in which a concept of language as "constitutive" rather than referential became our intellectual fetish—then psychoanalysis is the quintessential modernist discourse. To say this is to argue that psychoanalysis exemplified the coherency model of aesthetic high modernism; that it participated in the simultaneous erasure or "bracketing" of both individual and world in favor of its own symbolic process; and that it both reflected and generated a cultural trend by construing consciousness as an epiphenomenon of instinct. At the same time, however, and almost in spite of itself, psychoanalysis wove together the two views of language described above, namely the social and the personal, by theorizing culture as the symbolic enactment of psychical realities.

I may seem to risk stretching the category of "aesthetic modernity" beyond its breaking point to call psychoanalysis an aesthetic, but when I call it an aesthetic, I am not referring to the predilection of psychoanalytic hermeneutics for literary texts and works of art rather than, say, politics, but rather the fact that psychoanalytic truth itself tends to be judged according to standards of coherence and symbolic richness more often applied to works of art than to scientific theorems. It is customary to accuse psychoanalysis of treating texts as persons and persons as texts. But I suggest further that, as a discourse psychoanalysis has had much intrinsically in common with contemporary forms of art. What is more important, considering such similarities will help us to think of psychoanalysis as being of a piece with contemporary developments in that branch of our intellectual history having to do with the redefinition of language as "constitutive" of the real, rather than as a privileged objective discourse about human subjectivity, and as such uniquely capable of generating interpretations of works of art. There are good reasons, political as well as philosophical, why we should at this time upset this notion of language as "real," which psychoanalysis more than any other discourse has made into a scientific principle, and which poststructuralism has pried loose of its materialist basis in neurophysiology.

Psychoanalysis differs from other scientific discourses. In particular, in psychoanalysis, unlike in other sciences, the law of noncontradiction does not apply.[2] According to this law, "for any statement *p*, the statement '*p* and not-*p*'" must be false "as a matter of logical necessity."[3] Logically, a statement and its contradiction cannot both be true. In art, however, this rule does not apply. One could even argue, as did Oscar Wilde, that "a Truth in art is that whose contradictory is also true."[4] I admit that art has never been held to the same logical standards as science and philosophy; modernist art, however, went out of its way to declare its allegiance to the law of contradiction, to announce that it found the law of noncontradiction a bore. At about the same time, moreover, in *The Interpretation of Dreams* Freud was making a hermeneutical science out of the law of contradiction. According to Freud, truth in dreams—and, by extension, in the psyche as a whole and therefore in psychoanalysis as a whole—is that whose contradictory is also true.

---

[2] In her *Riddle of Freud: Jewish Influences on His Theory of Female Sexuality* (London: Tavistock, 1987), Estelle Roith reminds us that the conception of thought as "inherently" antithetical has been traced to talmudic tradition. She quotes Theodor Reik's statement that "the Talmudic texts treat punctuation and sentence structure very casually, so that a statement can be read in a positive or negative sense, can express an assertion as well as a doubt or a query" (67).

[3] This law or principle, proverbial in philosophy, is concisely defined thus in *A Dictionary of Philosophy* (London: Pan Books, 1979), s.v. "non-contradiction."

[4] Quoted by Peter Raby in *Oscar Wilde* (Cambridge: Cambridge University Press, 1988), 3.

Almost from the first, psychoanalysis has been taken to task for this because of how the law of contradiction made room for Freud's theory of patient "resistance." Thanks to the idea of resistance, even the patient who denies the truth or relevance of the analyst's interpretation of his symptoms may be understood to confirm that interpretation with his very denial, to signify his unconscious assent to its truth. Interpreting the patient's "no" to mean "yes" has made psychoanalysis seem to some of its critics an imperialist politics rather than a science or a therapy because of the power it gives the analyst over the analysand. In the late essay "Constructions in Analysis," Freud counters such criticism by "a certain well-known man of science" who claimed that "in giving interpretations to a patient [psychoanalysts] treat him upon the famous principle of 'Heads I win, tails you lose'": "That is to say, if the patient agrees with us, then the interpretation is right; but if he contradicts us, that is only a sign of his resistance, which again shows that we are right. In this way we are always in the right against the poor helpless wretch whom we are analyzing, no matter how he may respond to what we put forward."[5] It should come as no surprise that Freud felt this was not a fair assessment of psychoanalytic technique and took this opportunity "to give a detailed account of how we are accustomed to arrive at an assessment of the 'Yes' or 'No' of our patients during analytic treatment" (257).

Over the years Freud gave various accounts of this procedure (though none quite like that in this essay) and advised "the practicing analyst" that he "will naturally learn nothing in the course of this apologia that he does not know already." All these accounts rest, however, on the definition of "psychical reality" upon which psychoanalysis itself depends, and which is its ultimate referent. If we still largely accept, even if we question, the peculiar authority psychoanalysis has claimed for itself, we accept this authority to the degree that we hang on to the notion of "psychical reality" as psychoanalysis has defined it. During the modern period the notion

[5] Sigmund Freud, "Constructions in Analysis," in *SE* 23:257.

of psychical reality—that realm in which a truth and its contradictory are both true—already valorized by romantic and symbolist art and poetry and their descendants, and made into the object of scientific scrutiny by psychoanalysis, helped pry representation free from its nineteenth-century moral and religious contexts. To rephrase this in general terms, romanticism relocated language, as it were, so that it seemed to come from "inside" us, a natural expression of self and its dubious relatedness to all that was not-self, rather than from the "outside" as it had been understood, a reflection of an orderly world in which a "self" (conceived as "soul") had its small place. The materialist, biologistic impulse of Freudian psychoanalysis was to locate language squarely in the brain.

A current notion of language (among those who "do" theory) seems to combine the most extreme aspects of these two views, thanks in part to the semiotic view of language as a road that "does not go through to action." We see language as a totalized, undetermined yet determining world of significations without beginning or end, as a Heraclitean flux of meanings at once created by us without our control, and in control of us. Now, in the wake of post-Freudian poststructuralism, when psychical reality seems to have taken up existence, as it were, outside of us, and we have become its symbolic enactments rather than the other way around, might be a good time to reintroduce into our discourse the idea of individual agency (not to be confused with any fixed identity) for the sake of both politics and pedgagogy.[6] But for now I will stick to discussing the idea of "psychical reality" and how we have used it to erase individual agency in the name of subjectivism.

Psychical reality, like the "sensuous thought" described earlier as a favorite idealization of modernist poetry, is self-referential, self-validating, reflexive, and symbolic-and-there-

[6] It is in fact in reaction to this paradoxical erasure of the personal by the proliferation of cultural meanings that the "situated speaker" or "positioned subject" has begun to claim its place by announcing its affiliations and explaining its history as part of its critical discourse.

fore-real. Psychical reality, at once the subject and object of psychoanalysis, lends mind an object-like concreteness and language an ersatz substantiality. It gives psychoanalysis what Michel de Certeau calls its "truth-seemingness," that realism by means of which psychoanalysis both legitimizes its "references" and sets itself up as "the subject supposed to know."[7] Psychical reality is the name for what Freud invented when he revised the "seduction theory" of hysteria, and the logical, if irrational, linchpin in the theories of the unconscious and infant sexuality with which he replaced it. As Jacqueline Rose reminds us, "Freud's earliest work [1885–86] was under Charcot at the Salpetrière Clinic in Paris, a hospital for women," where were housed "five thousand neurotic indigents, epileptics, and insane patients, many of whom were deemed incurable."[8] Although Charcot redefined hysteria as a "specific and accredited neurological disease" rather than a moral "category of sexual malingering," he persisted in thinking of hysteria in terms of other categories of degeneration, albeit behavioral or genetic ones (96).

But in his article "Hysteria," written in 1888 and showing the influence on his thinking of both Charcot and Breuer, Freud began to articulate views that diverged from Charcot's. He pointed out, for example, that although the diagnosis of hysteria is "based wholly and entirely on physiological modifications of the nervous system," such modifications were, paradoxically, not accompanied by "perceptible changes in the nervous system," nor ought one expect "any refinement of anatomical techniques" to reveal such changes.[9] In other words, as I pointed out when discussing so-called representation paralysis, Freud began to realize the importance of psychical reality almost a decade before he revised the seduction theory. Freud had already understood by the late 1880s, for example, that the hysterical paralysis of an arm could result from a lesion in the patient's "idea" or conception of the arm

[7] Michel de Certeau, *Heterologies: Discourse on the Other*, trans. Brian Massumi (Minneapolis: University of Minnesota Press, 1986), 32–34.
[8] Jacqueline Rose, *Sexuality in the Field of Vision* (London: Verso, 1986), 96.
[9] Freud, "Hysteria," in *SE* 1:41.

rather than an organic lesion in the brain tissue.

But the more familiar history of "psychical reality" began on 21 April, 1896, when Freud presented his lecture "The Etiology of Hysteria" to a "select professional audience" of uncomprehending "donkeys" (as Freud called them) presided over by Richard von Krafft-Ebing, a lecture in which he claimed that all neurotics had been sexually abused as children. Neurotic symptoms, he asserted, were all traceable to "an actual irritation of the genitals (proceedings resembling coitus)" caused by a child's father, servant, brother, nurse-maid, or teacher.[10] By 1897, however, Freud came more or less to agree with the pronouncement of Krafft-Ebing that this explanation was "a scientific fairy tale" and, as is well known, responded to his own increasing doubts by revising his "seduction theory" of hysteria. Rather than locating the origin of hysterical symptoms in any historically actual event, Freud now identified such symptoms as concretizations of the child's own unconscious sexual wishes and fantasies. Hysteria was, in other words, a reaction to that which *seemed* and was *felt* to be, concrete, that which was experienced *as if* real, by the individual psyche, and which therefore was real. Psychical experiences could give rise to hysterical, somatically real, symptoms, whether or not they corresponded to anything that actually occurred "outside" the mind in the physical/social world. Dreams are Freud's favorite example of the psychically real, since virtually everybody dreams, experiences dreams most of the time as real while "in" them, and discovers upon waking that they are "only" dreams.

Validating psychical reality over historical fact gave license to a variety of subjectivisms (some more useful than others), which ultimately permitted the caricature of psychoanalysis itself, even by some of its own practitioners, as mere subjectivism. Subjectivism in art was already by the turn of the century outpacing realism as the preferred mode. The famous "Conclusion" (1868) to Walter Pater's *The Renaissance:*

---

[10] Quoted in Peter Gay, *Freud: A Life for Our Time* (New York: Norton, 1988), 93.

Studies in Art and Poetry, for example, is often cited as a watershed text at once linking painting to poetry, England to the Continent, and romanticism and symbolism to modernist impressionism.[11] Pater clung to a romantic faith in the innate creativity of the human imagination; according to this faith "each mind" even in its isolation "keep[s] as a solitary prisoner its own dream of a world" (188), even though "to regard all things and principles of things as inconstant modes or fashions has more and more become the tendency of modern thought" (186). In the "Conclusion" Pater tells us that "sharp and importunate reality," the "cohesive force" of "external objects" readily dissipates "in the mind of the observer" upon reflection. Each mind, he says, is solitary, "ringed round for each one of us by that thick wall of personality through which no real voice has ever pierced on its way to us, or from us to that which we can only conjecture to be without" (187). Within that wall we know only our own "impressions—colour, odour, texture"; these for all intents and purposes comprise "experience itself."

Even though these words may suggest the relativism and solipsism we sometimes associate with modernity, to Pater language seemed part of the outside world, the world outside "that thick wall of personality." To enter the individual "mind of the observer," he claimed, one must leave behind the world "of objects in the solidity with which language invests them" (187). Pater's view of the relation between "mind" and "world" then was classical in its assumption of the epistemological stability of the separate subject and object, even if the distance between the two seemed hopelessly attenuated. The romantic view of consciousness led not only to social relativism, but also to a complementary internal relativism as well, "the hypothesis of an unconscious, that is, of a mental activity being carried on within the human mind but without the knowledge of the consciousness and independently of it."[12] Freud "did not invent

[11] Walter Pater, *The Renaissance: Studies in Art and Poetry*, ed. Donald L. Hill (Berkeley and Los Angeles: University of California Press, 1980).
[12] Jean Pierrot, *The Decadent Imagination 1880–1900*, trans. Derek Coltman (Chicago: University of Chicago Press, 1981), 119.

the hypothesis of the unconscious," which was enjoying a fairly wide dissemination by the 1850s, according to Lancelot Whyte; but he "brought it to final fruition by making it the basic hypothesis of psychoanalysis."[13] Psychoanalysis, however, also made that solidity with which language invests objects a peculiar faculty of the unconscious, which thus creates out of language the truth-seemingness of our dreams of worlds. It was Freudian psychoanalysis, as Lacan has since emphasized, which theorized that the unconscious is structured like a language. In absolute contrast to Pater's view Freudian psychoanalysis denies that *any* part of the unconscious is "prior" to language.

This idea has had momentous consequences. Because of this solidity, this thing-ness, with which Freud realized we invest representation, the historical veracity of his patients' narratives ceased to matter. Because of the truth-seemingness of psychical reality—a reality comprised of language, since to Freud there is no place in the unconscious that is not always already engaged in producing representation—there was no longer any reason to distinguish between what was "outside" the individual and what "inside." This resolution of our heretofore basic epistemological dualism has proven to be both liberating and problematic, enabling and illusory. Certain of its problematic aspects, namely, those which render the concept of psychical reality itself potentially just another idealization, a fetish, effect an illusory resolution of epistemological dualism by pretending that one half of the dualism is irrelevant and exaggerating the importance of the other. For example, in reexamining Freud's revision of the seduction theory, Laplanche and Pontalis point out that Freud need not have worried about "verifying" the truth of the incestuous seductions his patients described to him; nor need we in general worry about the origins of any fantasy in the sense of discovering its "verifiable elements."[14]

[13] Lancelot Whyte, *The Unconscious before Freud* (London: Julian Friedmann, 1978), 62.

[14] Jean Laplanche and J.-B. Pontalis, "Fantasy and the Origins of Sexuality," *International Journal of Psychoanalysis* 49 (1968): 8. Laplanche and Pontalis argue that "psychical reality" was Freud's primary interest, even though despite himself he often "compromises" this interest by falling into biological realism.

Even for Freud, they claim, the idea of "primary process" is
just that, an idea: not a name for specifically physiological
activity, but merely for the theoretical priority of instinct.
Freud, they argue, uses the notion of primary process to
"cover up" the disjunction in his misleadingly dualistic conception of psychic process, to cover "the moment of separation between before and after [the rise of desire] whilst still
containing both: a mythical moment of disjunction between
the pacification of need and the fulfillment of desire, between
the two stages represented by real experience and its hallucinatory revival, between the object that satisfies and the sign
which describes both the object and its absence" (15). In the
essay from which this passage comes, "Fantasy and the
Origins of Sexuality" (1968), Laplanche and Pontalis address
the question of precisely what we ought to consider real in
the sexual microcosm of the psyche. The "mythical moment
of disjunction . . . between the two stages represented by real
experience and its hallucinatory revival" epitomizes, for
them, the dualism from which Freud was trying logically to
escape by means of his "biological realism." It is important
to emphasize that this disjunction is *constitutive* for psychoanalytic theory, before considering what happens when this
disjunction is made to seem "mythical," or a point of junc-
ture rather than disjuncture. Accordingly I turn here to a discussion of fetishism, symbolism, and the importance of disjunction, before returning to the specific subject of psychical
reality.

For Freud, fetishism is concerned with the fantasy of the
maternal penis and is the manifestation of entrenched oedipal conflict (as were all the pathologies he considered himself
to have figured out). This etiology implies that the fetishizing
subject was already on his way into the so-called genital
phase of his psychosexual development when he became fixated upon its "idealization." But since Freud psychoanalytic
revisions of the concept of fetishism have treated it as a more
primitive system of idealization and representation proper to
a pregenital, preoedipal state of conflict. Thus the castration
anxiety, which fetishism seeks to relieve, is less a male fear

of damage to the penis than the fear in either sex of narcissistic injury associated with the sudden, uncontrollable, unbearable loss of body integrity or beloved object. Fetishism reveals itself to represent the flight from other-directed genital sexuality and ego function in favor of a regression to an idealized union of "mother" and "me," a conflation of self and other, self and world, into an unrealistically and narcissistically enlarged self, characterized by the refusal to individuate, the lack of ego development, and an inability to use symbols to represent rather than to embody.

As a psychic symbol the fetish then (according to psychoanalytic theory) is taken to be the imaginative stand-in for the magical maternal phallus, the subject's own (possibly threatened) penis, the mother-vagina and breast, the parents' feces, the parents' "product," and therefore the child itself. But it is the manner in which the fetish symbolizes all these things together, reaching consummation in their happy indistinguishability, as it were, in the fetishist himself, whose very separateness is at the same time denied, rather than what in particular it symbolizes, that distinguishes the fetish. The fetish enacts an imaginative connection between bodies by masquerading as a compacted coitus, thus denying the metaphorization it performs. It is an abstraction masquerading as a concretion. The fetish acts as the "logical copula" in a fantastical equation by means of which the subject associates itself—equates itself—with the father's penis, the mother's breast and nipple, with its own and its parents' excrement, with its mother's real and possible children all lumped together, and all of these in turn with edible substances.[15]

But, to repeat Melanie Klein's important claim, this is as it should be, or at least, how it is "normally." The psychosexual appetite of the infant is enormous; it must satisfy the ravenous "metabolism of images" responsible for the growth

[15] Jacques Lacan refers to the phallus as the "logical copula" in "The Signification of the Phallus," in *Écrits: A Selection*, trans. Alan Sheridan (New York: Norton, 1977), 287. This essay also appears as "The Meaning of the Phallus," in *Feminine Sexuality: Jacques Lacan and the École Freudienne*, ed. Juliet Mitchell and Jacqueline Rose, trans. Jacqueline Rose (New York: Norton, 1982).

and development of individual consciousness and personality. And there is no reason to suppose that this appetite disappears before the child reaches adulthood; on the contrary, its
tastes merely become more cultivated and varied through
sublimation and the development of the ability to symbolize.
The phrase "metabolism of images" from Lacan and Granoff,
epitomizes the conflation of *soma* and *seme* typical of
fetishism and of how the unconscious, that dark cohabitation
of physical instinct and abstract intelligence, is supposed by
psychoanalysis to function. In "The Importance of Symbol-
Formation in the Development of the Ego," Klein explained
why, as Sandor Ferenczi first suggested, identification is the
forerunner of symbolism.[16] In "normal" development, Klein
writes, oedipal conflict begins earlier in infancy than Freud
supposed, "at a period when sadism predominates" and is
active "at all the various sources of libidinal pleasure" (219).
This early stage is inaugurated "by oral sadism (with which
urethral, muscular, and anal sadism associate themselves)"
(232). The child's dominant desire at this time is to destroy
the mother, to rip her open to find her imagined contents (i.e.
the father's penis, excrement, children, food) and also implicitly to destroy the father, whom it expects to find inside the
mother, as well as itself, who is also "inside" her. Not surprisingly, Klein tells us, the "earliest defense set up by the
ego is directed against the subject's own sadism and the
object attacked, both of these being regarded as sources of
danger" (232). This defense is conceived of as violent in
nature—a kind of defense by expulsion.

This is the normal story of those sadisms and anxieties
that, Klein argued, are necessary for the formation of the ego
and the symbolizing faculties peculiar to the healthy human.
Not only simple libidinal interest, but also the anxiety arising in this phase of oral/anal sadism, sets in motion the
mechanism of identification and, in turn, of symbol-formation. Symbol-formation turns out to be thus the "basis" not

[16] Melanie Klein, "The Importance of Symbol-Formation in the Development of the Ego" (1930), in *Love, Guilt, and Reparation and Other Works
1921–1945*, vol. 1 of *The Writings of Melanie Klein* (New York: Free Press,
1984), 220.

only of "all fantasy and sublimation" but also "of the subject's relation to the outside world and to reality in general"
(220). The child equates the mother's body with the world,
which becomes "the mother's body in an extended sense"
(232). To develop psychologically then requires "sadistic
appropriation and exploration of the mother's body and of the
outside world," which takes place via symbol-formation; the
subject must establish "symbolic relation to the things and
objects representing the contents of the mother's body and
hence . . . [its] relation [to its] environment and to reality"
(232). (This would be true for both males and females, despite
the fact that it is still "a man's world out there"; certainly,
access to the knowledge-world, has been jealously guarded by
her sons.)

What is relevant here about the passages quoted above is
that originally the sexual organs "stand for" the objects the
child imagines to be inside the mother, rather than the other
way around. In other words, one's own body parts are the first
symbols, and they stand for, and signify, imaginary referents,
or what Freud called "psychical objects." This analysis
reverses Freudian hermeneutics, which reduce all our signs
and symbols to one referent: the phallus (more precisely, following McDougall, the penis or, even more specifically, the
female penis). Freudian hermeneutics is a binary language
referring always to the unitary presence or absence of the
penis—equated finally with the presence or absence of a unitary mother. A Kleinian hermeneutics compared to Freud's
binary language is more variously transformable, more polymorphous. And because the symbol is privileged, prior even
to its referent, it is more literary. That is, it signals the movement of psychoanalysis across that disjunction from the
"real," or physiological, to the symbolic, to a new literary or
hermeneutic perspective from which the body itself looks
decidedly unreal.

To extend this logic, then, the imagination does not represent the body; the body expresses, stands for, the mind; body
is an extrusion of mind. Symbols do not represent the sublimation of sexuality; sexuality, rather, is for psychoanalysis

our primal discourse, perhaps that from which evolve other already sexualized discourses. Freud used the term "epistemophilia" to mean "the [pathological] eroticization of knowing," and linked it to the perversion "scopophilia," the eroticization of seeing. But Klein applied "epistemophilia" to the impulse to explore and appropriate objects by establishing symbolic relations to them. The natural curiosity of a child thus becomes an urgent need to scan the world for symbols. Epistemophilia enables the child to feel he knows things, even if in a reductive sense all he can know (according to Klein) is the fantasized content of his mother's body.

The reader may recall Krafft-Ebing's distinction between the normal or "physiological" fetishist and the abnormal or pathological one: the normal fetishist (Everymale) has a personal preference for certain parts of the female anatomy "having a direct relation" to "genital sex," whereas the pathological fetishist instead idealizes some contingent part that has no such relation. Early on, Freud more or less uncritically adopted this distinction so that it became a formative bit of psychiatric diagnostic dogma around the turn of the century. But Klein's healthy epistemophiliac (Everychild) is in a sense the inverse of Krafft-Ebing's "physiological" or normal fetishist. The healthy epistemophiliac is determined not by his relation to "real" bodies, but rather by his facility with symbols (in the most general sense, in which the world is seen as symbol), which to Krafft-Ebing were the stock-in-trade of perversion. Klein's epistemophiliac goes about the world finding and making ever new symbols by means of which to feel connected to his "environment and to reality."

A state of mental health encourages the development of "kindly imagos," that is, of highly individualized, even idiosyncratic, yet flexible and meaningful, symbols.[17] Based on how psychoanalysts describe the progress of their analysands, it would not be going too far to argue that according to psychoanalysis individuals cannot even have feelings about their experience until they are able to symbolize it, that is, to have

[17] Melanie Klein, "Personification in the Play of Children" (1929), in *Writings*, 1:209.

freely imaginative fantasies about it and verbalize those fantasies. If, generally speaking, before the turn of the century the "physiological" (specifically, the genital) was the sign of the normal and the ground of the real, by the 1910s and 1920s, in the psychoanalytic literature the sign of the normal and the ground of the real had shifted from the physiological to the mental or symbolic. In his "Preface to Reik's *Ritual: Psychoanalytic Studies*," Freud reminds us that "psychoanalysis was born out of medical necessity. It sprang from the need for bringing help to neurotic patients, who had found no relief through rest-cures, through the arts of hydropathy or through electricity. . . . Its further course led it away from the study of the somatic determinants of nervous disease to an extent that was bewildering to physicians. Instead, it was brought into contact with the mental substance of human lives—the lives not only of the sick, but of the healthy, the normal, and the supernormal."[18] Psychoanalysis had led itself "away" from the study of the somatic to "the mental substance of human lives" through the study of dreams and other symbolic human productions. Furthermore, to repeat a point made in connection with Klein, such symbolization, according to the logic peculiar to psychoanalysis, was not understood as the product of the body so much as in some obscure way its source. The symbolic does not refer to or stand in for the body but instead "speaks" it. In other words, to use a phrase of Lacan's from a different context ("The Mirror Stage"), the libidinal dynamism of psychoanalytic discourse itself had set off "in a fictional direction."

Psychoanalysis came to embody its own symbolist aesthetic. Like literary and artistic modernism more generally, psychoanalysis as it developed became increasingly self-referential as a discourse, but, unlike the artistic avant-garde, it represented itself as a science. For some analysts, philosophers, and scientists, this embrace of the "fictional" has been difficult to swallow. Donald P. Spence, for example, author of *Narrative Truth and Historical Truth* (1982), is obviously uncomfortable with how the internal coherence of what he

[18] Freud, "Preface to Reik's *Ritual: Psychoanalytic Studies*," in *SE* 17:259.

calls "narrative truth" takes precedence in psychoanalysis over "historical truth."[19] From a scientific point of view he finds this appalling, even though he admits that it is narrative truth, not historical truth, which heals the patient. Spence can find no logical explanation for this fact, which he seems to wish were not so, namely, that what seems to be basically an aesthetic practice has therapeutic efficacy. Psychoanalysis appears to Spence to be an aesthetic activity because it eschews provable facts in order to construct narrative truth out of "pattern matches," or formal "correspondence[s] between an anomalous happening and earlier events in the patient's history" (145). Language, which Spence describes as "infinitely flexible" to the purpose at hand, "plays a critical role" in creating these matches, which are then interpreted by the analyst as "indications of cause and effect" (145). "Formal similarity," then, replaces logic in establishing the "meaningful connection[s]" out of which the narrative truth of psychic reality is constructed.

Reconsidering Freud's revision of the seduction theory of hysteria, Laplanche and Pontalis, unlike Spence, suggest that Freud might as well have been more thoroughly modern than he was and made the discourse of psychoanalysis more like the avant-garde in its rejection of nineteenth-century realism and subject/object dualism. Their answer—from the early postmodern perspective of the late 1960s—to what they think was Freud's problem is a definition of psychical reality that further elides the theoretical disjunction between the physiological and the symbolic, a solution that seemed to make sense at the time. Psychical reality, according to Laplanche and Pontalis, is a term Freud uses but which, they feel, is not fully understood by psychoanalysts and is often compromised by Freud himself, who, unfortunately from their point of view, persistently "falls back" into biological realism. In place of biological realism they offer a different kind of realism, however, based on what to my mind is merely the same phenomenological dualism displaced inward

---

[19] Donald P. Spence, *Narrative Truth and Historical Truth: Meaning and Interpretation in Psychoanalysis* (New York: Norton, 1982).

where it distinguishes between what they call "structural fantasies" and secondary ones. Thereby they simply replace one kind of primary/secondary dichotomy with another. From my point of view (as I shall argue more pointedly in the next chapter) this is hardly surprising because any model that is not interactive can only recapitulate a hierarchical dualism. It is this larger, ultimately political problem in which I am most interested, but Laplanche and Pontalis's attempt to redefine psychical reality exclusively in its "own" terms exemplifies the inward movement in modernism in general and psychoanalysis in particular from the "somatic" to the "mental," from the "real" to the linguistic—that movement which through a series of subsequent displacements and idealizations "in a fictional direction" we now experience as a renewed interest in "cultural construction."

Laplanche and Pontalis argue, for example, that psychical reality refers not to subjectivity in general, or to the whole psychological field, but to "a heterogeneous nucleus within this field, a resistant element, alone truly real, in contrast with the majority of psychological phenomena" (3). This resistant element is a particular symbology consisting of three genres of "primal fantasies," which constitute the formal core of our psychical reality and exist, as it were, a priori. All three of these so-called primal fantasies are fantasies of origins: "The primal scene pictures the origin of the individual; fantasies of seduction, the origin and upsurge of sexuality; fantasies of castration, the origin of the difference between the sexes. Their themes therefore display, with redoubled significance, that original fantasies justify their status of being already there"(11). These three genres of primal fantasies and their unconscious elaborations constitute the human text psychoanalysis sees itself interpreting; the success of psychoanalysis depends on "the dialectic 'integration' of the fantasies as they emerge." In this essay Laplanche and Pontalis say that to accomplish this it is necessary to distinguish between "primal" or "original" fantasies, which are "structural," and others. They are not certain how to do this, but suggest that original fantasy includes a dramatis personae from which the subject is absent. (By saying this they are equating primal fantasies with masturbatory fantasies as psychoanalytic theory has defined them.)

Fantasy *(Phantasie)* here does not mean merely that which is not real: "This opposition antedates psychoanalysis by many centuries, but is liable to prove restrictive both to psychoanalytic theory and practice." They complain that psychoanalysis is often based on "a very elementary theory of reality" (1) that opposes the real to the imaginary and locates the unconscious somewhere in between, "between an inner world, where satisfaction is obtained through illusion, and an external world, which gradually, through the medium of perception, asserts the supremacy of the reality principle" (2). But, as Laplanche and Pontalis remind us, according to psychoanalysis the unconscious is not an intermediary; it is too "deep" for that. They argue that "material reality" is right where we think it is; that the "reality of intermediate thoughts," or the "psychological field" lies between material reality and psychical reality; and that, at the deepest level, we find "the reality of unconscious wishes and their 'truest shape[,]' fantasy"(3). This topology itself is almost absurdly simplistic and, worse still, privileges the unfathomable-yet-magically-true unconscious, which for all intents and purposes is synonymous with the psychically real. The psychical apparently derealizes itself in direct proportion to its distance from the deep "heterogeneous nucleus" (heterogeneous relative to what, one wonders?); the closer to the "material world" something psychical is—and the closer, one must assume, to the social—the less psychically real it is.

In this decadent version of the psychoanalytic model the old disjunction between psyche and world remains; it is just that both Cartesian doubt about the reality of the material, and Kantian confidence in the unknowability of the noumenal become trivial when compared to the psychically real, the transcendentally interior, subjectless subjectivity. Psychical reality is thus in one sense just the scientized version of modernist impressionism,"a subjectivity in which the sub-

ject has disappeared."[20] It represents the totalization of idealized mentality, sensuous thought. The body itself, reduced to
being an idea—and somebody else's idea at that—joins the
ranks of the unknowable. Jacques Lacan and Julia Kristeva,
like Melanie Klein, emphasize the mythic yet constitutive
disjunction—the "dehiscence" as Lacan has called it—
between the material world, as represented by the body of the
(m)other, and its hallucinatory revival in the realm of the
symbolic. For Lacan this disjunction separates the moments
"before" and "after" the mythic moment when the child
encounters its image in the mirror. For Kristeva this disjunction falls between the "semiotic" and the "symbolic." Insofar
as they don't dispense with the importance of "disjunction"
per se they continue the dualistic tradition of old-world
Freudianism; but insofar as they locate that disjunction within subjective consciousness, as it were, they "exalt" (as John
Donne might say) that dualism into a fetishization that
Freud's "discovery" of psychical reality helped along. I am
not concerned with figuring out who is a Freudian and who is
not, but with tracing the vicissitudes of the concept of psychical reality, its relation to the idealization of language, and
its contribution to a certain contemporary fetishization of
"discourse," as well as in trying to reclaim some of Freud's
commonsensical materialism for our current work. It is far
from clear that the "mythical moment of disjunction . . .
between the two stages represented by real experience and its
hallucinatory revival" is in fact the dualism from which
Freud was trying logically to escape by means of his "biological realism." As Frank Sulloway and others have argued,
Freud did not think of himself as "falling back" into biological realism. On the contrary, Freud *aspired to* biological realism. He did not think that psychical reality and biological
realism are mutually exclusive, or even contradictory.

In fact, in an effort to define "what 'the psychical' really
means," to define its "*nature,* or, as people sometimes say,

[20] Michael Levenson, *A Genealogy of Modernism: A Study of English
Literary Doctrine 1908–1922* (Cambridge: Cambridge Unversity Press, 1984),
119.

[its] *essence,"* Freud draws an analogy between himself and "a physicist" in "Some Elementary Lessons in Psycho-analysis" (1938):

> If an analogous question had been put to a physicist (as to the nature of electricity, for instance), his reply, until quite recently, would have been: "For the purpose of explaining certain phenomena, we assume the existence of electrical forces which are present in things and which emanate from them. We study these phenomena, discover the laws that govern them and even put them to practical use. This satisfies us provisionally. We do not know the *nature* of electricity. Perhaps we may discover it later, as our work goes on. It must be admitted that what we are ignorant of is precisely the most important and interesting part of the whole business, but for the moment that does not worry us. It is simply how things happen in the natural sciences."[21]

"Psychology, too, is a natural science," he adds. "What else can it be?" To Freud it was as logical for the psychologist to assume the existence of psychical reality before science could identify it physically as it had been for the physicist to study the effects of electricity before its nature had been discovered.

Freud is aware that at times he treats mental disease only "as if" he had the means to do so. At such times Freud idealizes, metaphorizes, perhaps fetishizes, his conception of physiology in order to reason away the opacity of the body. "Metapsychology" is the name Freud gives to the "conception of organic functions" with which he must make do when he cannot find "the chemical changes" he believes to be at work but which he is "at present unable to apprehend." Metapsychology is thus in a way the fantasmatic phallus of a science momentarily impotent, at the same time that it is a construction capable of expanding the range and applicability of psychoanalytic theory. Freud was aware that biology and metapsychology made strange bedfellows; accordingly he was insistent upon the former and apologetic about the latter. In "Analysis Terminable and Interminable" (1937), he raises the

[21] Freud, "Some Elementary Lessons in Psychoanalysis," in *SE* 23:282.

question of whether or not it is possible "for analysis permanently and definitively to resolve a conflict between instinct
and the ego," and suggests that, rather than hoping for a resolution of the conflict, we should aim at a taming of the
instinct."[22] Furthermore, if we are asked "how and by what
means this result is achieved, we do not find it easy to
answer. There is nothing for it but to 'summon help from the
Witch' [a quotation from Goethe's *Faust*]—the Witch Metapsychology. Without metapsychological speculation and theorizing—I had almost said 'fantasy'—we shall not get a step
further. Unfortunately, here as elsewhere, what our Witch
reveals is neither very clear nor very exact." (*SE* 23:225). In
the name of the witch metapsychology Freud offers us the
most tempting (and perhaps forbidden) fruit of psychoanalytic knowledge: the taming of instinctual demand. What is our
dearest wish? To tame our instinctual demands. "How and
by what means" shall we achieve this end? By means of
"speculation" and "theorizing"—by means, in other words,
of abstraction, or what Freud would like to call "fantasy." It
is only by indulging in that intellectual "fantasy" which
Freud discreetly names "metapsychology," and which he
conceives of as the feminine specter of a castrated Reason,
that we can imagine taming the untamable instincts.

Metapsychology, then, is itself a kind of sensuous thought,
that is, an idea or fantasy to which is attributed sensuous
reality. In psychoanalytic thought experiments metapsychology serves as a (magical) instrument. Further, metapsychology is to psychoanalysis what the fetish is to psychical reality:
an embodied idealization born of the wish for truth and
understanding, the wish to be privy to a special realm of
knowing and wholeness. The above passage, like the others
quoted from Freud's writing at about the same time, makes
clear both his awareness that his knowledge was provisional
and metaphorical, and his conviction that it nevertheless
qualified *as* knowledge. That he could consider both of these
contradictories true, even while expressing the sense of
absurdity about such a mode of proceeding, but not being, in

---

[22] Freud, "Analysis Terminable and Interminable," in *SE* 23:224–25.

turn, uncomfortable with that absurdity, indicates the special, privileged, logically invulnerable, paradoxical "ontology" Freud attributed to psychical reality. Here the law of
noncontradiction does not apply. Nevertheless, Freud used
the term "psychical reality" in a general way to indicate that
how we ourselves "conceive" of and represent our experience
turns out to *be* that experience.

In *The Interpretation of Dreams* Freud tells us that the
mind is by nature formal.[23] To determine what Freud might
mean by this, it is helpful to consider, first, that Freud does
not distinguish mind from brain and, second, consistent with
this first principle, the same formalism that he applies to the
dreams, images, and narratives applies as well to his own discourse. Literary critics appropriated psychoanalysis because
of its interest in personal stories and symbolic narratives and,
even more, because of how it seems, on account of its scientism, to prove that these narratives constitute individual and
cultural reality. But that Freud was first and foremost a neu-
rologist remains of more than biographical interest. Freud
suggested early on that memory was not a collection of complete images etched into brain tissue but a set of procedures
by means of which fragmentary impressions could be mobi-
lized to categorize information. "The full significance of this
discovery may have been missed by contemporary neurosci-
entists and psychobiologists," but, as current research shows,
Freud "was in effect describing the functioning of the limbic
system (a set of interconnected structures deep inside the
brain)," which since the 1930s has become increasingly cru-
cial to the understanding of memory and brain function in
general.[24]

Freud was not a brain/mind dualist because he was not a
mind/body dualist. Lancelot Whyte has even argued that
Freud's work constitutes only one phase of the long process
of "discovering" the unconscious, a discovery made inevitable by Descartes's "fundamental blunder" of postulating

[23] Freud, *The Interpretation of Dreams*, in *SE* 4:329.
[24] Israel Rosenfeld, *The Invention of Memory: A New View of the Brain*
(New York: Basic Books, 1988), 6.

"two separate realms of being, one of which is characterized by awareness" (26). Once one has ceased to believe in body and mind as separate realms, however, symptom and symbol, *soma* and *seme,* become indistinguishable. Freud was a person/world dualist, however, which accounts both for his optimistic view that there is nothing science cannot know, and his pessimistic view about the possibility of human happiness. For him the body was not just another object in the material world, but the physical voice of a tirelessly signifying physical subjectivity—not a text so much as an author, a speaker, a mouth. Freud was distressed that he lacked the medical technology to prove his theories; otherwise, for example, he perhaps could have located the "unconscious" as some current researchers think they have come close to doing. Freud was unable to substantiate his "biological realism," but he never doubted its validity. When he could not substantiate it, he felt he must "fall back" on mere "idea," on speculation and "metapsychology." (He never felt the reverse, that he was just falling back on biological realism when an idea failed him.) For example, Freud's theory of hysteria could not "point out that neuroses have an organic basis" because, as he admitted, there is no organic basis, no "substance," to point out. It is only "as if" there were. What Freud does have is an idea of this organic basis, an idea of the physiological, which he wishes he could locate, but cannot: "The theory [of hysteria] does not by any means fail to point out that neuroses have an organic basis—though it is true that it does not look for that basis in any pathological anatomical changes, and *provisionally substitutes the conception of organic functions for the chemical changes which we should expect to find but which we are at present unable to apprehend.*"[25] Freud himself was fully aware that he treated unconscious activity as if it were as plain as day, as perspicuous to the senses of its "observer" as speech or movement.

But he regarded this "as if" as if it were unproblematic, as

[25] Freud, "Fragment of an Analysis of a Case of Hysteria," in *SE* 7:113; my emphasis.

if it were merely a methodological curiosity that anyone (who wasn't a philosopher) who reflected a moment would find harmless. Only a philosopher, he implied, would be silly enough to criticize him for not being a sufficiently strict biological realist. More recently, psychoanalyst and physician Marshall Edelson has tried to quiet philosophers' qualms about psychoanalysis by arguing that strict biological realism is not necessary "because the development of theories of mind and brain has not advanced anywhere near the point where one could reasonably claim it is even possible for a proposition about the mind and a proposition about the brain to contradict each other."[26] Development of theories about mind and about brain, Edelson argues, "each with intended applications in its own quite different set of possible and actual domains, can and should be carried on independently," at least for now. According to Edelson, despite any neuroscientific discoveries about the location of the unconscious, we have no way of knowing whether the psychological domain "mind" and the biological domain "brain" could be described as "isomorphic." To claim them as isomorphic would mean "that at the least for every pair of individual entities in a psychological domain (whatever these entities may be), which are in some relation to each other (whatever the relation is), there is a corresponding pair of individual entities in a physical-biological domain (whatever these very different entities may be), which are in some relation to each other (whatever that very different relation is), and that the relation in one domain is the same kind of relation (for example, binary and symmetric) as the relation in the other domain" (112). Edelson's reasoning makes it painfully clear just how far apart neuroscience and psychology remain, philosophically as well as pragmatically. Nevertheless, as Lyotard put it, the legitimacy of one need not negate the legitimacy of the other, so that mind and brain, psychoanalysis and neuroscience, could be said to comprise a true differend, despite Freud's

---

[26] Marshall Edelson, *Hypothesis and Evidence in Psychoanalysis* (Chicago: University of Chicago Press, 1984), 110. Edelson is replying in part to Spence, *Narrative Truth and Historical Truth.*

mind/brain monism, and despite his faith in a science of the imagination.

To Freud it made sense to suggest that there is no place in the brain where representation is not always already at work. The unconscious reacts "to everything that is simultaneously present in the sleeping mind as currently active material" by manufacturing a certain kind of coherence (*SE* 4:228). The mind cannot do otherwise; manufacturing this coherence is a "necessity": "The dream-work is under the necessity of combining into a unity all instigations to dreaming which are active simultaneously" (*SE* 4:228). To some extent the mind peforms its dream work with the sensibility of an expressive artist. The sleeping mind will often "transvalue" its material by means of a kind of displacement which "usually results in a colourless and abstract expression in the dream-thought being exchanged for a pictorial and concrete one. A thing that is pictorial is, from the point of view of a dream, a thing that is *capable of being represented.*" (*SE* 5:339–40; Freud's emphasis). The unconscious, then, is driven by the need to represent itself as "concretely" and colorfully as possible, using displacement "in order, as it were, to facilitate its representation."

We must not, Freud says, underrate the role "considerations of representability [play] in the peculiar psychical material of which dreams make use" to this end (*SE* 5:344). Communicativeness is not one of these "considerations of representability," since dreams "are not made with the intention of being understood" (unless we think they are made to be understood by the conscious mind, or perhaps by the analyst) (*SE* 5:341).[27] They are, in primitive form, representation

----

[27] It is the thesis of the neuroscientist Jonathan Winson, in *Brain and Psyche: The Biology of the Unconscious* (New York: Vintage, 1985), that dreams in humans "are a window on the neural process whereby, from early childhood on, strategies for behavior are being set down, modified, or consulted" (209). In other words, REM sleep is a "process whereby the flow of recent events and past associations is tapped into and integrated into a guide for future behavior" (213). "When Freud dissected and analyzed dreams and from them constructed his concept of the unconscious, he was looking at this [neurological] process" (209). The fact that some of us remember our dreams is fortuitous, and not related to their function.

for its own sake, at the same time that they represent (or end up representing themselves in) the psychic, familial, and even cultural coherencies Freud spent his life defining. Freud emphasizes that dream images "instinctively" tend away from the colorless and the abstract toward the concrete, the pictorial, and the coherent and formed. The unconscious, in other words, is driven to "embody" rather than merely represent itself, preferring images less "like a language" and more like a concrete "memorial to itself."[28] As Ricoeur puts it, "The signifying factor [*le signifiant*] which he [Freud] finds in the unconscious and which he calls the 'instinctual representative' (ideational or affective) is of the order of images, as is evidenced moreover by the regression of the dream-thoughts to the fantasy stage. . . . As for the 'presentation' properly so-called [*Vorstellung*], this is not, in its specific texture, of the order of language; it is a 'presentation of things,' not a 'presentation of words.'"[29] This thingness itself is symptomatic: thought as thing. The "things" chosen by the unconscious for "presentation" (this word makes the unconscious act prior to "*re*presentation," which is an "intentional" act) are of course not actual "things" but images we experience in dreams (or psychosis) *as if* they were things because they possess for us psychical reality.

It is the concept of psychical reality that gives psychoanalysis both its truth-seemingness, and that organic seamlessness which makes it resemble the "coherency model" of high modernism. "Psychical reality" is the psychoanalytic equivalent of its poetic contemporary, the "sensuous thought" discussed in the preceding chapter. Sensuous thought, for both Yeats and Eliot, poets who otherwise conceived of their poetic missions quite differently, represented

---

[28] Freud, "Fetishism," in *SE* 21:154.

[29] Paul Ricoeur, *Freud and Philosophy: An Essay on Interpretation*, trans. Denis Savage (New Haven: Yale University Press), 398. Ricoeur nevertheless conflates what he calls the infra- and the supra-linguistic aspects of dream representation, claiming that this conflation itself is characteristic of dreams, again leaving the individual a kind of placeholder between the inside and the outside. Ricoeur thus treats the unconscious in precisely the same way as consciousness (see 398–400).

the ideal linguistic unity of thought and feeling, brain and body, an ideal which, they thought, the best poetry embodies in an impersonal way. Psychical reality, like sensuous thought, also denotes a unity of thought and feeling, but an internal one, best represented by how we literalize our dream thoughts in the form of dream images, which we experience as if they were real things, persons, and events.

Freud's assumption that culture in general was but the macrocosmic social enactment of this same psychical reality enabled him in good faith to concoct anthropological fairy tales such as *Totem and Taboo*, narratives that serve both as precedents for contemporary forms of culture analysis and as warnings in spite of themselves against problems of inadvertent wish-fulfillment inherent in such projects.[30] The notion of "psychical reality" gives mental life the status of the symbolic-and-therefore-real which we ascribed to it by increasing (or, one might say, inflating[31]) the value and significance of representation generally. Psychoanalysis deemed representation to be the equivalent of mental life, of psychic life, rather than the representation either of it or of some world "out there." Psychoanalysis thus was of a piece with the developing aestheticized view of language and representation in the modern world generally, insofar as it rejected the formerly prized naturalness of a world not made by man.

But although psychoanalysis was in a sense just one manifestation of paradigms shifting everywhere, at the same time it built a highly visible and relatively stable structure bridging the very fault lines that divide the nineteenth century from the twentieth. That revolutionary work, *The Interpretation of Dreams*, was completed in 1899 but publication was delayed until 1900 so it could usher in the new century. It was Freud's resolute and prolific scientism, his unproblemat-

[30] Joan Copjec begins the much-needed critique of certain serious limitations imposed upon film theory by the conflation of Lacanian psychoanalytic theory with Foucauldian social theory. See "The Orthopsychic Subject: Film Theory and the Reception of Lacan," *October* 49 (Summer 1989): 53–71.

[31] In *The Post-Modern Aura: The Act of Fiction in an Age of Inflation* (Evanston: Northwestern University Press, 1985), Charles Newman finds "inflation" the form of corruption endemic to postmodern theory.

ic acceptance of the person/world duality, which enabled him to feel he was doing classical science, and which ultimately gave objective status to his startling new formulation of the relations between person and world and person and self, as being primarily linguistic—and thus, in the old sense, not relations at all. In many ways his work suggests simple disbelief in a world comprised of pragmatic social interaction, or existential *engagement*. He was not, however (to repeat myself), a body/mind dualist, but a person/world dualist. It was epistemological dualism, of course, still fairly secure at the end of the nineteenth century, that permitted Freud to assume that *his* "utterance [could] be independent of the speaking subject," that is, independent of his own unconscious wishes and projections (26), unlike the utterances of those he analyzed. This model of idealized scientific objectivity, which ignores the extent to which the subject and object necessarily interact, has since of course been consigned to the epistemological attic. Similarly, what at first justified the claim of psychoanalysis to be a branch of medicine, was that it sought the causes of physical symptoms. But psychoanalysis reinscribed the body as symbol into the discourse of its own symptomology, in this case synecdochized, as a giant organ of speech susceptible to a "talking cure."

The Oedipus complex, the specimen romance of psychoanalysis, with its typical complications and idealized "solution," constitutes a personalized historical narrative that lends the status of science to the myth of the body's appropriation by its species. According to this myth, the child, handed over to civilization by its family at the time of potty training (if not sooner), grows up when it discovers that its sexuality, which during adolescence seemed to confer uniqueness, in reality makes it a mere "appendage to his germ plasm" (*SE* 14:78). According to Freud, growing up means discovering that one's feelings of connection with the world, whether experienced as religious faith or romantic love, are merely leftover oedipal wishes, derived from infantile fantasies of merger with Mother. Despite our willingness to see in Freud's work the possibility that through such compensatory mechanisms as sublimation and repression we can to some degree reconcile our wishes with the real world, there really is no middle ground in Freud: his theories allow no interaction between the person and the world. Individuals inhabit the seethingly passionate un/consciousnesses they enclose, bits of which escape uncontrollably to form an "outside" world, which mirrors back to us, in almost unrecognizable but uncannily familiar form, our own imaginations. Self and world in Freud are polarized equivalents that do not affect and change each other in those ways we now consider to be characteristic of our lives as creatures of culture. Perhaps it is because of this polarization, and the lack of interaction between person and world in Freud's theory, that Freud's followers dispensed with the "world" and equated the psychical with the real, just as we tend to describe the high modernists doing.

Kantian, if not Cartesian, dualism structures both those Freudian myths which seem to be about "father" and related constructs such as the ego ideal and those "about" mother and preoedipal instincts and identifications. The romanticized, reified quality of this dualism of self and world—it too is an idealization—comes home to us when we read works such as *Totem and Taboo* (1912–13) or *The Future of an Illusion* (1927). Even if we share their atheistic, materialistic assumptions, Freud's scientific myths about the origin and nature of society may seem to us a bizarre fantasia of Freud's unconscious (to paraphrase D. H. Lawrence). *Civilization and its Discontents* (1930) can be depressing because it expresses a cynicism born of the conviction that, like the prelapsarian perfection of Eden and its corrupt counterpart after the Fall, the self with its insatiable wishes and the world from which the self seeks satisfaction remain incommensurable halves of an unrecoverable unity at the center of which is absence.

As an institution, then, psychoanalysis reflects the life of that oxymoronic entity, a bourgeois institution in its own right, the "private individual." In Freudian psychoanalysis what mediates between self and world is language; in Lacanian psychoanalysis the polymorphous omnipresence of language renders inconsequential the Freudian disjunction between self and world. Here language unites self and world by constituting them. The idea of language-as-symbolic-process mediates between self and world even as it begs certain questions about their relation. This explains why literary criticism found psychoanalytic hermeneutics as useful as psychoanalysis found literary texts; they shared an interest in "intermediate thought" and used each other to remain in that intermediate realm while seeming to be doing something concrete.

Nevertheless, to reiterate an important point, I am not arguing against language in favor of something more "real"; that would be silly. Thanks in part to psychoanalysis we have gotten used to the idea that interaction as such, and perhaps even the activities of knowing generally, take place always through language in myriad forms. But I argue that our idea of language remains too cut off from the particularity of its speakers and contexts and thus is complicit in the erasure of agency per se, rendering it in some ways a highly apolitical notion, despite the fact that we think we have rejected what we took to be the apoliticalism of aesthetic modernity. This is especially and ironically so in the realm of literary studies. Recently, as for example in the ethnography of Renato Rosaldo, self-conscious authors have been attempting to account even in their theoretical writing for the effect on what they are saying of their "personal" situations, backgrounds, attitudes, and assumptions.[32] Elsewhere in the humanities similar efforts are opening up fields to subject matters and thinking subjects heretofore "invisible" and inaudible. These efforts, representing as they do a renewed interest in personal "identities," hark back to how Freud's science combined a stubborn ontological materialism with a wittily appreciative psychological formalism. "Psychical reality" names both a living space and its inhabitant, that mind-body totality of the symbolizing-and-therefore-real individual we know by the linguistic tracks it leaves.

Ironically, both the efficacy of psychoanalysis as a "talking

---

[32] Renato Rosaldo, *Culture and Truth: The Remaking of Social Analysis* (Boston: Beacon Press, 1989).

cure," and its usefulness from the point of view of postmodern thinking, is precisely that it dispenses with the distinction between representation and that which it represents. If aesthetic modernity reconceived human relations as formal relations, postmodernity pushes this understanding of language to its logical extreme, moving from the idea of language as self-referential to the notion that it is nonreferential. Today in English studies a revivified historicism strives to reconnect this supposedly nonreferential language to some practically and politically real world without closing its eyes to how explanatory narratives participate in the construction of that world. As Jean-Joseph Goux put it, we know we must now ask ourselves, "How can this permanently slipped gear be re-engaged?"[33] Psychoanalysis did not cause the fetishization of language, various versions of which were, as suggested earlier, already circulating, but rather participated in a phenomenon that was culture-wide, if not always self-consciously so.

But if in some ways psychoanalytic theory helped to alienate the mind from the social materiality of its world, in other ways it has made possible exciting new conceptions of their relation. In his brilliant theoretical work, Lacanian Slavoj Žižek decisively deconstructs the antithesis of psyche and culture. In the last section of his *Looking Awry: An Introduction to Jacques Lacan through Popular Culture,* Žižek responds to Richard Rorty's premise that we must "'drop the demand for a theory which unifies the public and private' and 'be content to treat the demands of self-creation and of human solidarity as equally valid, yet forever incommensurable.'"[34] For Žižek the incommensurability of the public and the private is a "liberal dream," invalid not for the Marxist reason that the public/private split is the historical "product of a specific social structure," but for the psychoanalytic reason called "the *superego*." A liberal could concede

[33] Jean-Joseph Goux, *Symbolic Economies: After Marx and Freud*, trans. Jennifer Curtiss Gage (Ithaca: Cornell University Press, 1990), 210.
[34] Slavoj Žižek, *Looking Awry: An Introduction to Jacques Lacan through Popular Culture* (Cambridge: MIT Press, 1991), 159. See also Žižek, *The Sublime Object of Ideology* (London: Verso, 1989).

the Marxist's point, but

> The real impasse runs in the opposite direction: the very social
> law that, as a kind of neutral set of rules, should limit our aes-
> thetic self-creation and deprive us of a part of our enjoyment on
> behalf of solidarity, is always already penetrated by an obscene,
> "pathological," surplus enjoyment. The point is thus not that
> the split public/private is not possible, but that it is possible
> only on condition that the very domain of the public law is
> "smeared" by an obscene dimension of "private" enjoyment:
> public law draws the "energy" for the pressure it exerts on the
> subject from the very enjoyment of which it deprives him by
> acting as an agency of prohibition. (159)

Žižek refuses the disjunction of psyche and world, except as a
gap across which we persistently misrecognize, misread, and
misconstrue the reality of our own doings. For Žižek, Lacan
has made it possible to read culture, its politics, and poetics,
as Freud a century ago read "the subject" afflicted by "representation paralysis."

It is no wonder that some of Freud's colleagues were un-
easy when he at once asserted "that neuroses have an organic
basis" and claimed he could use speech to cure them.
Psychoanalysis, as a modernist discourse, participates in the
move toward the mystification of the object in a way exemplified by Ricoeur in his book on Freud when he wrote that
"consciousness is first of all an intending of the other, and
not self-presence or self-possession."[35] In some ways this
statement sums up the conception psychoanalysis has come
to represent for us: paradoxically, psychoanalysis has led to
the triumph not of the subject, but of what Regis Durand has
called the "triumph of the object."[36] Durand seeks in the
modern era the genealogy of a subject not to be defined in
relation to an object, and thinks to have found one in the

---

[35] Ricoeur, *Freud and Philosophy*, 378. Here Ricoeur is exploring the
affinities between Husserlian phenomenology and Freudian psychoanalysis.

[36] Regis Durand, "On *Aphanisis:* A Note on the Dramaturgy of the Subject
in Narrative Analysis," in *Lacan and Narration*, ed. Robert Con Davis
(Baltimore: Johns Hopkins University Press, 1983), 865.

concept of *aphanisis*, or disappearance, located "on the very borderline between psychoanalytic and literary theory," and between zero and one.

That Freud was a biological realist—as well as a male chauvinist—is part of his Old World bourgeois identity. That Freud had a commonsensical notion of the therapeutic interaction (which has its problematic aspects) between two persons is likewise true. But that Freud regarded language, and an instinctual need for symbolic self-representation, as hardwired into the human brain, is modern; furthermore, these ideas are now fundamental to our understanding of ourselves both as biological individuals and as social creatures. But as it has been interpreted by and incorporated into modern and postmodern literary discourse (to repeat and elaborate what I have been saying), psychoanalysis has become increasingly detached from its commonsensical notions of its own referentiality, notions it does not pay to leave behind. When symbols symbolize only other symbols, they become by definition self-referential and cease, paradoxically, to represent selves or worlds. In his essay "Mom," Andrew Parker argues that psychoanalysis reaches "an impasse within the discipline when it traces hysteria to an unconscious realm both prior to and other than the body."[37] Freud, as I pointed out earlier, does not locate the unconscious in a realm prior to or other than the body. But other psychoanalysts since Freud, such as Melanie Klein, seem to, arguing, like Lacan, and Laplanche and Pontalis, that sexuality begins at the moment autoerotism moves away from "any natural object" and "into the field of fantasy."

It is a seemingly paradoxical principle of psychoanalysis that this move away from the natural object is most natural. But Parker argues that "sexuality is less a solution than the name of a problem for psychoanalytic theory," which "paradoxically confers on the body something like the status of a 'literary' text"—and vice versa (102). Sexuality is thus the name of a general problem of reference that in its psychoana-

[37] Andrew Parker, "Mom," in *Sexual Difference*, Special Issue of the *Oxford Literary Review* 8, nos. 1-2 (1986): 98.

lytic formulation sacrifices the natural object in the name of the subject, but which as a consequence also sacrifices the credibility of the subject by mystifying the object. The object becomes more a miracle than a symbol (something ineffable rather than an object present to human understanding). To make this point Parker invokes Julia Kristeva's concept of "the abject," namely, "that which the superego seeks to expel in order to conserve its precarious self-identity" but which invariably reasserts itself one way or another (101). In the case of post-Freudian psychoanalysis, the body itself is this abject: "Reference to the body forms the *abject of Lacanian theory*, that very 'something' which it cannot recognize as a thing and still preserve its disciplinary integrity. This attempted abjection of the body—a prerequisite for Lacan's assumption of the semiotic character of his object— nonetheless cannot fully succeed in that the body never stops haunting the presumed autonomy of the unconscious, never stops littering the field of psychoanalysis" (102; Parker's emphasis). Parker stresses "the irreducibility of reference to the body" in psychoanalysis not in order "to reground sexuality in a natural corporeal presence" but rather to sugggest that we view *"representation as the malady of psychoanalysis"* (98; Parker's emphasis). This malady, I would add, operates by intellectual abstraction as well as psychological denial. Abstraction can be a form of denial, or rather, a denial achieved through the use of form; for example, to give the body the semiotic character of the Lacanian object is to cognize it as diverse conjugable forms rather than to recognize it as a thing.

Parker implies that psychoanalysis itself suffers from pathological fetishism: fetishism is that form of "mental work" (Freud's phrase) which substitutes representation for that which it represents. In this "mythical moment of disjunction between the pacification of need and the fulfillment of desire" autoerotism becomes sexuality, "disengaged from any natural object," moving instead "into the field of fantasy."[38] But in this mythical moment sexuality as well becomes mythical:

[38] Lapalanche and Pontalis, "Fantasy," 16.

when the sign replaces the "natural" object it describes, the desiring subject becomes equally fantasmatic. The dialectical poles of ambiguous desire thus collapse into each other, fusing into a composite fantasmatic subject-object made of discourse and fantasy, deprived of reference and intentionality, neither me nor not-me; an image-thing; a fetish.

Theoretically, that "archaeology of the subject" which is psychoanalysis can recapture the mythical moment of disjunction and bridge the mythical discontinuity between need and desire. If this were true, one could repossess every lost connection—every lost continuity—between the me and the not-me. But this is the case only in the world of the fetishist: "The fetish is the deposit of all the part objects lost during the subject's development. As is obvious through the acts of constriction often performed (the corset or shoe fetishes), the fetish is both content and container. Thus the link between the object and the erotogenic zone is re-established (the nipple in the mouth, the stool in the rectum) and the primal scene is mimed as a pregenital relationship."[39] An overvalued psychic reality, like the fetish, is simultaneously a "natural" object and the hallucinatory replacement that serves to make its naturalness irrelevant. Psychoanalysis ceases to concern itself with the actuality of the events described by patients insofar as it deems reality to be continuous, if not synonymous, with psychical reality, and not, as a Kantian epistemology would have it, because material reality lies on the far side of an unbridgeable epistemological abyss. But to acknowledge this abyss as real "owns" the epistemophilia of the inquiring mind, creative yet realistic, ever establishing, renewing, and revising its symbolic relations to reality and its contents.

Denying this necessary "disjunction" is the characteristic act of someone we could call the "epistemophobe," one who is afraid to know, and who therefore limits knowledge by overvaluing, overinterpreting, oversignifying one object—filling it with meaning until it seems to be both "content and

---

[39] Janine Chasseguet-Smirgel, *Creativity and Perversion* (New York: Norton, 1984), 87.

container," more meaningful than its owner/user—whether that object be the unconscious, a corset, a discourse, a faith, or "great" works of literature. By this definition Lacanian psychoanalysis—and the New Criticism—and deconstruction—are epistemophobic. Freud's writing, by comparison, even with its notable moments of epistemophobia, reveals an almost tireless epistemophilia, a hungry scanning of the world for symbols. Freud does not try to cover up the disjunction between before and after, between need and desire, or between "the object that satisfies and the sign which describes both the object and its absence." In fact this disjunction and its endless variations are essential to psychoanalysis as he defines it; he describes it and puzzles over it again and again. Disjunction and our need to conceptualize it is what makes psychoanalysis necessary, not because psychoanalysis can eradicate or cover up or deny it, but rather because in the course of analysis we can learn that this disjunction is not "just in our heads." It is the real.

The disjunction between need and desire is, for Freud, the fact of the matter until science has figured everything out, made psyche equivalent to brain, come up with a construction adequate to the facts and made possible the end of psychoanalytic inquiry. On that hypothetical day psychical reality will have become so perspicuous to the inquiring mind that it too will be known to be part of the "material world."[40] In effect this ideal perspicacity of the seemingly inaccessible is the dream of psychoanalysis; in this dream that which is by definition negative (the unconscious) becomes positive, accessible to positivist investigation. As such Freud's understanding of the scientific process was entirely Newtonian, and his conception of subject/object relations entirely unproblematical.[41] Freud held an uncom-

[40] The theory and practice of contemporary neuroscience has traveled a long way on that road already, for better and worse. For "popular" accounts of this phenomenon, see, for example, Jonathan Winson, *Brain and Psyche*, and, perhaps, the offensively reductive *Molecules of the Mind* by Jon Franklin (New York: Athenaeum, 1987).

[41] "The decidedness of my attitude on the subject of the unconscious is perhaps specially likely to cause offense, for I handle unconscious ideas, un-

plicated view of the human unconscious as an object of study. Nor did he view primary process as a metaphor despite the fact that he lacked the technology to locate the unconscious or trace physically the fluctuations of desire. At the same time Freud need not have worried about locating the referents for his new terms and ideas. If we cannot verify what in the material world corresponds to our ideas about it, and since we act on the basis of these ideas anyway, we may as well concern ourselves with the interior, erotolinguistic world, the world of the symbolic-and-therefore-real. It is not far from this to psychoanalysis in its postmodern incarnation, in which the symbolic constitutes rather than represents: the interior world of signs is not only indistinguishable from any other world we may feel we know but is always already that world. There is no other—all is self.

Ironically, this inversion is analogous to the regressive idealization of instinct characteristic of perversion. Valorization of a psychical reality that is "alone truly real" accomplishes just what the fetish is designed to do, "[namely, to] give us, for a while, the feeling that a world not ruled by our common laws does exist, a marvelous and uncanny world."[42] This feeling may be precious, and the world may at times seem marvelous, because, no doubt, symbolic activity constitutes something, if not everything. The point here is that from how Freudian psychoanalysis has been appropriated by literary studies, we can learn something about modernism, postmodernism, contemporary cultural discourse, and the academic literary enterprise in general that should make us a bit more suspicious than we are of our interest in language. We do not take as seriously as we claim to do the constitutive, imaginative, and political power of discourse and theory if we do not base our understanding of its power on the significance and

conscious trains of thought, and unconscious emotional tendencies as though they were no less valid and unimpeachable psychological data than conscious ones. But of this I am certain—that any one who sets out to investigate the same region of phenomena and employs the same method will find himself compelled to take up the same position, however much philosophers may expostulate" (*SE* 7:113).

[42] Chasseguet-Smirgel, *Creativity and Perversion*, 88.

responsibility of the discoursing "I," the individual speaker/writer, as much as the impersonal unconscious. What literary theory has found most useful about psychoanalysis has to do not with its litany of complexes, oedipal or otherwise, or syndromes (including fetishism), but rather with its valorization of symbolic process. But at its extreme, this valorization veers into what Parker calls semiosis—the hypertrophic overvaluation of representation as if it were a something-in-itself.

This diagnosis applies even more broadly: postmodernist literary theory as a discourse succumbs to intellectual fetishism because it fears, even as it insists upon, the loss of its own referentiality, which it claims already to have sacrificed to aesthetic anti-foundationalism. To make this point rather crudely obvious I want to place here following Freud's definition of fetishism (below) as rooted in castration anxiety, a slight revision of that analysis so that it applies to post-Freudian poststructuralist psychoanalytic discourse (that which proclaims the rule of "the signifier") as a whole. Freud has said that in the mind of the fetishist "the woman *has* got a penis, in spite of everything; but this penis is no longer the same as it was before. Something else has taken its place, has been appointed its substitute, as it were, and now inherits the interest which was formerly directed to its predecessor. But this interest suffers an extraordinary increase as well, because *the horror of castration has set up a memorial to itself* in the creation of this substitute" (*SE* 21:154; my emphasis). Similarly (I am arguing), in the mind of the post-Freudian Freudian, the poststructuralist discourse-fetishist, "language *has* got a 'reference,' in spite of everything; but this reference is no longer the same as it was before. Something else has taken its place, has been appointed its substitute, as it were, and now inherits the interest which was formerly directed to its predecessor. But this interest suffers an extraordinary increase as well, because *the horror of objectlessness has set up a memorial to itself* in the creation of this substitute." This "substitute," this "memorial" to its own lack of referentiality, is discourse disconnected from its subject and object, a discourse expected to enact in the abstract the dialectic of presence and absence (the game of *fort/da*) by serving as "the locution and link of exchange." This is the irony of phallocentrism: that its alternative to self-referentiality is only non-referentiality. In other words, when we relieve art and discourse of their mimetic mission—art need not (indeed, cannot) represent, and language need not (indeed, cannot) refer— the result is not necessarily greater particularity and concreteness (as opposed to metaphysical or transcendent value) but rather increased abstraction and "abjection." Discourse can grow full of itself only in a pejorative sense. Even Freud sensed in the end that a metapsychology of discourse that took into account more than the self-enclosed psychoanalytic couple (analyst and analysand) was necessary if the theory of language implied by psychoanalysis were to be of lasting use as an instrument of cultural analysis.

Positively Mental: On the Supposed Materiality of Language

Herein lies the "last secret" of dialectical speculation: not in the dialectical mediation-sublimation of all contingent, empirical reality, not in the deduction of all reality from the mediating movement of absolute negativity, but in the fact that this very negativity, to attain its "being-for-itself," must embody itself again in some miserable, radically contingent corporeal leftover.

—Slavoj Žižek

Our experience is not that of affective smoochy-woochy.

—Jacques Lacan

Herein lies the paradoxical legacy of psychoanalytic modernism: the idealization of language as material; the conflation of the biological with the linguistic; and the abjection of the subject as immaterial so that the body itself comes to seem like some "miserable, radically contingent corporeal leftover" in relation to which the category of bodily experience is construed as "affective smoochy-woochy."[1] To put this another way, what began in the late nineteenth century as an attempt by psychoanalysis to alleviate the physical symptoms of neurotic patients through the medical "arts of

[1] Slavoj Žižek, *The Sublime Object of Ideology* (London: Verso, 1989), 207; Jacques Lacan, *The Seminar of Jacques Lacan: Book I, Freud's Papers on Technique (1953–1954)*, ed. Jacques-Alain Miller, trans. John Forrester (New York: Norton, 1988), 55.

hydropathy or through electricity" led "away from the somatic determinants of nervous disease" into the "mental substance of human lives" and thence, by the end of the twentieth, into variously politicized theories of semiotic materialism.[2] These days we tend to conceive of the psyche as "like a language" in structure, and of the subject as its syntactically organized cultural persona. We theorize the subject as the historically malleable precipitate of thwarted desires and intersecting identifications, rather than as any totality of natural, essential, or psychological identities. The modern understanding of consciousness as destabilized and decentered, then, prefigured its compensatory postmodern theorization as constructed from top to toe. We have put the subject back together, in a way, but this time as a sort of "formatted" tabula rasa, an electronic simulacrum of its former self.

Conversely, this theorization of the subject as constructed presumes that representation is sufficiently material and perdurable for things (like subjects) to be made of it, for sociopolitical superstructures (like hegemonic capitalism) to persist because of it. Today these ideas may seem relatively tame to academic theorists although, even if they no longer seem as radical as they did twenty-five years ago, they can still polarize a group discussion at the drop of a hat. This is especially so when such a discussion turns political, or raises the question of whether or not changing representation can affect, constitute, or cause political or social change. By itself the notion that language is material is neither salutary nor pernicious, political nor apolitical. But, insofar as it may or may not serve as a foundational assumption for practices as various as presidential campaigning and psychobiology, religious fundamentalism and deconstruction, art and advertising, it deserves to be scrutinized again and again, in any context in which it figures significantly.

I can only reiterate, although with a slightly different emphasis, some reasons why the idea that language is materi-

[2] The quoted phrases here are from Sigmund Freud, "Preface to Reik's *Ritual: Psychoanalytic Studies*," in *SE* 17:257.

al seems problematic, at times counterintuitive or even coun-
terproductive, if at others exciting or emancipatory. In this
chapter I "problematize" the idea that language is material,
or at least try to make it seem less commonsensical, by
rejecting Lacan's claim that his project was a "return to
Freud." To reject this claim is to reject that mystification of
language as "immaterial body," which is no uniquely postmodern idea, but on the contrary a form of religious magical
thinking with an ancient genealogy. From my point of view
to sentimentalize language this way is to indulge in "affective smoochy-woochy." Instead, I suggest that we distinguish
Freudian from Lacanian psychoanalytic theory on the basis,
for example, of the sociopolitical implications of their different attitudes toward the materiality of the body and of language. In this chapter I sound a more cynical note than in
those preceding, as the following textual anecdote will at
once make clear. I would point out first, however, that to say
language is material is not the same as saying that ideas have
material origins and consequences; the latter statement
seems empirically undeniable, whereas the former seems
essentially mystical.

Now for the anecdote. Once upon a time, in 1966, a student of philosophy asked Lacan to compare the "subject" as
it is conceived by Marxist theory with the "subject" as it is
constituted by psychoanalysis.[3] "What is the relation," the
student asked, "between the subject of a revolutionary praxis
aiming at going beyond its alienated labor and the subject of
alienated desire?" "What," in other words, "is, according to
you, the theory of language implied by Marxism?" Lacan
answered at considerable length and, with his barbed tongue
characteristically in his cheek, suggested that the only possible relation between the two subjects would be that phantasm of relation Marx had called the fetish. "It is a matter of

[3] Jacques Lacan, *Television: A Challenge to the Psychoanalytic Establish-
ment*, trans. Denis Hollier, Rosalind Krauss, and Annette Michelson, ed. Joan
Copjec (New York: Norton, 1990), 110–111 (for all quotations in this para-
graph). The discussion of *Television* that follows was first presented at the
Rutgers/Princeton Conference, "Culture in Contest," Princeton University,
March 1991.

common knowledge," Lacan said, "that Marxists are not very adept" at "calling into question the category of dialectical materialism." But they really should be, he averred; revolutionary theory ought to leave "empty the function of truth as cause" and recognize that the subject "is nothing"—a mere "sham plausibility." With these words Lacan thus returned the question, unopened, to its asker, when he replied. "In what way can one go beyond the alienation of his labor? It is as though you wanted to go beyond the alienation of discourse," Lacan remarked, implying that one could no more go beyond the alienation of discourse than swim to the moon.

For Lacan, there is no distinction, no difference, between labor and discourse. Lacan believed that it ought to be obvious to everyone (except to the neurotic, whose problem is the refusal to see this as true) that one *cannot* "go beyond the alienation of discourse." There is no "place" else to go, not even to those biological spaces of our everyday selves which we tend to think of as our most material habitation: not to the body, whose Heideggerian essence dwells in language; not to affect ("affective smoochy-woochy"), which in Lacan's view merely sports a "question-begging appeal to the concrete"; and not to the libido, which Lacan calls a "fluidic myth" that conglomerates like "sheep" where it doesn't belong.[4] For Lacan what is truly material is the sign, language, the mathematics of the signifier.[5] To our friend the philosophy student, he asserted: "My theory of language is true whatever be the adequacy of Marxism. . . . The least you can accord me concerning my theory of language is, should it interest you, that it is materialist. The signifier is matter transcending itself in language."[6] Here I wish to pause in

---

[4] Jacques Lacan, *Television*, 23; "The Signification of the Phallus," in *Écrits, A Selection*, trans. Alan Sheridan (New York: Norton, 1977), 285; and "The Function and Field of Speech and Language in Psychoanalysis," in *Écrits*, 105.

[5] See Lacan, *Television*, xxiv: "No discovery since 1931 has been more important in mathematical logic than that impossibility [of formally demonstrating both *A* and not-*A*], related to the handling of signs which are entirely material."

[6] Lacan, *Television*, 112.

order to emphasize that this concept remains for me a puzzle worth puzzling over: what does it mean, what does it imply, to say that language is material, that the signifier is "matter"? (Whether or not matter transcends itself in language is a theological question.) Is this nonsense, a Lacanian delusion, an exercise in what David Macey has called Lacan's "curious ontolinguistics?"[7] Or is this assumption rather more deeply entrenched in our thinking and feeling than we might care to acknowledge? Hasn't this notion—that language is material—and its corollaries, that language is the stuff of which culture is made, and that we ourselves are made of culture— become the foundational assumption of a postmodern, post- psychoanalytic age, as hard to shake as the Oedipus complex, and as well worth shaking, insofar as thinking this way keeps us (the cultural workers, the intellectuals, the educators) politically, practically ineffectual?

All of our many questions about language, its ontology, its meaning, its function, its purpose, have their own histories— whether, for example, God is the Word or the Word is God, and what, in relation to so magnificent an identity, is left for "man" to be. From the point of view of Freudian psycho- analysis, the reality of God, like that of other symbolic con- structs including words, is a function of unconscious libidi- nal wishes and affects active in the psyche since infancy. It is in the primitive unconscious, Freud states in *The Interpre- tation of Dreams,* that we experience "words" as "things," a fact that explains both the seeming concreteness of our dreams and the sexiness of our thoughts. Conversely, from the point of view of Lacanian psychoanalysis, the illusory reality of the psyche with its wishes and affects is, from earli- est infancy, an effect of the language "always already" sover- eign. Both points of view have limitations: Freud's insights into the instinctual oedipality of the private imagination do not "translate" easily to the intersubjective realm of culture, whereas Lacan's paranoiac intuition that the private mind is no such thing does not help us realize our own or one anoth- er's individuality. We do and no doubt will, however, contin-

[7] David Macey, *Lacan in Contexts* (London: Verso, 1988), 175.

ue to take seriously the notion that human beings are creatures of language; that we inhabit, although we may struggle against it, a psychical reality constructed of language; and that this language paradoxically makes even private reality a shared and fluid social space.

Does this make language material or immaterial? Does language connect us to the world and to each other; does it "speak" our world and ourselves; does it perhaps isolate us, as Walter Pater suggested, within our own dream of a world? Or have we perhaps reached a point where the undecidability of these questions has ceased to matter, if only because if the thinking subject doesn't get a grip on our culture's media-arsenal and educational system s/he risks being "alienated" out of existence? For Marx and Engels in *The German Ideology* (1846) the history of "man" is in part the history of the "materialistic connection of men with one another . . . which is as old as men themselves." The changing form of this connection "presents a 'history' independently of the existence of any political or religious nonsense which may in addition hold men together."[8] For them one form of the material connection of "men" with each other is, perhaps surprisingly, "consciousness" understood as having material dimension in language. Consciousness for Marx and Engels is "not inherent, not 'pure' consciousness," but that which is "afflicted with the curse of being 'burdened' with matter, which here makes its appearance in the form of agitated layers of air, sounds, in short of language" (50–51). By pretending to be squeamish about the idea that language is impure, agitated, "'burdened' with matter," they dismiss the moralist's mistrust of language as inevitably "fallen." On the contrary, from their point of view, language as material consciousness deconstructs the fundamentally false antithesis of nature and history because "consciousness is . . . from the very beginning a social product" (59) arising, like language, "from the need, the necessity, of intercourse with other men" (51). "Language," they assert, "is as old as consciousness . . . lan-

---

[8] Karl Marx and Friedrich Engels, *The German Ideology, Part I*, ed. C. J. Arthur (New York: International Publishers, 1970), 50–51.

guage *is* practical consciousness" (51).

Other prominent modern theorists (Freud not among them), however, conserve the sublime ontology of the Word by representing its materiality as equivocal, mystical, paradoxical, or otherwise miraculous.[9] For Ferdinand de Saussure, language is both material and immaterial, as a result of which he describes language and speech contradictorily in his *Course in General Linguistics*.[10] Language, he says, for example, is "a complex physiological-psychological unit" articulated by the vocal organs and received by the ear in measurable ways; yet at the same time it is "only the instrument of thought" (8–9). Language is an institution with a history, yet it is only "a form and not a substance" (122). All speakers participate in discourse, writes Saussure, but the brain has its own "associative life" outside of discourse (123). When in 1969 Louis Althusser reworked some of the ideas in *The German Ideology*, he used the concept of "ideology" in much the same ways his predecessors used the concept of language, or of capital.[11] Althusser finds both Marx and Freud useful, asserting both, following Marx, that "ideology has a material existence" to be found in "an [ideological] apparatus, and its practice, or practices" (165-66), and that, following Freud, "*ideology is eternal*, exactly like the unconscious," that is, "omnipresent, transhistorical, and therefore immutable"

[9] In *Freud and Man's Soul* (New York: Vintage, 1982), Bruno Bettelheim argues against what he calls the general Anglo-American "positivistic-pragmatic" corruption of psychoanalysis. Bettelheim finds support for this argument in the English translation of the *Standard Edition*, which eliminates the many instances where Freud refers to the soul [*die Seele*] as opposed to the mind or psyche, eliminating at the same time Freud's sense of the "tragic conflict" experienced by the "I" and the paradoxical richness that an awareness of such conflict brings in the course of "maturation." I agree with Bettelheim that for Freud emotion and consciousness ought to be coextensive (the neurotic tries to keep them apart), a point that academic theorists often neglect, but I think Freud consistently rejected religion and metaphysics intellectually and temperamentally.
[10] Ferdinand de Saussure, *Course in General Linguistics (Cours de Linguistique Générale* [1915]), trans. Wade Baskin (New York: Philosophical Library, 1959; New York: McGraw Hill, 1966).
[11] Louis Althusser, "Ideology and Ideological Apparatuses," in *Lenin and Philosophy*, trans. Ben Brewster (London: Verso, 1971).

(161; Althusser's emphasis). Althusser thus seems here, more like Saussure than like Marx, relatively comfortable with a dualistic understanding of symbolic process as at once intersubjective and metapsychological, demystified and idealized. Thanks to the ambiguous ontology of Althusser's notion of "ideology," for us the question of its materiality or immateriality remains equivocal although, admittedly, ideology could be said to be most effective in the "world" when it most ruthlessly exploits this equivocation.

In his essay "Freud and Lacan" (1964), Althusser fiercely defends first Freud, as the inventor of a genuinely revolutionary science, and then Lacan, as a hero who "thinks nothing but Freud's concepts" and who defends those concepts in language wrongly criticized for "artifice," "strangeness," "hermeticism," and "abstraction."[12] On the contrary Lacan's language is, Althusser argues, "a dumbshow equivalent of the language of the unconscious" marked by *Witz*, "contained passion," and "passionate contention" (204); it is language "unable to live or survive except in a state of alert and accusation: the language of a man of the besieged vanguard" (203). Lacan is on the alert to defend *"the irreducibility of* [the] *object"* (203; Althusser's emphasis) of psychoanalysis, namely, the unconscious, against those who will only "conclude a pact of peaceful coexistence with psychoanalysis after years of non-recognition, contempt and insults . . . on condition of annexing it to its own sciences or myths: to psychology, whether behaviorist . . . phenemonological . . . or existentialist; to . . . bio-neurology[;] to 'sociology' of the 'culturalist' or 'anthropological' type . . . and to philosophy" (201). Such praise would be inspiring if it did not seem rather misplaced, or perhaps displaced, and based upon a willful misreading of Lacan designed to suggest (and who could object to this?) that research into "the ideological formations that govern paternity, maternity, conjugality and childhood" is "a task for *historical materialism"* (211; Althusser's emphasis).

The astonishing process by which Althusser turns Lacan into a cultural materialist merits a more thorough contextual

[12] Althusser, "Freud and Lacan," in *Lenin and Philosophy*, 215, 204.

reading than this chapter can provide. It is nevertheless relevant to point out here that Althusser accomplishes this transformation in five steps, which reenact what I have been arguing is the itinerary over the past century of the so-called linguistic turn, comprising the apotheosis of materialism, its occultation in language, and its sublimation as what Lacan will call an immaterial body. What follows is a summary of Althusser's argument in "Freud and Lacan." First, in unique "theoretical solitude" Freud invents a science of the unconscious weighed down by "homemade concepts . . . borrowed from the sciences as they existed, and, it should be said, from within the horizons of the ideological world in which these concepts swam" (197). Next, Lacan "intervenes," thanks to "Saussure and . . . the linguistics that descends from him," to save the science of "the unconscious and its effects" from "the temporary opacity of the shadow cast on Freudian theory by the model of Helmholtz and Maxwell's thermodynamic physics" (203, 207–8). Third, Lacan introduces us "to the paradox, formally familiar to linguistics, of a double yet single discourse, unconscious yet verbal, having for its double field only a single field, with no beyond except in itself: the field of the 'Signifying Chain'" (208). Fourth, combining two of Lacan's many "natural" tropes (the chimpanzee and the migratory locust) into a more grotesque image than any Lacan comes up with, Althusser paraphrases Lacan as narrativizing the "humanization of the small biological creature that results from human parturition" obliged to take "the long forced march which makes mammiferous larvae into human children, *masculine* or *feminine* subjects" (205–6; Althusser's emphasis).

Finally, in a move neither Lacanian nor Freudian, Althusser invokes a trinitarian model of culture that paradoxically (and quite conventionally) equates the semiotic with the cultural by erasing the biological. Indeed, writes Althusser, "any reduction of childhood traumas to a balance of 'biological frustrations' alone, is in principle erroneous, since the Law that covers them, as a Law, abstracts from all contents, exists and acts as a Law only in and by this abstraction" (212). But

Freud does not ever wholly dismiss biological determinism;
nor does he credit any abstraction with its own ontology.
Lacan, on the other hand, does not equate "the symbolic"
with what Althusser first calls the "order of the human signifier" and then equates in the following passage with "the
Law of Culture": "This [the Law] is the beginning, and has
always been the beginning, even where there is no living
father, of the official presence of the Father (who is Law),
hence of the Order of the human signifier, i.e. of the Law of
Culture: this discourse, the absolute precondition of any discourse, this discourse present at the top, i.e. absent in the
depths, in all verbal discourse, the discourse of this Order,
this discourse of the Other, of the great Third, which is this
Order itself: *the discourse of the unconscious*" (212; Althusser's emphasis). The churchly rhythm of this catechism of
the unconscious is unmistakable, as is its theologizing of the
ineffable and absolute Law of the Father.

What Althusser is enlisting on behalf of his own cause
("ideology") is thus not Lacan's cultural materialism, but his
semiotic immaterialism. For Lacan "language is not immaterial. It is a subtle body, but body it is."[13] In Chapter 1 I offered a reading of Freud's use of Weismann's germ-plasm theory to suggest how completely Freud's theories of sexuality,
narcissism, mourning, and melancholy were rooted in his
self-conscious love and dread of the flesh. In Lacan's formulation, however, even the germ plasm and Freud's interest in it
become, on the one hand, quasi-platonic idealization and, on
the other, mere stupid animalism. In his tenth seminar, "The
Two Narcissisms," Lacan reminds his listeners that, according to Weismann, the germ-plasm theory "posits the existence of an immortal substance made up of sexual cells" that
"preserves the existence of the species" from one individual,
and one generation, to the next.[14] In relation to the germ
plasm, the individual is a kind of parasite the sole aim of
whose sexuality is to be "the vehicle for the eternal germ-
plasm" (120). This theory implies, Lacan points out, "that

[13] Lacan, "Function and Field," 87.
[14] Lacan, *Seminar I*, 120.

from the point of view of the species, individuals are, if one can put it this way, already dead. An individual is worth nothing alongside the immortal substance hidden deep inside it" (121). The individual, in other words, "doesn't reproduce as an individual, but as a type. . . . It isn't this or that horse, but the prop, the embodiment of something which is *The Horse*. If the concept of species is valid, if natural history exists, it is because there are not only horses, but also *The Horse*" (121). And this the human species has in common with all other animate species: that what sets in motion "the gigantic sexual mechanism" is not "the existence of the sexual partner, the particularity of one individual, but something which has an extremely intimate relation with what I have been calling the type, namely an image" (121).

I have no quarrel with Lacan's analysis of love as hallucination, or of sex as by definition mindless; one could easily argue besides that these analyses accord with Freud's. It is, for lack of a better way to put it, Lacan's cynical beatification of logos as the basis for "the great fantasy of *natura* mater, the very idea of nature" to which I object as a kind of bad faith (149). Theologizing the image seems too reactionary a move to serve as foundational assumption for any supposed theory of historical materialism. In his twelfth seminar, *Zeitlich-Entwicklungsgeschichte,* Lacan makes explicit the theo-logic of his theory. He explains "behavior of the instinctual type," whether in animals or humans, as "a thickening, a condensation, a dulling" of the perception of the external world, such that the subject becomes "stuck within a number of imaginary conditions." The human subject, however, as far as we can tell is unlike the animal in that it can distance itself from its own libido far enough to see itself "as body" from the point of view of the desired other (146–7). The subject's tendency to want to "agglutinate" with the body of the other "has an irremediably fatal significance for the individual, in so far as it is subjected to the x of eternal life"(217) in its confrontation with "his image of the master, which is what he sees in the form of the specular image, [and which] becomes confused in him with the image of death.

Man can be in the presence of the absolute master. He is in his presence from the beginning, whether he has been taught this or not, in so far as he is subjected to this image" (148–49). To be a human subject is thus to inhabit a world founded on "paranoiac knowledge" in which one can only distinguish between the image glimpsed in the intraorganic mirror of primary narcissism and the "absolute master" by an act of peculiarly human *méconnaissance*.

In his famous case study of Dr. Schreber, Freud defined paranoia as repressed homosexual desire, as a man's unconscious desire to be phallically "hunted out" and penetrated. This desire manifested itself, in Schreber's case, in an elaborately symbolical imaginary scenario dramatizing the paranoid subject's fearful fantasy that he may be invaded and taken over not just by the body of the other, but by the entire system of signification peculiar to (constitutive of) the other. Paranoia thus enacts itself psychically as a conflict between signifying systems both of which may, at bottom, belong to one ambivalent psyche. Paranoia may in turn be understood as the ambivalent twin of fetishism. If fetishism is a pleasurable fantasy of total fusion with the other (whether person, shoe, or signifier) in a phantasmic whole to the extent that all sense of separate self is pleasurably subsumed in the perfection of the other; paranoia, on the other hand is the fear of that same loss of self in the overwhelming potency of the other. Relief from either of these extremes may only be possible at the moment (to which psychoanalysis aspires) when the subject learns to apprehend himself as object, that comforting illusion of objectivity that Lacan calls at the end of "The Mirror Stage" "the ecstatic limit of the '*Thou art that*', in which is revealed to him the cipher of his mortal destiny."[15] At this point it becomes evident that in Lacanian theory the moment when the subject apprehends himself as object is the same moment as when he is in the "presence of the absolute master," giving a virtually cosmic significance to primary narcissism as a circle whose periphery is nowhere and whose center is everywhere.

[15] Lacan, "The Mirror Stage," in *Écrits*, 7.

Fortunately, from our present theoretical perspective the repetitious impossibility of deciding between the material and the immaterial natures of language may indicate that this opposition constitutes yet one more factitious binary. As Judith Butler recently put it, "It is of course necessary to state quite plainly that the options for theory are not exhausted by *presuming* materiality, on the one hand, and *negating* materiality, on the other."[16] Other theoretical options might include, for example, Freud's notion of "construction," to which I shall return; James Clifford's notion of semiotic realism; and the dynamic model of democracy Ernesto Laclau and Chantal Mouffe have articulated. Each of these models assumes that how we conceive of language, and of ourselves as producers and products of language, affects how we think about "culture," and how, and whether, we see ourselves as able to take part in it, as teachers in the academy, or as citizens outside the classroom.

The question of "agency," of the individual as cause, waited patiently on the theoretical back burner during the sixties, seventies, and early eighties while we turned up the deconstructive heat under the crockpot of the so-called stable subject. But this question has resurfaced with new urgency insofar as it has gradually dawned on us, as Butler put it, that "the death of that subject is not the end of agency, speech or of political debate," nor, one might add, of our need for these. Agency was and "is always and only a political prerogative" and not a formal category (13); it "belongs to a way of thinking about persons as instrumental actors who confront an external political field" and not to the implied activity of the subject confronting his own interiority (16). Feminists, African-Americanists, postcolonialists, Marxists, humanists, theorists, and critics of many political and even anti-political "stripes" alike have had occasion to wonder aloud: given that we now understand the subject in (Christian white bourgeois male) Western discourse to be its ideological effect rather

[16] Judith Butler, "Feminism and the Question of Postmodernism" (Paper delivered at the Greater Philadelphia Philosophy Consortium, 22 September 1990), 22.

than its efficient cause, how can we reconceive of ourselves as agents for political change? One weakly pragmatic solution to this has been our version of that moment when Descartes pauses to say that, all idealism aside, of course he doesn't waste time in radical doubt every morning when he wakes up and goes to put his feet on the floor—he does not reconstitute reality every morning from the ontological ground up. Like Descartes we too teach the ideas of radical doubt and social construction, but otherwise we have to go about the business of life as usual.

Have we ever really considered ourselves to be the mere effects of representation, and if so, just how disingenuously solid were we when we did so? Contrariwise, what if, as we went around speaking of ourselves as culturally constructed, by which we generally meant, I suspect, rather that *other* people were culturally constructed, what if we have all the while really been coming apart at the seams, allowing to leak out our belief in ourselves as political agents, even as others grew perniciously more solid? The "subject" in that case would have functioned as a MacGuffin for poststructuralist theory, as a pretext for rumors about its own sublimation into the gaseous refinements of semiotics. Lacan presided with glee at the funeral of the *sujet supposé savoir* as though he had dispatched the dear departed personally. But as William Kerrigan argues in a brilliant essay on Lacan as a "sonuvabitch" who buried Freud prematurely in his "murky, sometimes outrageous metaphysics," Lacan merely "denounc[ed] the bonds of narcissism while flagrantly surrendering to his own"; "in his published texts he played no other role but the all-knowing master."[17] "Lacan did one thing well," writes Kerrigan, something which "needed doing at his historical moment" and which he did so well "that we probably need not do it again." This was to "psychoanalyze[ ] several hundred years of French intellectual history. The ego on his couch was Descartes" (1005).

Lacan mismanaged Descartes's case, however:

[17] William Kerrigan, "Terminating Lacan," *South Atlantic Quarterly* 88 (Fall 1989): 998, 999, 1000. I thank Bill Dowling for this reference.

[Lacan] kept losing sight of the surrealism of his own interpretations. He entertained the seductive thought that his patient was
Everyman, and claimed that the human ego was through and
through narcissistic. He embarked on the countertransferential
venture of making psychoanalysis into a system in the metaphysical sense, and welcomed into his system the work of
philosophers apparently opposed to Descartes, such as Hegel
and Heidegger, using them in such a way as to bring out their
latent solidarity with the Cartesian tradition. Denouncing the
living Cartesianism of phenomenology, he took from it everything he could use. He invested deeply, fatally, in the re-
trenched rationalism of the linguistic structuralists. (1006–7)

Lacan was a surreal Cartesian who pretended to be a materialist. But we need not lose sight of the surrealism of Lacan's
interpretations just because he did; the cost for us would be
too great. And, although I am not exactly arguing that Lacan
has directly influenced politics, I am arguing first, that
Lacanian theory is an exemplary postmodern MacGuffinizer
of the subject, that is, of you and me; and, second, that those
of us who similarly MacGuffinize may be, like Lacan, invest-
ing deeply, fatally in a phallogocentric rationalism at least as
old as Descartes.

Psychoanalysis in a sense from its beginnings rendered the
subject abject by valorizing the patient's "speech" as the privileged bearer and locus of the patient's meaningfulness.
Psychoanalysis "bracketed" the suffering patient so that his
or her unique symbology could be isolated and objectively
(that is, like an object) interpreted. "Anna O.," Breuer's famous hysteric, aptly nicknamed psychoanalysis—in English—"the talking cure" and the name stuck.[18] This epithet
makes it sound not only as if the patient would be cured by
talking, but as if the "cure" could itself talk—a surreal sug-
gestion. Lacan uses this pun in a new way when, as part of
the epigram at the beginning of part one of "The Function
and Field of Speech and Language in Psychoanalysis," he
includes the imperative *"Cause toujours,"* parenthetically

[18] "Anna O." is Bertha Pappenheim, lively feminist and socialist.

said to be the "motto of causalist thought?" (40). Lacan enjoys the punning connotations here of the verb *causer*, which means both "to cause" and "to chat," uniting, therefore, the portentous and formal with the trivial and colloquial, the causal with the casual. The psychoanalyst must rummage around in the patient's chit-chat in search of the "cause" of his suffering, because, as Lacan somewhat wearily tells us, "psychoanalysis has only a single medium: the patient's speech" (40).

In the "talking cure" it is less a question of whether the patient or the doctor is "talking"; rather, the talking is talking, and it is a talking that can, for example, at once mimic and express the unconscious, since "the unconscious is structured like a language." And it can "cause" effects; that is, a deranged discourse is not only a symptom but also, according to the dream logic of psychoanalysis, a cause of mental derangement. The patient's speech therefore may be all we have, but we must not take it lightly; it is more real than the patient. The "talking cure" was designed for the "talking body," for the body that produces speech. The body in question is necessarily a symbolic, symbol-producing body: "Speech is in fact a gift of language, and language is not immaterial. It is a subtle body, but body it is" (87).[19] "Language is not immaterial"; with these words Lacan coyly conflates like the canonical fetishist the "physiologic" with the "ideal." Language, Lacan is saying obliquely in order to make his outrageous illogic seem more playful than it is, is material. This is absurd—and yet, in a way, it is "true." It is at least the case that psychoanalysis depends entirely on the functional truth of this statement: language is not immaterial; language is, and is not "material."

Because the human being does not make its symbols, "man" is the talking animal who needs a talking cure. "Man speaks . . . because the symbol has made him man" (65).

---

[19] Interesting in this regard is Žižek's article in *October* 38 (Fall 1986) about Hitchcock's film *The Trouble with Harry*, in which Žižek distinguishes between what he calls "the sublime body," which dies an infinite number of "symbolic deaths," and the physical body, which loses "the whole game" when it dies.

"The concept . . . engenders the thing," writes Lacan.[20] But even this counterintuitive idealism is not extreme enough: "For it is still not enough to say that the concept is the thing itself. . . . It is the world of words that creates the world of things" (65). But the human being does not even make this "world of words," this speech. If anything is to be learned in the course of this analysis, it is this post-Saussurean lesson. Language makes speech, and "it is from language that speech must be delivered" (59). The subject that thinks it "speaks" either its speech or language or owns any such semi-stable ontological entity as an "ego," an "I," or even a localizable subjecthood, is deluded. The "decisive function" of the analyst's reply to the subject's "stories" is not to accept or reject, but "really to recognize . . . or to abolish [it] as subject" (87).

Based on Lacan's writing, this is an understatement. The analyst does not merely make or break, "recognize" or "abolish," the subject "as subject," although this sounds violent enough. Lacan fetishizes the speech of the subject, as if it were the phallus making possible "intercourse" with the subject, and transforming the subject into a partial object magically created by the speech it must not regard as its own. It is something that comes between the analyst and the patient. As Lacan says (and a comparison of this passage with Freud's "Constructions in Analysis" to be discussed below will show how extreme is his difference from Freud): "Analysis is . . . the relation of two bodies between which is established a phantasmic communication in which the analyst teaches the subject to apprehend himself as an object; subjectivity is admitted into it only within the parentheses of the illusion, and speech is placed on the index of a search for the lived experience that becomes its supreme aim" (90–91). This passage makes it clear that Lacan accords the subject very little freedom "within the parentheses of the illusion," wedged, as it were, between speech and language, the prisoner of a "discourse without escape" (41). The physical relation between two bodies, which was for Freud the basis of communication, and of the participatory interaction of co-construction, is for

---

[20] Lacan, "Function and Field," 65.

Lacan an illusion and a phantasm. So what could be "the lived experience" that is the "supreme aim" of this subject-become-object? The answer is not "life" in any usual sense. The "lived experience" for the "subject" of Lacanian psychoanalysis is itself an idealization: what Lacan calls "full speech." "Full speech," as Lacan tells us, is what psychoanalysis gives us instead of "reality": "I might as well be categorical: in psychoanalytic anamnesis, it is not a question of reality, but of truth, because the effect of full speech is to reorder past contingencies by conferring on them the sense of necessities to come, such as they are constituted by the little freedom through which the subject makes them present"(48). The "little freedom" of the subject then consists in creating a sense of the "present" by connecting the "past" with what is "to come" (again eliding himself in the process). "Full speech" must be understood as the fleeting, healing union of "speech" with "language," a fetish connection in a magical semiotic realm, a realm barely distinguishable from ideology.

"We always come back," Lacan points out, "to our double reference to speech and to language": "In order to free the subject's speech, we introduce him into the language of his desire, that is to say, into the *primary language* in which, beyond what he tells us of himself, he is already talking to us unknown to himself, and, in the first place, in the symbols of the symptom" (81; Lacan's emphasis). Here Lacan suggests that the subject has a "primary" language, comprised of symbols and symptoms, and a secondary one, namely trammeled speech. Freud is the one, Lacan reminds us, who taught us about this double reference. Freud "insists" that a "double meaning" is the "minimum of over-determination" required before a "symptom" can be considered psychopathology. This double meaning combines in the symptom the "symbol of a conflict long dead" with "its function in a *no less symbolic present conflict*" (59; Lacan's emphasis). The way to deliver speech from language, is to trace the "ramification of the symbolic lineage in the text of the patient's free associations" in search of "nodal points" where its "verbal forms" intersect with "its structure" (59).

At these nodal points "the symptom resolves itself entirely in an analysis of language, because the symptom is itself structured like a language"(59). "What is more," Lacan says, reminding us of Rat Man and Wolf Man, "words themselves can undergo symbolic lesions and accomplish imaginary acts of which the patient is the subject" (87). Lacan is, of course, correct to name Freud (with Breuer) as discoverer of the connection between symbol and symptom in the course of his first "talking cures." But Freud was too much the materialist, too little the idealist, to claim that words cause wounds. Freud may have discovered, as Lacan says, that man's "relations to the symbolic order" have "effects"; that to understand man we must trace the meaning of these relations "right back to the most radical agencies of symbolization in being"; and that putting into words the meaning of these relations could perhaps free him from his psychopathological symptoms. But it is significant that, for Lacan, what heals the subject undergoing the "talking cure" of symptoms caused by a traumatic "truth" is not so much catharsis, not remembering and reliving and claiming the truth, nor the *prise de conscience* that accompanies the remembering, but rather the fact that "he has verbalized it."

To verbalize, then, according to this logic, is briefly to create a certain plenitude, to enact a union of speech with language, logos with Logos: to embody "full speech." To connect language with speech is to fashion the Lacanian version of sensuous thought, an objective correlative for the phantasm of self. Freud, like Lacan, may not be certain where the boundary is between the "physiological" and the "ideal," or if there is one worth talking about; but when Lacan thinks he gets hold of it he uses it as a weapon to beat up on the subject. Furthermore, "subject" here means "victim," not "autonomous ego" or "individuated consciousness": the subject is the captive of language, "captivated" by "corporeal images" (87), "subject" to "an ever-growing dispossession of that being of his [in the course of analysis], concerning which—by dint of sincere portraits which leave its idea no less incoherent, of rectifications that do not succeed in freeing its essence, of stays and defenses that do not prevent his statue from tottering, of narcissistic embraces that become like a puff of air in animating it—he ends up by recognizing that this being has never been anything more than his construct in the imaginary and that this construct disappoints all his certainties" (42). The subject of psychoanalysis discovers perforce not "certainties" but "the fundamental alienation" that enables the mistaking of mere puffs of air for "narcissistic embraces." Even the subject's self-love is an illusion, because the subject too is a "mere puff of air." "That being of his," as Lacan puts it, is only a "construct."

"Construct" for Lacan seems to be a term of derision for the substantiality we accord mere "puffs of air," whereas for Freud a "construction" is the stuff of which the future is made. Still, the difference between the two may be mostly a matter of attitude; Lacan's idealism expresses itself as a corrosive sardonic cynicism, whereas Freud's relative materialism leaves something to work with, namely our ability to communicate, and something to work for, namely a culture that is not pure phantasm. For this reason it seems to me that insofar as literary theorists today turn to psychoanalytic writing, we ought to turn to Freud rather than Lacan. Is it so very useful to conclude, with Lacan, that to psychoanalysis we owe our understanding that subjectivity is an illusion? Lacan recognizes certain "moments" of Hegelian phenomenology as "structuring" for psychoanalysis, especially the master-slave dialectic, and Hegel's "insistence on the fundamental identity of the particular and the universal." But, he asserts, it is to psychoanalysis that we owe the realization that "identity" is "disjunctive of the subject, and without appeal to any tomorrow." Do we want to believe that we have no such appeal?

What does this mean? Mainly that for Lacan there is no alternative to those fantasies of "totality" that incapacitate us: "Let me simply say that this is what leads me to object to any reference to totality in the individual, as well as into the collectivity that is his equivalent. Psychoanalysis is properly that which reveals both the one and the other to be no more than mirages" (80). The task of psychoanalysis, in Lacanian terms, is not to deliver the subject from its unconscious (that is impossible; the unconscious can never be the subject's in the first place), but to deliver "speech" from "language." Slavoj Žižek may be the first to have made political use and political sense, as well as hermeneutic use and hermeneutic sense, of Lacan's conceptual "puffs," two examples of which, to reemphasize this point, are apparently "the individual" and "the collectivity that is his equivalent." Žižek's definition, for example, of Stalinism as "the big Other," as, in other words, a seemingly autonomous symbolic economy in relation to which the individual experiences his alienation in and from discourse, makes sense, at least to a paranoid American taught in the 1950s to think of communism in just those ways.[21]

But when it comes to defining the "subject" of democracy, Lacanian theory is less convincing, even in Žižek's capable hands. "Who is the subject of democracy?" Žižek asks:

> The Lacanian answer is unequivocal: the subject of democracy is not a human person, "man" in all the richness of his needs, interests, and beliefs. The subject of democracy, like the subject of psychoanalysis, is none other than the Cartesian subject in all its abstraction, the empty punctuality we reach after subtracting all its particular contents. In other words, there is a structural homology between the Cartesian procedure of radical doubt that produces the *cogito*, an empty point or reflective self-reference as a remainder, and the preamble of every democractic proclamation "all people *without regard* to (race, sex, religion, wealth, social status)." [22]

The unequivocal Lacanian answer to the question "Who is the subject of democracy?" is thus no different from the unequivocal Lacanian answer to the question "Who is the subject of Stalinism?" or "Who is the subject of Labor?" The Lacanian answer to any question of who the subject is is always the same: the subject alienated in and from discourse,

[21] See, for example, Žižek, *Sublime Object,* 197.
[22] Slavoj Žižek, *Looking Awry: An Introduction to Jacques Lacan through Popular Culture* (Cambridge: MIT Press, 1991), 163.

the phantasm, the puff of air, "the Cartesian subject in all its abstraction, the empty punctuality we reach after subtracting all its particular contents." It is not surprising that, having thus emptied the subject, Žižek accounts for the ethnic and material particularity of the democratic subject as an "excess," a "smear," a "certain 'pathological' stain" (165).[23] It would be more apt to argue that democracy fails to be democracy precisely when it views subjects in this way, as formal abstractions stained by their histories. It is not the historicity, but the Cartesianism that Žižek is astute enough to detect in our Constitution which constitutes its pathology. This Cartesianism is a function of the aristocratic paternalism of its authors, not the ground of the racial, sexual, religious, economic, or social heterogeneity that daily subverts its spurious universalism.

Lacanian postmodernism thus accounts for culture tautologically or perhaps even total-logically: the individual constitutes the collective, which constitutes the individual; discourse constitutes the individual, which constitutes discourse; discourse constitutes culture, which constitutes discourse. Postmodern consciousness is taken to be oxymoronic, like the postmodern subject, and stands accused of being *essentially* a fabrication, that is, deeply and absolutely shallow. Meanwhile, what we thought of as the individual, not only the source and center of lyrical human consciousness but also the destroyer of graven images and the creator of revolutionary new ones, becomes "a construct" in a pejorative, and finally uninteresting, sense. It is of course possible to romanticize, to idealize, even the sociohistorical. But there need not be a struggle for dominance between accounts privileging "culture" over those privileging a notion of "the subject" because when put into merely dialectical relation with each other, their Cartesian ambivalence emerges and one becomes master, the other becomes the slave. For Lacan Freud's revolutionary insight that the unconscious is structured like a language made it possible to dispense with the

[23] Žižek reformulates "stain" as pleasure or enjoyment in *For They Know Not What They Do: Enjoyment as Political Factor* (London: Verso, 1991).

body per se, except as symbol and symptom, a slave to language; to view the body not as the cause, but as an "effect of
signification."[24] This differs fundamentally from Freud's biologistic yet humanistic orientation. Whereas "people, idiosyncratic people, drop out in the work of Lacan," and whereas
"in Lacan there are no people, just theory," Freud offers by
contrast "a postphilosophical and postreligious morality,"
"in certain respects a stoic vision."[25] But it is a profoundly
social vision I wish to emphasize here, because it is based on
the affective material reality of the individual as *common
sense*.

Lacan has encouraged us to forget that which Freud in 1937
already felt the need to reiterate: that psychoanalysis "is carried on in two separate localities" and "involves two people."
What makes shared experience possible for Freud is finally
the shared biology, which makes us able to feel, to respond
emotionally, not just intellectually, to each other. The work
of construction, which constitutes "the link between" two
separate localities, depends on interaction, an interaction
seemingly unthinkable for Lacan. We forget that, as Freud
took pains to remind us, psychoanalysis involves two persons
who together fashion something of practical as well as symbolic value: a construction. When we forget this bit of common sense, we not only ignore the persons involved in the
psychoanalytic relation, about whom we certainly have no
reason to care, but we also by implication deny our own status as individual speakers, and thus discursively institutionalize a kind of "impotence of despair."[26] We write as if we
fancy ourselves the "locution and link of exchange" between
other, bigger realities outside of ourselves—say, "history"
and "culture"—which we believe romantically to be composed of something other than individuals. And it is this
notion which we sometimes use psychoanalysis to justify
and which I wish to criticize (again). Because Freud and Lacan

[24] Andrew Parker, "Mom," in *Sexual Difference*, Special Issue of the
Oxford Literary Review 8, nos. 1–2 (1986): 99.
[25] Kerrigan, "Terminating Lacan," 1002–3.
[26] Mary Shelley, *Frankenstein, or, the Modern Prometheus* (1818; London:
Penguin, 1985), 181.

think about persons and language and meaning differently, they think about psychoanalysis differently. Freud is a semiotic materialist, for whom the final arbiter of the meanings generated by psychoanalysis must be the analysand him/herself. But Lacan is an idealist for whom language alone is real, or rather, constitutive, and the analysand is more or less an "effect," the virtual image, of language.

Literary critics still tend to believe Lacan when he claims to be a Freudian. This, it seems to me, is because for many literary critics too language alone is "real"; they feel quite at home with this idea, treating language as being "real" and ignoring the consequences of this notion. One of Freud's ongoing missions throughout his career was to parry assaults on the authority of psychoanalysis, and justify its ways to humanity. One such rebuttal was the late essay, "Constructions in Analysis" (1937), which reveals how un-Freudian, even antiFreudian, is Lacan's notion (discussed above) of the psychoanalytic situation as a "relation of two bodies between which is established a phantasmic communication." Freud's essay uses the idea of construction to argue against the claim that in the dualistic encounter of analyst with analysand, the analyst inevitably triumphs, and the analysand is inevitably overwhelmed by the analyst's authority, reinscribed, as it were, within the analyst's own discourse.[27] In "Constructions in Analysis" Freud responds to "an opinion upon analytic technique" expressed by "a certain well-known man of science," which he feels to be "at once derogatory and unjust" (*SE* 23:257). This man claimed that, in the psychoanalytic situation, the analyst manages to be "always in the right against the poor helpless wretch whom [he is] analyzing, no matter how he [the patient] may respond" to the interpretation offered (*SE* 23:257). The analyst, he said, treats the patient "upon the famous principle of 'Heads I win, tails you lose'" because, "if the patient agrees with us, then the interpretation is right; but if he contradicts us, that is only a sign of his resistance, which again shows that we are right" (*SE* 23:257).

In response to this critique, Freud takes pains to explain

---

[27]Freud, "Constructions in Analysis," in *SE* 23:257–69. This essay has figured recently in Peter Brooks, "The Idea of a Psychoanalytic Literary Criticism," in *The Trials of Psychoanalysis*, ed. Francoise Meltzer (Chicago: University of Chicago Press, 1987), and Jane Gallop, *Thinking through the Body* (New York: Columbia University Press, 1988), as well as by implication in Julia Kristeva, but they do not emphasize the point which I wish to argue here.

that the task of the analyst is to induce the patient "to remember something that has been experienced by him and repressed," and that the way for the analyst "to make out what has been forgotten . . . [is] to *construct* it" rather than interpret it (*SE* 23:258-59; Freud's emphasis). The goal of psychoanalysis, Freud first of all reminds his reader, is "inducing the patient to give up the repressions (using the word in the widest sense) belonging to his early development and to replace them by reactions of a sort that would correspond to a psychically mature condition" (*SE* 23:257). With this goal in mind the analyst must bring the patient "to recollect certain experiences and the affective impulses up called by them" with the aid of certain kinds of material that the patient puts at the analyst's disposal. What sort of material is this? "All kinds of things. He gives us fragments of these memories in his dreams, invaluable in themselves but seriously distorted as a rule by all the factors concerned in the formation of dreams. Again, he produces ideas if he gives himself up to 'free association,' in which we can discover allusions to the repressed experiences and derivative of the suppressed affective impulses as well as of the reactions against them. And finally, there are hints of repetitions of the affects belonging to the repressed material to be found in actions performed by the patient . . . both inside and outside the analytic situation" (*SE* 23:258). The "things" the patient gives the analyst to work with are all of the symbolic, poetic, iconic order: memories, dreams, ideas, affects. These "things" which Freud in this article calls "psychical objects," and which I called earlier, following *The Interpretation of Dreams* "image-things," are the building blocks of which psychoanalytic constructions are made.[28]

Freud points out that, since the analyst has "neither experienced nor repressed any of the material under consideration," "his task cannot be to remember anything. What then is his task?" The analyst's task is to construct what has been for-

[28] I use this cliché despite its tiresomeness because in this essay Freud explores at length that comparison of which he was so fond between the construction performed by the psychoanalyst and that performed by the archaeologist. Freud considers the former by far the more "real."

gotten and to convey these constructions to the patient: "The time and manner in which he conveys his constructions to the person who is being analysed, as well as the explanations with which he accompanies them, constitute the link between the two portions of the work of analysis, between his own part and that of the patient" (*SE* 23:259). Construction, in other words, is inseparable from interaction. On the one hand, the time and manner of the "conveying" of the analyst's constructions, and the explanations in which they are imbedded "constitutes the link" between the analyst and the patient. On the other hand, as Freud will go on to say, the patient's response forms another and indissoluble part of that link. Freud feels the need to remind us that the work of analysis "is carried on in two separate localities" and "involves two people, to each of whom a distinct task is assigned" (*SE* 23:258). The fact that a construction constitutes the link between two separate localities, two people, is what distinguishes it from an "interpretation," a point that Freud goes on to clarify.

The analyst must construct, from traces it left behind, that which has been forgotten: "It is a 'construction' when one lays before the subject of an analysis a piece of his early history that he has forgotten, in some such way as this: 'Up to your nth year you regarded yourself as the sole and unlimited possessor of your mother; then came another baby and brought you grave disillusionment. Your mother left you for some time, and even after her reappearance she was never again devoted to you exclusively. Your feelings towards your mother became ambivalent, your father gained a new importance for you,' . . . and so on" (*SE* 23:261). The above story is a construction; the word "'interpretation' applies to something that one does to some single element of the material, such as an association or a parapraxis." An interpretation would test the significance of an idea or affect in order to determine its place in a construction, whose shape it would change accordingly. Interpretation and construction go on simultaneously, with the latter always a little ahead of the former, precisely because interpretation is an instrument used in construction.

To seem valid or be of use interpretations, unlike constructions, do not require "two separate localities" or persons (this point will become significant when applied to discourse in general). An interpretation is a narrative that gives extension and "makeshift duration" (Henry James's phrase) to an image or idea. It is a hypothesis in that it need not be "real" even in the sense of the symbolic-and-therefore-real characteristic of psychical reality. An interpretation or narrative can remain entirely internal to its creator, as in the case of conversations we might imagine having with someone we are about to meet for lunch, or theories we concoct in our minds about what we are reading, or a rationalization we offer ourselves of some faux pas perpetrated in public the day before. An interpretation is an intentional object in that it is an object for consciousness, and as such may generate affects or ideas, but until it is part of an utterance, written or spoken, to be communicated to another person (or other persons) it is not a construction.

Furthermore, a construction communicates by touching its recipient or audience. Freud tells us that patients often respond to single interpretations with "indirect forms of confirmation" such as "'I didn't ever think' (or 'I shouldn't ever have thought') 'that' (or 'of that')" which "can be translated without any hesitation into: 'Yes, you're right this time—about my unconscious" (*SE* 23:263). This unequivocal response occurs much more rarely to an extensive construction. Even so only once in a while does the analyst produce "false combinations" of interpretations in a valueless construction. On such occasions "what in fact occurs . . . is that the patient remains as though he were untouched by what has been said and reacts to it with neither a 'Yes' nor a 'No'" (*SE* 23:261). It is true, Freud admits, that, as said the "man of science" to whom the essay "Constructions in Analysis" is addressed, the analyst does "not accept the 'No' of a person under analysis at its face value; but neither do we allow his 'Yes' to pass," because this plain "Yes" may indeed be intended unconsciously by the patient to avoid the discovery of some painful truth (*SE* 23:262).

On the contrary, for a construction to be valid it must "touch" the person for whom it is designed; he must not remain "as though he were untouched by what has been said." And the sign that the construction has touched the person is that he responds by expanding upon the construction, adding new affect-bearing bits: "The 'yes' [of assent by a patient to the construction offered] has no value unless it is followed by indirect confirmations, unless the patient, immediately after his 'Yes,' produces new memories which complete and extend the construction. Only in such an event do we consider that the 'Yes' has dealt completely with the subject under discussion" (262). Patients' reactions to constructions offered by the analyst are "rarely unambiguous and give no opportunity for a final judgment. Only the further course of the analysis enables us to decide whether our constructions are correct or unserviceable": "We do not pretend that an individual construction is anything more than a conjecture which awaits examination, confirmation or rejection. . . . In short, we conduct ourselves on the model of a familiar figure in one of Nestroy's farces—the manservant who has a single answer on his lips to every question or objection: 'It will all become clear in the course of future developments'" (265). "Construction" as Freud defines it is itself an admirable and useful construction. It provides the model in this text, which to some extent proposes a psychopathology of discourse, of what discourse should be and do—that is, to take it out of the realm of fetishism into that of construction, the realm of "future developments."

To some extent, a construction is that which generates more constructions; Marx's exploration of "commodity fetishism," for example, is a construction that continues to provoke engaged and involved response in the critical writing of others generations later. That multifarious discourse we call "culture" is comprised of innumerable such constructions or, perhaps more accurately, co-constructions, in a variety of verbal and nonverbal media. A construction unites image and interpretation, symbol and history, icon and narrative in a conception that moves its audience to "complete and extend the construction"; it is in this sense that construction adds to the richness of its perceiver's life by leaving him not "untouched." Being touched in this sense makes it possible for individuals—and perhaps therefore for society, though more slowly—"to give up repressions (using the word in the widest sense) belonging to [their] early development and to replace them by reactions of a sort that would correspond to a psychically mature condition." If a discourse that acknowledges the extent to which it is constructed can do for a society what psychoanalytic construction can do for an individual, then it matters what values we endorse in our critical writing, whether we are sexist, elitist, irrational, sentimental, or otherwise backward. To acknowledge that our discursive constructions are not mysterious emanations with lives of their own, but rather what Edward Said calls "willed human work," would be to acknowledge the communities of contestation and constraint within which we work together—and which we construct.[29]

The explicit purpose of Freud's essay "Constructions in Analysis" was to defend psychoanalysis against the charge that it was a form of intimate medical imperialism. But beyond this, as I have tried to show, the essay makes at least two other implicit claims: one, that Freud was himself aware that the psychoanalytic couple was engaged not only in an intimate conversation, but in a larger project that, as communication, at the same time had its own social, discursive dimension; and two, that this discursive dimension must inevitably carry psychoanalysis forward in time, out of Freud's control and into the "future." Recent research in neuroscience indicates that the unconscious may process information in a way quite different from what Freud described. According to Israel Rosenfeld, we restructure the past in terms of the present in order to get things done because "we need not stored images but procedures."[30] Although in the

---

[29] Edward Said, *Orientalism* (New York: Vintage, 1979), 15.
[30] Israel Rosenfeld, *The Invention of Memory: A New View of the Brain* (New York: Basic Books, 1988), 8. See also, Gerald M. Edelman, *Neural Darwinism: The Theory of Neuronal Group Selection* (New York: Basic Books, 1987).

end Freud felt the power of psychoanalysis to change our lives to be profoundly limited, his own idea of "constructions in analysis" could, had he thought of its hopeful implications for the efficacy of human beings in the world, given him cause to feel cheerier.

INDEX

Substitution (*cont.*)
43, 46, 125. *See also* Equivalence effect
Superego, 197
Surrealism: of Lacanianism, 220; as situated art, 76–78. *See also* Avant-garde movements
Symbolism: in Baudelaire, 147–48; body parts as first symbols, 179–80; in commodity fetishism, 80, 82; culture as symbolic discourse, 64; of female genitality, 92–93; of fetish, 88; in hysteria, 43, 50; imagos, 47; in modernism, 154; of phallus, 28; as the real, 150–52, 179, 204; in surrealism, 77–78. *See also* Autosymbolism

Talking cure, 220–21
Totalization, 39, 125, 166, 227. *See also* Equivalence effect
Triangulation, 129–33
Tzara, Tristan, 74–76, 153

Umbilical cord, 21–22, 29–40, 44

Unconscious, 118–20, 178, 184, 189–93, 195, 203, 215, 221; in Freud, 108; in Lawrence, 110. *See also* Psychical reality

Vagina, 92
Vaihinger, Hans, 150
Van Ghent, Dorothy, 152

Weininger, Otto, 3
Weismann, August, 14, 26
Weltanschauung, 56–58
Wilde, Oscar, 145–46, 169
Wilson, Edmund, 154
Winson, Jonathan, 191n
Woolf, Virginia, 123–24, 125
Wordsworth, William: "Lines Composed a Few Miles Above Tintern Abbey," 156–60

Yeats, William Butler, 144–45, 155

Žižek, 197–98, 206, 221n, 226
Zweig, Paul, 126, 128

Library of Congress Cataloging-in-Publication Data

Ian, Marcia, 1950–
  Remembering the phallic mother : psychoanalysis, modernism, and the
  fetish / Marcia Ian.
      p. cm.
  Includes bibliographical references and index.
  ISBN 0–8014–2637–5. — ISBN 0–8014–9941–0 (pbk.)
  1. Psychoanalysis and literature. 2. Mothers in literature. 3. Femininity
  (Psychology) in literature. 4. Bisexuality in literature. 5. Fetishism in liter-
  ature. 6. Modernism (Literature) 7. Feminism and literature. 8. Literature,
  Modern—History and criticism. I. Title.
PN56.P92I36 1993
801'.92—dc20   92–33381